Archaeologies of Food in Australia

TOM AUSTEN BROWN STUDIES IN AUSTRALASIAN ARCHAEOLOGY

Dr Tristen Jones, Series Editor

The Tom Austen Brown Studies in Australasian Archaeology series publishes new research on the archaeology of Australia and the adjacent regions. It aims to develop our understanding of Australasia's human past, with particular focus on the archaeology of Aboriginal and Torres Strait Islander peoples during both prehistoric and contact periods.

Animal Bones in Australian Archaeology: A Field Guide to Common Native and Introduced Species
Melanie Fillios and Natalie Blake

Archaeologies of Food in Australia
Edited by Madeline Shanahan

Between the Murray and the Sea: Aboriginal Archaeology in Southeastern Australia
David Frankel

Crafting Country: Aboriginal Archaeology in the Eastern Chichester Range, North-West Australia
Caroline Bird and James W. Rhoads

Jakarda Wuka (Too Many Stories): Narratives of Rock Art from Yanyuwa Country in Northern Australia's Gulf of Carpentaria
li-Yanyuwa li-Wirdiwalangu (Yanyuwa Elders), Liam M. Brady, John Bradley and Amanda Kearney

Photogrammetry for Archaeological Objects: A Manual
Madeline G.P. Robinson

Archaeologies of Food in Australia

Edited by Madeline Shanahan

SYDNEY UNIVERSITY PRESS

A catalogue record for this book is available from the National Library of Australia.

NATIONAL
LIBRARY
OF AUSTRALIA

ISBN 9781761540493 paperback
ISBN 9781761540509 hardback
ISBN 9781761540479 epub
ISBN 9781761540486 pdf

Cover images: (Top) Nineteenth-century cutlery. Courtesy of Extent Heritage, 2025; (Centre) Macroblade (Leilira) Knife made by the Aranda people, Northern Territory. Courtesy of Michael Curry. Moore, Mark W. 2020. Museum of Stone Tools, UNE. Retrieved 14 July 2025, from https://une.pedestal3d.com/r/EMXgjoqr49; (Bottom) Qing Dynasty plate. Image courtesy of Brian Shanahan 2025.

We acknowledge the traditional owners of the lands on which Sydney University Press is located, the Gadigal people of the Eora Nation, and we pay our respects to the knowledge embedded forever within the Aboriginal Custodianship of Country.

Some quotations from scholarly sources may contain terms or views that were considered acceptable within mainstream Australian society when they were written, but may no longer be considered appropriate. The wording in these quotes does not necessarily reflect the views of Sydney University Press or the editors.

Contents

List of figures

List of tables

Foreword

Karen Metheny

As a food studies scholar working across a range of disciplines, including archaeology and anthropology, it is a great pleasure to see this volume come to fruition. As Madeline Shanahan notes in her introduction, there is both great potential but also a critical need for food-focused studies in Australian archaeology. I would argue that an archaeology of food is of critical importance for *all* archaeologists, because food has the ability to bring all aspects of society and culture into focus.

There is interpretive power in a food lens. As this volume clearly demonstrates, archaeologists can connect food-related evidence to meaningful socio-cultural practice, from subsistence strategies and food systems, to the social and symbolic, to the economic and the political, across a range of temporalities and geographies. By highlighting the diverse food-related practices of Australia's original inhabitants, as well as those of the many groups of colonists, migrants, immigrants, and labourers who settled here, the authors also draw our attention to the vast range of outcomes that may result from cultural encounter and exchange.

In each chapter, whether examining prehistoric or historical contexts, the authors incorporate into their analyses the core concept of foodways – defined as the range of cultural, social, material, technological and economic practices related to the production and consumption of food, from production, procurement and preparation to presentation, consumption and disposal. This is a term that is well known to historical archaeologists and anthropologists, but Chapters 1–3 are particularly notable for their contributors' engagement with the concept of foodways in prehistoric contexts, connecting the evidence for food resources and food choices to cultural, social, and even symbolic practice.

In Chapter 1, Tim Owen links prehistoric subsistence strategies to the concepts of foodways and cuisine. This type of interpretive lens is still rare in archaeological literature from around the globe, so to think about foodways and culture in deep time is both exciting and powerful. That the author is successful in doing so here suggests the strength of multidisciplinary approaches that incorporate multiple lines of evidence, including traditional knowledge, to build those connections.

In Chapter 2, Dilkes-Hall, Davis and Malo draw heavily on the concept of ecological knowledge to examine and interpret the evidence for Aboriginal plant use dating back 47,000 years. The choice to view archaeobotanical evidence through this lens deliberately extends the discussion of food as part of a subsistence strategy to consider the *cultural* choices behind the selection of certain resources and decisions to prepare and consume them in a certain way (*foodways*).

In Chapter 3, Disspain, Manne and Lambrides shift the focus from plants to the ecological, social, and cultural significance of fishing in Australia. They provide an overview of the archaeological evidence for fishing across the continent, from 42,000 years ago to the present. These three chapters should prompt important discussion and new interpretations of the Aboriginal past, particularly as the material, archaeobotanical, and zooarchaeological evidence for food extends far back in time. The use of oral tradition and ecological knowledge further expands and deepens our interpretations. Together, the authors provide compelling evidence for how the Australian landscape has shaped and been shaped for millennia by its original inhabitants.

The effects of colonialism, capitalism, and globalisation, though comparatively recent and rapid in development and impact, have also been wide-ranging and profound, altering the landscape in ways that will continue to be felt well into the future. Archaeologists are on more familiar ground here when discussing foodways, given the abundance of textual, material, and archaeological evidence of past lifeways in the historical period. The chapters that follow are nonetheless quite revelatory, demonstrating the important contributions offered by a food-focused lens but also highlighting the profound impacts that foods and food practices can have in a variety of socio-cultural contexts. In Chapter 4, for example, Nussbaumer and Fillios provide an excellent overview and discussion of the social and ecological dynamics of colonisation with specific focus on the introduction of domesticated animals to Australia, beginning in 1788. The authors highlight the archaeological evidence for both short-term cultural encounter and extended contact through colonisation, noting variations in both responses and actions, as well as the long-term consequences of these encounters.

The study of institutional food by Connor in Chapter 5 is extremely important, highlighting as it does the fact that food represents and is used as an implement of power, and those who control access to food can exert their power over others in a variety of social, economic, and cultural contexts. Two types of institutional contexts are examined with respect to food: rationing, for example through the British Navy, the carceral system, the many work camps organised within extractive industries, the fisheries, and the agricultural sector, as well as mission sites; and institutional provisioning and dining through prisons, hospitals, and schools. Connor draws from archaeological and historical evidence to outline the varied contexts of institutional food provisioning in Australia, distinguishing not only between institutions and provisioning systems, but also between voluntary residents and those subject to coercive practices; the author also demonstrates the varied impacts of institutional provisioning on the basis of gender, ethnicity, and indigeneity.

In Chapter 6, Grimwade explores changing foodways practice in the Chinese diaspora to Australia through the documentation of large stone ovens that were built to roast pigs and were a frequent feature of Chinese immigrant communities. The chapter provides a typology of ovens, spatial distribution of documented examples, a brief examination of the ritual importance of the pig in Chinese religion, and an overview of preparation methods and contexts of consumption in Australia. Grimwade demonstrates that this traditional foodway, though steeped in ritual and religion, nonetheless changed over time to become increasingly secular in practice.

Newling's emphasis in Chapter 7 on cooking processes in historic-period domestic kitchens provides critical background to understanding both daily practice as well as changes to those practices with the introduction of new technologies and material goods. As the author notes, there is plenty in the literature on British and American kitchens, but it is important to describe the construction and technologies specific to Australian kitchens beginning with the colonial period. This chapter serves as a primer for any historical archaeologist, historian, or site interpreter working with food and foodways.

Finally, in Chapter 8, Harris, Woff, and O'Donohue discuss the importance of glass and ceramic bottles and containers as diagnostic artifacts and as essential forms of food-related material culture that give insight into domestic foodways practices. This chapter offers an introduction to food preservation technologies of the historical period and links the material evidence for these containers to specific food preservation methods. But the authors connect these bottles and containers to larger questions around food choice and food consumption as well, noting that vessel selection and use were also influenced by and reflected aspects of identity in relation to ethnicity, social class, and economic status. Further complicating their history, the choice of vessels and how to use them also reflected differences between urban and rural households, access to changing technologies, as well as the degree of participation in an increasingly global economy. For this reason, the authors stress the value in determining the context of a vessel's use or re-use to better understand foodways practiced in the home.

Shanahan argues that many archaeologists in Australia are hesitant to engage with or are unaware of the potential for a food-focused archaeology. If that is the case, this volume provides an excellent demonstration of its methodological and interpretive power, whether researchers use existing data and collections or embark on new research endeavors. The volume will prove to be a critical resource for Australian archaeologists. The contributors have highlighted a wide range of datasets and methods with respect to the study of plants, animals, fish and shellfish, but also wild and domesticated food sources, and the range of choices made with respect to foraging, husbandry, cultivation, importation, and domestic manufacture. They review a wide range of material and technological evidence, providing detailed discussions of food processing and preparation methods across time and space. They also have made their work accessible, and readers will see how to usefully apply a food lens to their own area of study. Finally, the detailed citations and references will be an important – even critical – resource, particularly the inclusion of gray literature where large amounts of data are to be found.

This volume serves to emphasise the applicability of a food lens to a broad range of time periods, from deep time to the colonial era to the present day. Critically, in her role as editor, Shanahan emphasises the public's interest in food and suggests this interest makes a food-focused archaeology both relevant and exciting. Given both scholarly interest in and public discourse about identity and multicultural exchange, but also the need to critically redress the biases and inequalities linked to colonialism, capitalism, industrialisation, and globalisation, Shanahan's observation is prescient. Notably, several authors in this volume draw on their research data to discuss issues regarding sustainability, environmental degradation, and the loss of resources. Questions of access to and control of food resources are also critical topics today and will be in the future. The contributors to this volume demonstrate clearly that these issues have a deep history, however, and are often multifaceted in origin and nuanced in their outcome. As such the authors demonstrate the relevance of a food-focused archaeology to future policy and planning.

This volume, then, provides a compelling foundation for an area of research that should prove essential to understanding both past and present in Australian archaeology, and will make an important contribution to the field of archaeology more broadly, demonstrating the potential for a food-focused archaeology. But this volume will also excite the interest of the public. As the contributors show, not only can each food or ingredient or recipe have different methods of preparation and consumption depending on place and time, but each culture and even each generation within the same culture can develop different preferences for foods and make different choices as to the best ingredients, methods of preparation, and ways of consumption—that is, what is "good" to eat. That is something to which we can all relate. And that too suggests the power of food archaeology.

Karen Bescherer Metheny
Master Lecturer in Gastronomy and Archaeology
Boston University

Introduction

Food for thought

Madeline Shanahan

Far more than simple sustenance, food is – and always has been – central to human culture, society and identity. It bonds individuals and communities together, strengthening collective identities through shared experience and memory. Food can be used to define boundaries between groups by highlighting differences and underlining culinary orthodoxies or taboos, from the foodstuffs consumed, to the manner and methods of dining (Twiss 2007, 1–10). Food also connects us to place. Climate, terrain, soils and seasons all shape the resources, produce and flavours of a region. The material impact that our relationship with food has had on the world is also significant, meaning that it is a subject that archaeologists are uniquely well situated to explore. Changing settlement patterns, domestication of both plant and animal species, environmental degradation, conflicts, migrations, demographic flux, technological revolutions, and evolving gender and domestic roles have all been both driven and shaped by our insatiable hunger, and they have all left a tangible imprint.

This volume draws together a series of chapters addressing the archaeology of food in Australia. It highlights the range of culinary stories the discipline can tell, from deep time to the more recent past. As outlined in more detail below, considerable scholarship has been devoted to the archaeological study of food overseas, but this thematic approach is in its infancy in Australia, a fact that is surprising when we consider the role that food plays in wider national discourse. Twenty-first century Australia is a nation somewhat obsessed with food. From almost every media forum, we are bombarded with discussions of what and how to eat (Bannerman 2011, 49–51). At its most superficial, this food fixation stems from consumer culture and is influenced by changing fashions and fads, however, in other ways it reflects a more profound national discourse. Food is a key component of culture, and for a diverse nation like Australia, it has been central to identity maintenance and construction. While food historians have picked up this gauntlet (see for example, Santich 2012; Symons 1982; Van Reyk 2021) and contributed to thematic discussions and overviews of the development of food cultures, there has been a relative silence from archaeologists in Australia about a subject on which the discipline has so much to offer, and which communities care so much about.

Why does the archaeology of food matter?

In recent years, we have seen this national food focus in Australia connect directly with debates relating to archaeology and we have witnessed people actively looking to the past for answers. Most notably, we witnessed intense discourse surrounding Bruce Pascoe's *Dark Emu* (2018), which re-examined Aboriginal food procurement, arguing that the "mythology" of hunter-gathering has obscured the complexity and sophistication of pre-colonial economies. The book triggered fierce public and scholarly debate, which in turn connected to key issues we are grappling with as a postcolonial society. While much of this discourse was divisive, what it highlighted was the intense interest that wider Australian society has in history and archaeology, and importantly, the relevance of food in these debates. What is clear is that discussions of our gastronomic pasts hold resonance today – connecting with issues such as colonisation, climate change and environmental sustainability.

Looking to contemporary discourse once more, we also see the public's interest in health and nutrition, and the way in which the past can be used (and abused) by the diet industry in the promotion of products and approaches harnessing the alleged habits of our ancestors. The Paleo diet is the most iconic of these, drawing upon the concept of a supposedly "natural" idealised diet of the past to answer contemporary health issues. As an archaeology volume, this work does not comment on the efficacy of such regimes, but it is concerning to see the Palaeolithic misrepresented as some form of Eden in which our ancestors lived an existence free from concerns around health and nutrition. It also demonstrates a concerning degree of "presentism" in which the complexity and diversity of Palaeolithic food cultures globally are misrepresented. There was, of course, no single "Paleo diet", and as archaeologists it is our job to reveal the past in all its glorious diversity, rather than to accept these reductive idealised narratives about people who were every bit as complex as we are today. The Paleo diet is the most extreme of these diets drawing on the supposedly "natural state" of the species, but fasting routines, gluten-free diets and a range of other regimes trending at any one time or another frequently use rhetoric around the benefits of a return to our origins. Rigorous analysis of the distant past provides the opportunity to contribute meaningfully, scientifically and factually to these contemporary discussions, but also helps curb the mythmaking.

The other key contribution archaeology can make is to assist in the development of more nuanced discussions of diversity in the past. Australia's extraordinary range of cuisines, drawn from every corner of the globe, is frequently cited as one of the most significant contributions of multiculturalism, with the range of offerings reflecting the diversity of our communities. The role of food in experiences of migration is a theme that resonates today, with a past that deserves recognition. In recent decades though, the connection between food and multiculturalism has also been critiqued, with scholars such as Ghassan Hage highlighting the othering and consumptive nature of rhetoric relating to so-called "ethnic cuisines". Hage (1997) argues that "ethnic" food is consumed by the white middle class in restaurants, without truly creating intercultural understanding. In particular, Hage (1998; 1997) criticises this "cosmo-multiculturalism" and the inherently consumptive sanitised nature of the transaction. While being cognisant of this body of literature and the complexity of the issue, archaeology provides the opportunity to critically examine the material markers of change, diversity and migration experiences in the past. To date, archaeological studies of ethnicity have been all too few in Australia, but food provides a critical framework to engage with these discussions and consider experiences of food and community from multiple chapters of our history. Gordon Grimwade's chapter on Chinese roast pork in this volume (Chapter 6) is an invaluable contribution, highlighting that there are many methodological approaches to understanding culinary diversity in the past more consistently and comprehensively.

Looking globally

While the archaeology of food has received limited dedicated focus in Australia, it has attracted considerable attention from scholars globally. These studies have shown that much of what archaeologists excavate – such as faunal remains, ceramics and cesspits – can collectively tell the story of food culture when drawn together and considered as a whole. The following section will review some of the main focus areas for the archaeology of food globally. It is not intended to be a detailed literature review of all global archaeologies of food (see Twiss 2019) but rather, is intended to do two things. First, to highlight the potential of the subject as demonstrated in global studies and by extension the need to progress comparable research in Australia. Second, it is intended to highlight the disciplinary diversity of approaches to the subject and the need to draw multiple perspectives together to shed light on food and foodways in the past.

Before presenting an overview of the subdisciplines and methodological approaches to individual aspects of food, it is useful to highlight global thematic studies which draw together multiple strands of evidence and perspectives. The work of scholars such as Hastorf (2018), Metheny and Beaudry (2016), Scarry, Hutchinson and Arbuckle (2023) and Twiss (2019), in synthesising multiple strands of evidence on food from diverse sites both globally and temporally, demonstrates the potential for thematic volumes on food. Looking at these syntheses and thematic global studies, two key issues emerge, both of which have a bearing on the current volume and its value.

The first issue that emerges from the global studies is that Australia is rarely if ever mentioned. When we consider the extraordinary length of occupation in Australia – itself a continent – coupled with the many decades of work undertaken across academic and consulting archaeology, the omission of this part of the human food story surely needs rectifying. This dedicated volume on the subject in Australia will begin to correct this absence and, in the process, highlight the many varied contributions that scholars have made to the subject. It will also demonstrate that there are key issues and questions distinct to our shores, which only focused scholarship here can address.

The second issue that emerges from these global studies which is of relevance to the current volume is the value in drawing the contributions of many varied subdisciplines together to better understand the story of change and complexity of food cultures in the past. To understand food in the past, we cannot focus solely on lithics without also considering related categories of evidence, such as hearth sites, hunting strategies, residue and pollen analysis. In isolation, these studies tell us about artefact or evidential categories and typologies, but when pieced back together and viewed collectively, they will tell us about food culture. Archaeologists in Australia have, to date, excelled in the former, but have only rarely rejoined the puzzle pieces and looked at the latter. These global studies also highlight that archaeology is indeed a "broad church", with researchers spanning from the sciences through to the humanities, all of which have the potential to shed light on the subject. Some of us work in the laboratory, analysing the most microscopic forms of evidence and drawing on the new technologies at our disposal in the twenty-first century, while others interrogate culture and society, seeking answers to questions about the nature of identity, experience and community.

With the potential of this "broad church" in mind, the following section will outline some of the primary categories of evidence, methodologies and approaches to the archaeology of food that have been pursued to date. While many of these are already regularly being used in Australia – as this volume will demonstrate – it is useful to review approaches elsewhere to highlight the progress that has been made and provide a context for the contents of this volume. This discussion also highlights the potential for the archaeology of food in Australia, which is still in its infancy, but it also demonstrates some key differences and unique aspects of our past that require additional focus. The following is not intended to be a detailed review of studies relating to each subdiscipline, but rather, it is intended to outline the diversity of datasets and perspectives, and the many varied tools at our disposal.

Plant foods

The information that can be gleaned from the analysis of plant remains, known as archaeobotany, has grown exponentially in recent years through scientific innovation. Unlike animal remains (such as bones and shells), plant remains do not typically survive as well in the archaeological record. When they do survive, they are often fragmentary or much smaller. This means that our ability to both gather and analyse plant materials is more challenging, but has progressed significantly in recent decades, providing critical insight into the complexity of diets in the past.

Plant remains come in a range of forms, some of which can be collected relatively easily while others require more sophisticated techniques. Macrobotanical remains are remnants of plants that can be detected with either the naked eye or low-powered magnification. These include elements such as seeds, pods, nutshells or chaff. These can be collected by hand if large enough but are also commonly recovered through flotation of soil samples. By studying these palaeobotanical assemblages, researchers are able to gather information on diets from even the most distant periods in the past. The famous Acheulian site, Gesher Benot Ya'aqov (Israel), dating to the early to mid Pleistocene, provided an extraordinary palaeobotanical assemblage in which 129 species of fruits, nuts and seeds (including almonds, figs, grapes, olives, juniper, pistachios, acorns and water chestnuts) were represented. Importantly, the assemblage included toxic species, which required cooking to make them edible, and hard nuts requiring tools to open them. Analysis of the palaeobotanical assemblage provided a rare insight into the diet of early hominins, as well as critical information on their food processing capability and technology (Goren-Inbar et al. 2002).

Microbotanical remains (such as pollens, phytoliths and starches) can also be detected through more complex forms of analysis, providing a more rounded view of the range of species consumed, including those that do not preserve as well (such as tubers). These can be detected through soil sampling on sites, as well as through residue analysis of artefacts (discussed in more detail below). These testing regimes help us to understand the foods consumed, and they can also shed light on how spaces were used for processing, cooking and dining, based on variable concentrations of different substances such as pollen. For example, a storage or food processing area will have comparatively more pollen present than a habitation space (Kelso 2015, 399).

Information that can help us to reconstruct the wider environment and plant species present – even if not directly consumed – can also help us to understand food procurement and harvesting practices. For example, the presence of certain weed species can indicate the development of agriculture in a region, as well as methods of crop-processing such as threshing, winnowing and sieving (Riehl 2015, 31). A key focus for the subdiscipline of archaeobotany globally has also been tracing the domestication of plants (Zohary, Hopf and Weiss 2012). For example, sites such as Franchthi Cave in the southern Peloponnese (Greece) contained extensive evidence relating to the transition to agriculture. Weed species that were indicative of cultivated fields, domestic emmer wheat, two-row barley and lentil seed size increase were key indicators pointing to the shift to the cultivation of domesticated plant foods. The contemporaneous zooarchaeological assemblage also indicated a shift from wild prey to domestic sheep and goats (Hansen 1991).

Meat, fish and shellfish

Animal bones, analysed by vertebrate zooarchaeologists, and shells, analysed by archaeomalacologists, provide a range of information relating to species consumed and also to procurement, processing and cookery. Bones and shells have traditionally been easier to recover in most environments than seeds or pollen, but again, new techniques have unlocked potential avenues in recent decades, allowing for more complex analysis. These developments mean that we have moved beyond simply stating which species were consumed and in what quantities, and can now ask more detailed questions relating to food and foodways. Zooarchaeologists can determine not simply which species were eaten but also factors such as age and sex of animals. This information can help us to understand more about ancient hunting and farming practices. Were older animals eaten to maximise yield? Were young male animals slaughtered, suggesting that females were kept for dairying and breeding? The season in which an animal was killed is also informative. This can shed light on patterns of mobility in hunter-gatherer societies, as well as provide information on farming cycles in agrarian societies.

Importantly, analysis of bones can also show us far more than simply which species were being slaughtered. The morphology and location of tool marks on bones provides important information on hunting, processing and cookery methods. The materiality of the tool (whether stone or metal) and nature of the cutting technique (chopping, sawing, cutting) can be established through analysis of the marks (Fisher

1995). The cuts of meat favoured also tell us a great deal about dining and food cultures. For example, in the post medieval North Atlantic world we notice the gradual shift in elite households from communally shared joints of meat, or cuts suitable for stews, towards individual portions. This illuminates not just what people were eating, but also how dining and cookery practices were changing. American historical archaeologist James Deetz highlights the significance of this shift in butchery, as traditional chopping methods that produced large joints of meat were eventually replaced by sawing methods, so that individual portions of steak and chops and so on could be served. Deetz argues that this change indicates an increased desire to mask the origins of food, as well as an increased emphasis on the individual (Deetz 1996 [1977]). Matthew Johnson similarly observes this shift in a European early modern context, as medieval stews and soups gradually gave way to more differentiated and individualised styles of cooking and eating (Johnson 1996, 175–6). The bones we find on sites can tell us far more than just which species were being eaten; they can also be used to understand significant cultural and culinary change.

Human remains and waste

From the late twentieth century on, the range of techniques available for the study of human remains and waste increased, meaning that we can now understand the food stories of both individuals and populations more than ever before. This capability ranges from extraordinary opportunities to capture information on an individual's consumption at a moment in time, to large datasets allowing us to look at change in a population over long periods of time. For example, bog bodies from north-western Europe reveal ritual meals consumed prior to human sacrifice. Analysis of the stomach contents of Tollund Man, the bog body from Early Iron Age Denmark, shows that in the hours before he was killed, he ate a porridge containing barley, pale persicaria and flax, and probably some fish (Nielsen et al. 2021). Examinations of the 5,300-year-old frozen mummy known as the Tyrolean Iceman indicated that he died with a full stomach, having dined on grain and fatty species of wild game such as deer and ibex shortly before his death (Gostner, Pernter and Bonatti 2011).

Analysis of skeletal remains provides more information relating to the food story of individuals over a longer period. Stable isotope analysis of bone or tooth enamel provides extraordinary information about the food stories of individuals and populations over time. Through stable isotope analysis, archaeologists can determine at what age a person was weaned, where they moved over the course of their life, and what staple foods underpinned their diet in different phases. This allows us to understand an individual's life story, but when looking at larger datasets, we can also begin to understand dietary change and patterns of migration for populations over long periods. For example, analysis of stable isotopes from Mesolithic cemeteries in coastal France indicated that the women represented had generally consumed less fish in the early parts of their lives than their male counterparts. One theory around why this may be the case is that women were moving to the coastal region from further inland upon marriage (Schulting and Richards 2001). Isotopic analysis of later medieval skeletons from Whithorn Cathedral Priory (Scotland) on the other hand demonstrated that high-ranking clergy and bishops consumed considerably more fish than the lay community. This can be interpreted as evidence demonstrating adherence to religious dietary restrictions and the maintenance of fast days (Müldner et al. 2009).

The formation of bones is also indicative, with diets either lacking or overly rich in essential nutrients having an impact on the formation of human skeletons and growth rates. Harris lines (thin encircling lines near the ends of arm and leg bones) can indicate periods of malnutrition during childhood (Waldron 2006). Equally, bones can be used to demonstrate signs of excessive food consumption. Analysis of skeletal remains from medieval monasteries indicate that the chubby Friar Tuck character was not without some factual basis. Arthritis in key joints suggests obesity, and a medical condition known now as DISH (diffuse idiopathic skeletal hyperostosis) triggered by overeating and a rich diet has been detected across multiple sites, pointing to a lush lifestyle and abundant food (Rogers and Waldron 2001).

Dental health also has much to reveal. Like bone formation, dental hypoplasia (pitting or grooves of the teeth) can be a sign of malnutrition (Sutton 2015, 383). Food consumption also influences the oral microbiome. Higher sugar consumption promotes the growth of bacteria, increasing the risk of cavities (Warinner et al. 2015). As with stable isotope analysis, looking at large datasets over time can help us to understand changes in diet, as well as health outcomes in populations over time. Cavity-causing mouth bacteria increased during the Neolithic period in Europe with the introduction of agriculture and increased consumption of carbohydrates. There was an even more marked increase in cavity-producing bacteria during the early modern period, when refined grains and sugar became yet more prominent (Adler et al. 2013). Wear on teeth is also significant, with grit in grain processing contributing to distinctive patterns of tooth wear while other foods lead to scratching or pitting. Dental calculus is also an extraordinary resource, trapping evidence of health issues, past meals and parasites. For example, phytoliths and starch grains were extracted from dental calculus at the Palaeolithic site Shanidar III (Iraq), indicating that Neanderthals prepared and consumed wild barley and other species over 44,000 years ago (Henry, Brooks and Piperno 1999).

The study of human faeces is equally telling. Cess pits, coprolites and the contents of preserved intestines can be analysed using a range of techniques. Faecal material can tell us about the foods being consumed, but also the underlying health of individuals. Botanical and faunal specimens of partially or undigested food can often be retrieved directly. Pollens and phytoliths can also be recovered and chemical analysis undertaken to detect proteins. Parasites can be identified, telling us about health and hygiene, as well as providing information on cooking practices, and particularly the consumption of raw or undercooked food (Sutton 2015, 375).

Residue and chemical analysis

As mentioned above, a range of scientific methods can be used to detect traces in artefacts, soils and human waste, indicating the presence of various categories of foods from the past. Residue analysis allows us to determine foodstuffs present at a site, as well as the tools and techniques used to process them. Lipids (fats, waxes and resins), along with other organic residues, can be absorbed into soils, hearths and vessels, or found on the surface of stone tools and other artefacts. Analysis of these can indicate the presence of various plant and animal products, including milk, particular species of meat and fish, alcohol and beeswax. This technique has been used on sites from diverse periods and locations. For example, lipid analysis has demonstrated that ceramic pots stored a range of foodstuffs including meat and dairy products in Indus settlements during the Mature Harappan period (c. 2600/2500 to 1900 BC). The same technique has also shown that a meal of corn and meat (likely venison) helped feed colonists facing starvation in early modern Jamestown, Virginia (Straube 2001).

Testing of soils within sites can also hint at the functions of areas and help us to understand how and where food was prepared and consumed. For example, chemical analyses of floor samples taken from the medieval site of San Genesio in Pisa, Italy, confirmed the use of the building as a tavern. There, testing aimed to detect phosphates related to organic material, fatty acids and protein residues. The concentrations of these phosphates indicated that the site was likely a tavern rather than a domestic space due to the vast quantities of food being prepared and consumed on site. Further analysis of concentrations across the site indicated the locations of kitchens, dining and storage areas (Inserra and Pacci 2011).

Artefact analysis

Artefacts themselves are of course a critical resource. The form and fabric of artefacts indicate the requirements of past peoples in food procurement, processing, cookery, storage and dining. What can the form of a stone tool tell us about whether it was used for cutting, scraping or grinding? Was a ceramic vessel used for storage, dairying, cookery or serving? Was a dish utilitarian, or was it a fashionable item used in table service? Can the shape of a bottle tell us what it once held? Looking more closely again, beyond form and fabric, the past uses of an artefact also leave traces. Patterns of use-wear, visible to the naked eye or microscope, can assist in finding answers to these questions. Does a stone tool show patterns of wear suggesting it was used to grind grain? Does a blade show chips indicative of chopping through bone? Does a dish show signs that cutlery was being regularly used? Vessels may also show characteristic signs of exposure to heat, indicating that the item was used in the process of cookery. Importantly, analysis of indicative markers may also be able to determine if its use changed over time. Retouch, repair and other varied signs show that objects could have had multiple uses simultaneously, or over their lifecycles.

Artefacts, and especially those associated with food preparation and dining, should not simply be analysed scientifically but also need to be understood culturally. What do specific forms say about cookery and dining in the past? This has been a core focus for post medievalists interrogating the shift from communal to more individualistic norms in the early modern period. Already touched on in relation to butchery practices, this shift was also characterised by a proliferation of goods in kitchens and dining rooms in the wake of incipient capitalism. There was a shift from dining in a relatively public hall where participants are seated on benches, drinking from a shared tankard and eating primarily with hands and limited cutlery from communal dishes, to a markedly different experience. A relatively short span of time sees the emergence of the private Georgian dining room, with its separate chairs, individual place settings and proliferation of highly specialised vessels and utensils, such as gravy boats, asparagus tongs and oyster forks. The identification of these artefacts not only tells us what people were eating and how, but also demonstrates a shift in the experience of the meal that is connected to wider socio-political, economic and ideological change (Johnson 1996; Leone 1999, 211; Shackel 1993).

Buildings and landscapes

Finally, it is also necessary to consider the importance of buildings and cultural landscapes in the story of food – site types that have been the key focus for the discipline since its development. While the focus of the archaeology of food can often prioritise the micro, it is critical to recognise that buildings, landscapes and settlements can also be understood through the lens of food. What does the location of an early hearth next to a river tell us about food practices in a hunter-gatherer society? What does soil sampling tell us about environmental degradation caused by clearance and farming? What can settlement patterns and field boundaries tell us about development in agriculture? How does the changing place of the hearth inside a house influence and in turn reflect changing cooking practices? How was space being used on allotments to grow vegetables and keep chickens or pigs? What does the location of markets, shops and inns tell us about food distribution in an urban centre? Archaeologists have pursued such questions across a range of sites and time periods. Among the most famous case studies is the extraordinary information yielded for Herculaneum and Pompeii, where the complexity of food distribution in these urban centres has been illustrated in detail. Bakeries with large brick ovens have been found across the cities, some of which boasted their own flour mills. Shops lining the streets have been excavated, some of which had vending counters inset with large storage jars for serving food. Restaurants have been identified, marked by the presence of built-in tables and benches (Allison 2015, 39). Collectively, these sites highlight a complex distribution network and culinary culture. While Pompeii and Herculaneum provide a level of preservation rarely encountered, by analysing sites and landscapes with a view to understanding food production and consumption, archaeologists can add people and experience back into their interpretations of the past.

What about Australia?

Despite this international interest in the study of food, to date, no major works have been published addressing the archaeology of food in Australia. Australian archaeologists have tended to focus on either site-specific analyses, or distinct categories of evidence (such as those outlined above), but they have not yet contributed substantially to the developing picture of Australia's gastronomic past. While Australian archaeologists frequently discuss components of the broader subject, such as meat consumption or table settings (see for example, Davies 2006; Gibbs 2005a; Howell Muers 2000; Lampard 2006; Lawrence 2001; Lawrence and Davies 2011, 281–306; Lawrence and Tucker 2002; Simons and Maitri 2006), comprehensive archaeological studies of Australia's culinary past drawing multiple strands together have not yet been attempted. Consequently, while historians have addressed Australian food consistently (Bannerman 1996; Bannerman 2008; Beckett 1984; Fahey 2005, 2002; Gollan 1978; Santich 2011, 2012; Singly 2012; Symons 1982), archaeologists have been somewhat silent on debates that they are well placed to contribute to. This means that while food historians have articulated one part of the culinary narrative of the nation, the archaeological picture has yet to be established. Issues of particular relevance in food history scholarship have included the degree to which colonists consumed native foodstuffs (Bannerman

2006; Blainey 2003, 206–8; Craw 2012; Fahey 2005, 88–9; Santich 2011), a subject that archaeological data should be able to contribute to as just one example of the many lines of potential inquiry. Despite early investigations of this subject at Wybalenna, for example, limited scholarship has progressed on these critical questions (Birmingham and Wilson 2010).

To begin this conversation, this book draws together a range of chapters addressing the archaeology of food in Australia – from deep time to the recent past. It showcases the many varied approaches to the study of food here, from the archaeological sciences (such as zooarchaeology and archaeobotanical analysis described above), through to historically grounded explorations of material culture and kitchens. The chapters collectively demonstrate the vast range and breadth of archaeological food research being undertaken here, and in doing so, they address critical questions about diet, cookery, dining and food culture over many millennia. As these chapters demonstrate, archaeology has the potential to answer a range of questions about food and foodways, from the most basic issues such as dietary composition and food processing, through to more complex issues relating to identity. So, archaeology can carry us from a simple understanding of what people ate, to a more nuanced understanding of what their patterns of consumption said about them as individuals, their identity, and ultimately, their worldview.

The first chapter in the volume, by Tim Owen, presents an overview of Aboriginal food cultures, continuity and change during the Holocene in south-eastern temperate Australia. While subsequent chapters look more closely at specific regions, time periods or evidential categories, this wide sweeping overview starts the book with a big-picture approach. In doing so, the extraordinary depth of Aboriginal occupation and food cultures in Australia are recognised from the outset. Owen's chapter also examines how the complex relationship between Country, climate and culture shape food and foodways, moving beyond the simple economic and technological models that have predominated in archaeological discourse to create a more nuanced understanding.

Moving from this high-level context, India Ella Dilkes-Hall, June Davis and Helen Malo then provide an overview of the role of archaeobotany in the study of food in Australia (Chapter 2). As has been outlined above internationally, information obtained from archaeobotanical assemblages contributes greatly to our understanding of diet, subsistence, resource use, environment and climate in the past. The chapter is also a critical reminder that a considerable proportion of Australian Aboriginal diets in the past stemmed from plant foods – a reality that is to some degree obscured by the relative durability and visibility of bone in the archaeological record. This chapter provides a brief overview of Australian archaeobotany before focusing on research in the Kimberley region of Western Australia, which has revealed a rich and complex record of Aboriginal plant use spanning over 47,000 years of occupation.

Staying on the theme of individual food types, Morgan Disspain, Tiina Manne and Ariana Lambrides examine the importance of fish over many millennia in Australia (Chapter 3). Beginning with evidence of fishing just to the north of Australia 42,000 years ago, and ending with data relating to early nineteenth-century colonisation, Disspain, Manne and Lambrides provide a critical overview of what the archaeological record tells us about the role of fish in Australia's past, and the methods used to analyse assemblages. As well as highlighting the historical significance of fish as food, the chapter also provides information on past native fish populations. These records provide invaluable data for conservation biologists and fisheries, highlighting the contribution of the research to wider conversations around sustainability.

On the subject of staple foods and their relation to diet and identity, Tanja Nussbaumer and Melanie Fillios examine the colonial reliance on and relationship to introduced meat species, and sheep specifically (Chapter 4). Their chapter argues that the preference for consuming mutton over more readily available native species, such as kangaroo, was a way of maintaining ties to British heritage and social identity. It also examines how the subsequent intensive sheep husbandry resulted in devastating and lasting environmental consequences – impacts intrinsically linked to colonialism. This theme of environmental destruction and the role of archaeology in examining change over time is a resonant one throughout multiple chapters, highlighting the role of the discipline in contemporary discourse around sustainable food futures.

The next series of chapters then look more closely at the connection between food and place. Kimberley Connor considers food experiences in that most iconic of Australian historical sites – the institution (Chapter 5). The chapter considers the use and abuse of food in institutions, providing an overview of the current state of research on the subject in Australia from the convict rationing system to Aboriginal missions and quarantine stations. It considers both the role of food in violence, coercion and control, as well as the power of illicit food practices in resistance. Importantly, the chapter argues that, as with other aspects of Australian culture and society, institutional experiences of food in the colonial period have had an impact on the development of food and foodways more broadly.

Gordon Grimwade's chapter then examines the importance of roast pork for Chinese diaspora communities in the nineteenth century and the role that it played in maintaining culture and connections (Chapter 6). Looking at purpose-built ovens from sites across Australia and New Zealand, Grimwade explains the process of roasting entire pigs to perfection over several hours, drawing on archaeological evidence, as well as observations from contemporary practice. Importantly, the chapter moves beyond a geographical and morphological overview and considers what their distribution tells us about the wider community at the time and cross-cultural shared culinary experiences. Grimwade's chapter provides not just a critical contribution highlighting the diversity of Australia's community in the nineteenth century, but it also demonstrates the multiple approaches to the archaeological study of ethnicities in Australia. While urban historical archaeology has primarily focused on assemblage analysis from stratified deposits, and thus struggled to pursue the study of ethnicity consistently, Grimwade's chapter demonstrates that a landscape approach and wider scale can provide alternative pathways for representing diversity in Australia's past.

Following the theme of place and experiences of cooking, Jacqui Newling provides a critical overview of historic kitchens, detailing how ovens, appliances and techniques changed over time (Chapter 7). In addition to expanding our understanding of Australian kitchens and experiences of food preparation, the chapter provides a context for archaeologists that will help to make meaning of historic assemblages. Understanding the experiences, challenges and material culture of kitchens should provide context for assemblage analysis. The chapter approaches the kitchen itself as an assemblage, with an aim to provide an understanding of cooking facilities and culinary material culture in domestic settings, as well as a detailed discussion of how they were used. Like Grimwade's chapter, it also encourages archaeologists to think more broadly about the boundaries of our datasets and discipline, and to situate our assemblages within place more meaningfully – be it the pig roasting oven of a goldfield or the open hearth of a historic house.

Picking up the theme of objects in the kitchen, E. Jeanne Harris, Bronwyn Woff and Peter O'Donohue provide a detailed review of the historic bottles regularly found on Australian historic sites (Chapter 8). In doing so, they explain the history and importance of food preservation technologies in the colonial period. The only focused study of an artefact type in the volume, this chapter demonstrates the importance of close and deep consideration of artefacts commonly found on sites and provides a framework that will assist archaeologists in assessing the significance and meaning of assemblages and the range of questions they can and should be asking.

This series of eight food stories from Australia's past have been selected to help open the door to so many more and to so many questions. The great depth of time and diversity in Australian archaeology, when coupled with the broad range of skills in the discipline, present unbridled potential for further research. A key aim of this volume is to create an opportunity for consulting and university-based researchers to come together to showcase this potential and to encourage more work along this line of inquiry. These thematic discussions provide a means and mechanism for the discipline to enter the public discourse more actively, contributing to questions of place, identity, postcoloniality, health and sustainability.

References

Adler, C.J., K. Dobney, L.S. Weyrich, J. Kaidonis, A.W. Walker, W. Haak et al. (2013). Sequencing ancient calcified dental plaque shows changes in oral microbiota with dietary shifts of the Neolithic and Industrial revolutions. *Nature Genetics* 45: 450–5.

Bannerman, C. (2011). Making Australian food. *History Australian Humanities Review* 51: 49–63.

Bannerman, C. (2008). *Seed cake and honey prawns: fashion and fad in Australian food*. Canberra: National Library of Australia.

Bannerman, C. (2006). Indigenous food and cookery books: redefining Aboriginal cuisine. *Journal of Australian Studies* 30(87): 19–36.

Bannerman, C. (1996). *A friend in the kitchen: old Australian cookery books*. Sydney: Kangaroo Press.

Beckett, R. (1984). *Convicted tastes: food in Australia*. Sydney: George Allen & Unwin.

Birmingham, J. and A. Wilson (2010). Archaeologies of cultural interaction: Wybalenna Settlement and Killalpaninna Mission. *International Journal of Historical Archaeology* 4(1): 15–38.

Blainey, G. (2003). *Black kettle full moon: daily life in a vanished Australia*. Melbourne: Viking.

Craw, C. (2012). Gustatory redemption? Colonial appetites, historical tales and the contemporary consumption of Australian native foods. *International Journal of Critical Indigenous Studies* 5(2): 13–24.

Davies, P. (2006). Mapping commodities at Casselden Place, Melbourne. *International Journal of Historical Archaeology* 10(4): 343–55.

Deetz, J. (1996 [1977]). *In small things forgotten: an archaeology of early American life*. New York: Anchor Press.

Fahey, W. (2005). *Tucker track: the curious history of food in Australia*. Sydney: ABC Books.

Fahey, W. (2002). *When Mabel laid the table: the folklore of eating and drinking in Australia*. Sydney: State Library of NSW Press.

Fisher, J.W. (1995). Bone surface modifications in zooarchaeology. *Journal of Archaeological Method and Theory* 2(1): 7–68.

Gibbs, M. (2005). The archaeology of subsistence on the maritime frontier: faunal analysis of the Cheyne Beach Whaling Station 1845–1877. *Australasian Historical Archaeology* 23: 115–22.

Gollan, A. (1978). *The tradition of Australian cooking*. Canberra: Australian National University Press.

Goren-Inbar, N., G. Sharon, Y. Melamed and M. Kislev (2002). Nuts, nut-cracking, and pitted stones at Gesher Benot Ya'aqov. *Proceedings of the National Academy of Sciences USA* 99(4): 2455–60.

Gostner, P., P. Pernter, G. Bonatti, A. Graefen and A.R. Zink (2011). New radiological insights into the life and death of the Tyrolean Iceman. *Journal of Archaeological Science* 38(12): 3425–31.

Henry, A.G., A.S. Brooks and D.R. Piperno (2011). Microfossils in calculus demonstrate consumption of plants and cooked food in Neanderthal diets (Shandir III, Iraq; Spy I and II, Belgium). *Proceedings of the National Academy of Sciences USA* 108(2): 486–91.

Howell Meurs, S. (2000). Nineteenth century diet in Victoria: the faunal remains from Viewbank. *Australasian Historical Archaeology* 18: 39–46.

Hage, G. (1998). *White nation: fantasies of White supremacy in a multicultural society*. Sydney: Pluto Press.

Hage, G. (1997). At home in the entrails of the west: multiculturalism, ethnic food and migrant home-building. In H. Grace, G. Hage, L. Johnson, J. Langsworth and M. Symonds, eds. *Home/world: space, community and marginality in Sydney's west*, 99–153. Sydney: Pluto Press.

Hansen, J.M. (1991). *The paleoethnobotany of Franchthi Cave: excavations at Franchthi Cave, Greece, Fascicle 7*. Bloomington: Indiana University Press.

Hastorf, C. (2018). *The social archaeology of food: thinking about eating from prehistory to the present*. New York: Cambridge University Press.

Inserra, F. and A. Pecci (2011). Chemical analyses of floors at San Genesio (San Miniato, Pisa): a medieval tavern. In Isabella Turbanti-Memmi, ed. *Proceedings of the 37th International Symposium on Archaeometry, Siena, Italy*, 459–64. Berlin: Springer.

Johnson, M. (1996). *The archaeology of capitalism*. Oxford: Blackwell.

Kelso, G.K., K. Bescherer Metheny and M.C. Beaudry (2015). Palynology. In K.B. Metheny and M.C. Beaudry, eds. *Archaeology of food: an encyclopedia, vol. 2*. Lanham: Rowman & Littlefield.

Lampard, S. (2006). Approaches to faunal analysis: a Port Adelaide comparative case study. *The Artefact* 29: 22–33.

Lawrence, S. (2001). Foodways on two colonial whaling stations: archaeological and historical evidence for diet in nineteenth-century Tasmania. *Journal of the Royal Australian Historical Society* 87(2): 209–29.

Lawrence, S. and P. Davies (2011). *An archaeology of Australia since 1788*. New York: Springer.

Lawrence, S. and C. Tucker (2002). Sources of meat in colonial diets: faunal evidence from two nineteenth century whaling stations. *Environmental Archaeology* 7: 23–34.

Leone, M.P. (1999). Ceramics from Annapolis, Maryland: a measure of time routines and work discipline. In M.P. Leone and P.B. Potter Jr., eds. *Historical archaeologies of capitalism,* 195–216. New York: Kluwer Academic and Plenum Publishers.

Metheny, K.B. and M.C. Beaudry, eds (2016). *Archaeology of food: an encyclopedia (2 vols)*. Lanham: Rowman & Littlefield.

Müldner, G., J. Montgomery, G. Cook, R. Ellam, A. Gledhill and C. Lowe (2009). Isotopes and individuals: diet and mobility among the medieval bishops of Whithorn. *Antiquity* 83: 1–15.

Nielsen, N.H., P.S. Henriksen, M.F. Mortensen, R. Enevold, M.N. Mortensen, C. Scavenius and J.J. Enghild (2021). The last meal of Tollund Man: new analyses of his gut content. *Antiquity* 95(383): 1195–212.

Pascoe, B. (2018). *Dark emu: Aboriginal Australia and the birth of agriculture*. Broome: Magabala Books.

Rogers, J. and T. Waldron (2001). DISH and the monastic way of life. *International Journal of Osteoarchaeology* 11: 357–65. DOI: 10.1002/oa.574.

Suryanarayan, A., M. Cubas, O.E. Craig, C.P. Heron, V.S. Shinde, R.N. Singh et al. (2021). Lipid residues in pottery from the Indus Civilisation in northwest India. *Journal of Archaeological Science* 125: 1–16.

Sutton, M.Q. (2015). Paleonutrition. In K.B. Metheny and M.C. Beaudry, eds. *Archaeology of food: an encyclopedia*. Lanham: Rowman & Littlefield.

Shackel, P.A. (1993). *Personal discipline and material culture: An archaeology of Annapolis, Maryland, 1685–1870*. Knoxville: University of Tennessee Press.

Straube, B.A. (2001). But their victuals are their chiefest riches. In W.M. Kelso, J.E. Deetz, S.W. Mallios, and B.A. Straube, eds. *Jamestown rediscovery VIII 35–52*. Richmond, VA: Association for the Preservation of Virginia Antiques.

Schulting, R.J. and M.P. Richards (2001). Dating women and becoming farmers: new Paleo dietary and AMS dating evidence from Breton Mesolithic Cemeteries of Téviec and Hoëdic. *Journal of Anthropological Archaeology* 20(3): 314–44.

Santich, B. (2012). *Bold palates: Australia's gastronomic heritage.* Kent Town: Wakefield Press.

Santich, B. (2011). Nineteenth-century experimentation and the role of Indigenous foods in Australian food culture. *Australian Humanities Review* 51: 65–78.

Simons, A. and M. Maitri (2006). The food remains from Casselden Place, Melbourne, Australia. *International Journal of Historical Archaeology* 10(4): 357–74.

Singley, B. (2012). Hardly anything fit for man to eat: food and colonialism in Australia. *History Australia* 9(3): 27–42.

Symons, M. (1982). *One continuous picnic: A history of eating in Australia.* Adelaide: Duck Press.

Scarry, M., D. Hutchinson and B. Arbuckle, eds (2023). *Ancient foodways: integrative approaches to understanding subsistence and society,* 1st edn. Gainesville, FL: University Press of Florida.

Twiss, K.C. (2019). *The archaeology of food: identity, politics and ideology in the Prehistoric and Historic past.* Cambridge: Cambridge University Press.

Twiss, K.C. (2007). We are what we eat. In K. C. Twiss, ed. *The archaeology of food and identity,* 1–15. Southern Illinois University: Center for Archaeological Investigation.

Van Reyk, P. (2021). *True to the land.* London: Reaktion Books.

Waldron, T. (2006). Nutrition and the skeleton. In C. Woolgar, D. Serjeantson and T. Waldron, eds. *Food in Medieval England: history and archaeology,* 254–66. Oxbow: Oxford University Press.

Warinner, C., C. Speller, M.J. Collins and C. M. Lewis Jr (2015). Ancient human microbiomes. *Journal of Human Evolution* 79: 125–136.

Zohary, D., M. Hopf and E. Weiss (2012). *Domestication of Plants in the Old World.* 4th edition. Oxbow: Oxford University Press.

1

Aboriginal traditions of food
Investigating Holocene dietary changes in southern Australia

Tim Owen

Introduction

Australian Aboriginal culture is underpinned by long-term traditions connected with food – from procurement, to processing, consumption and eventual disposal. Food as an essential item could be seen as an output of the local environment, where any and all foodstuffs that can be sourced by an Aboriginal group comprise the basis of a "local" diet. Throughout this chapter, I consider that diet represents the long-term aggregate of food consumed over the course of decades, thereby accounting for the yearly cycle of food availability as the seasons changed, or shorter-term climatic effects (such as drought), which could have temporarily altered the availability of foodstuff. Diet should not be seen as static, but rather intrinsically connected and responsive to patterns that impact politics, culture and economy more broadly. Importantly, the complexities and subtleties surrounding any Aboriginal food system cannot be described by a simple framework listing the range of foods available within an ecosystem. Rather, continued cultural practices and social and oral knowledge, handed down through generations, combined with anthropological and archaeological investigations, allows insight into the complexities of the long-term food systems.

Australia as a continent has changed substantially over the course of human occupation. Global climatic change through the late and Terminal Pleistocene (40,000 years ago [ka] to around 9 ka) culminated in a major reduction in the land mass available for habitation (Williams et al. 2018). These changes continued to a lesser, but still significant degree through the Holocene (9 ka to present). From an ecological perspective, a changing climate affects three fundamentals which underpin the bioavailability of foods: rainfall, temperature and soil. Changes in the Holocene climatic patterns are generally described in three ways, with alterations in sea level (relative to our level today), temperature (which is described as warmer or colder than today) and rainfall (described as wetter or drier than today). These changes affected the environment and frequently caused geomorphological changes to soils and sediments resulting in changes to landforms. Continuous aeolian (wind), alluvial and fluvial (water) and colluvial (gravitational) processes moved, shifted, eroded and deposited soils, sands and sediments, altering soil landscapes and landforms, and thus the ecological communities that grew.

Concurrent with the environmental changes, throughout the Holocene Aboriginal demography, society and economies also changed (Lourandos 1997). Demography altered, with increasing population levels over the Holocene culminating in greater densities in the late Holocene (Williams 2013). Archaeological patterns (evident through materials such as lithics) suggest these changes had local and regional influences on human movements, use of Country, and trade mechanisms associated with goods and materials (White 2018). Through the late Holocene, Aboriginal societies exhibited increasing levels of complexity associated with aspects such as defined territorial boundaries (and the ability to move across these boundaries), locations used for habitation, spirituality, law, lore, belief, ritual, trade, descent and hereditary systems (Attenbrow 2006). Some of these changes can be identified through the study of material culture, such as stone artefacts (Hiscock and Attenbrow 2005; White 2017) or refuse from food consumption (e.g. middens comprising shell and animal bone) (Brockwell et al. 2017).

Some of these changes may be described within frameworks of "intensification". Substantial debate into what intensification means for hunter-gathers often cites "increased productivity" or "increased economic output" becoming intertwined with any form of specialisation, diversification and innovation. Alternative models examine "labor investment [that] drives the engine of economic output, but that this comes at a cost of declining efficiency" (Morgan 2015, 198).

Within the southern Australian context, this chapter seeks to identify and examine some systems of late Holocene specialisation, diversification and innovation, and determine how alteration to food systems culminated in the diets consumed by Aboriginal men, women and children. Addressing these aspects should present further insight into the intensification debate, and notably the Australia hunter-gather/farmer debate (e.g. Morgan 2015; Sutton and Walsh 2021).

The range of foodstuff

Many aspects of Aboriginal peoples' traditions, practices, society and economy are connected to their cultural landscapes, which in turn become imbued with meaning, law, lore, spirituality and practice. Food and foodways fall within this complex system, and therefore can be regulated in terms of access, processing, consumption and disposal.

Holocene period south-eastern Australia can be described as temperate, with a diverse array of waterways, flood plains, lagoons, swamps, plains, mountains and the ancient coastline formed during the Terminal Pleistocene. This landscape is rich with a diversity of ecologies, providing an extensive range of foodstuffs from both the land and water. It is generally thought that Aboriginal populations flourished throughout the Holocene, with a growth in population density underpinned by a dynamic system of understanding passed through intergenerational equity (e.g. Attenbrow 2010a; Morgan 2015). The ecosystem had sufficient long-term viability that allowed Aboriginal peoples to practice modes of subsistence where preferred foods could be consumed on a cyclical basis applying the minimum of labour expenditure. This is the opposite system from traditional agrarian systems practised elsewhere, where extensive labour had to be invested to obtain marginal increases in land productivity.

Generally, only limited information on food and foodways is included in literature on Aboriginal cultural heritage. Where information is included, details provided are frequently non-specific, without attention to regional variability, or consideration that diet could be influenced intra group by age, gender and/or individual group norms, customs, traditions or power dynamics. Discussion in texts can outline that Aboriginal groups consumed food staples such as "grain", "yams" or "tubers", but provide little detail on the mechanics or traditions connected with the social economies of the foodstuffs (e.g. Pascoe 2014, 19–50).

When examining the range of foodstuff within any territory, the breadth and variety of foods available for consumption means that classification of specific food staples is difficult. For instance, plant foods alone need to be considered under broad categories of fruits, seeds, exudates (e.g. nectar and gum), "greens" and everything growing underground (yams, tubers, rhizomes, bulbs and roots). Historical texts understate the sheer breadth and variety of foodstuffs available as part of Aboriginal traditional diets, which could originate from the colonial or European misunderstanding of Australia and its ecological systems. Many early (non-Aboriginal) accounts include only highly simplistic descriptions of Aboriginal food systems. For example, Watkin Tench (1789) provides one of the earliest accounts of the food practices of Aboriginal peoples local to Sydney. On foods consumed, he focuses on fishing, describing the fishing materials and methods and even the gender roles. While fish undoubtedly played a key role in the diet of coastal Dharug people, his observations insinuate an over reliance that in turn masks the resilience and adaptability of the Cadigal people of Sydney:

> When prevented by tempestuous weather or any other cause, from fishing, these people suffer severely. They have then no resource but to pick up shellfish, which may happen to cling to the rocks and be cast on the beach, to hunt particular reptiles and small animals, which are scarce, to dig fern root in the swamps or to gather a few berries, destitute of flavour and nutrition, which the woods afford (Tench 1789, 260).

Written only three years after invasion, the unseen effects wrought by British land use practices impacted the traditional food bank around Sydney Harbour, likely played out through Tench's observations. Many similar and often quoted accounts abound, serving only to diminish knowledge on the range and breadth of foodstuffs consumed. However, detailed anthologies such as Val Attenbrow's (2010) *Sydney's Aboriginal Past* contain a breadth of traditional knowledge on food and plant use, and systems of procurement, connected to processing methods. Some detailed works and compilations delve deep into procurement, processing, consumption and disposal. For instance, Berndt and Berndt's (1993) compendium, *A World That Was,* contains very detailed accounts of food and food systems for the Yalradi on the Murray River, at Murray Bridge (South Australia). Works such as Philip Clarke's (2012) *Australian Plants as Aboriginal Tools* provide an understanding of Aboriginal food systems from a botanical basis, with consideration of ecological communities, species lists, and a connection to edible and/or medicinal plants. An investigation into *Aboriginal Biocultural Knowledge in South-Eastern Australia* by Cahir and colleagues (2018) describes the knowledge of Aboriginal peoples, languages and cultures within their environments, with sections on water, plant and animal food, and presents food systems within a full sphere of cultural tradition.

Some works compile extensive food lists, including fauna, flora, fish and shellfish – these can be used to commence further investigations into local Aboriginal diets. Lists of foods represent baselines from which any associated traditions and complexity inherent within the food systems can be investigated. Food lists are generally static, reflective of a single time period; although archaeological consideration may be able to assist in describing changes through time. For instance, stratigraphical investigations of shell midden species composition can demonstrate a change in species present, which may be indicative of changing ecological conditions (e.g. the shellfish habitat of sand flats changing to mangroves). This type of contextualisation is regularly undertaken for technical objects such as lithics like the Eastern Regional Sequence (Hiscock and Attenbrow 2005) but rarely considered for food systems. Consideration of changes and alterations through time are important because Aboriginal economies, demographies and societies were/are not static, rather everchanging, unfixed and fluid.

Terminology and debate

A perennial discussion on the terminology associated with Aboriginal food systems exists within archaeology, anthropology, history and biological disciplines. The debate focuses on notions of "hunting", "gathering", "farming", "agriculture" and "agrarian development", where the terms used and applied have been associated with systems of social and civil "advancement" or a type of social hierarchy, suggesting that categorisation under one group is somehow better than another (Australian Archaeology 2021; Pascoe 2014; Sutton and Walsh 2021).

Whilst not the intent of this chapter to delve into the etymology of these terms or their implied usage, two key matters are apparent. Firstly, the terms are constructs from northern hemisphere systems of food procurement and production. Within this debate there appear to be few terms applicable to Australian First Nations peoples because the food systems across the continent and over many millennia are not directly comparable. For example, south-eastern Australia late Holocene systems cannot be compared to pre–Last Glacial Maximum (LGM) Pleistocene systems in northern Australia. Given this diversity within Australia, it is even more problematic to compare food systems here with those of Asia and Europe. Rather than seeking inappropriate geographic, cultural and temporal comparisons with European models of land tenure and farming, more focus should be given to understanding the unique and varied nature of Aboriginal practices and economies, and significantly, how these changed over time.

Secondly, the terms and terminology have focused on Aboriginal traditions connected with food procurement, and some modes of processing. The debate thus far has directed little thought or discussion towards food consumption or food discard, with all its inherent and nuanced complexities. Without considering the whole food system (from procurement through to discard), terminological discussions on Aboriginal methods of procurement appear incomplete.

These terms should be considered an impediment to recognising the complexity of Aboriginal food systems. Academic debate has started to move beyond the restrictive terminology with the adoption of the term "Aboriginal Biocultural Knowledge", which is being used to "encourage cross-cultural awareness and to solve communication problems between Indigenous people and the broad group of researchers and public servants who are involved in land management" (Cahir et al. 2018, xix).

Holocene food systems

Broad regional investigations into long-term Holocene food systems can be undertaken through various archaeological methods. One technique is the physical investigation of archaeological sites and resources within a place or site. For instance, earth mounds ("habitation" locations comprising raised platforms of soil and organic material, often located in flood prone areas) provide a means for investigating adaptation to environmental and demographic change, and the connected Aboriginal social and economic responses to that change (Brockwell et al. 2017; Ó Foghlú 2021). An investigation into the composition of mounds can include the detail about the methods of food processing and cooking (including analysis of hearths and their carbon, ground ovens and clay cooking balls) and food disposal (through identification of bones, shell, seeds, pollen and spores) (Littleton et al. 2013; Westell and Wood 2014).

These modes of archaeological investigation are an indirect assessment of past diet – an examination of what is left behind, or what remains once foods have been processed, cooked and consumed. The analysis provides an understanding of the types (species) of foods consumed but does not examine complete or long-term diet. The outcomes present a snapshot of consumption, at a single point in time or place in the temporal and cultural landscape, not specifics on the proportions of vegetables, meats and seafood consumed. The analysis misses insight on gender or age preferences, inference on rules and traditions, and whether diet has changed over time. Bioarchaeological analysis involving an assessment of stable isotopes held in the organic and inorganic portions of bone may provide the basis for such interpretation. Isotope studies can be powerful with multifunctional analysis of the organic and inorganic portions of bone and tooth dentine and enamel, providing insight into not just diet, but also human migration between regions and countries (e.g. Adams et al. 2022).

For the purposes of this chapter, we will focus on the stable isotopes of carbon and nitrogen, held within the organic portion of bone collagen. All foodstuffs consumed contain stable isotopes of carbon and nitrogen. The ratio of carbon (C12 against C13) or nitrogen (N14 against N15) stable isotopes within a plant, fish, animal or shellfish species are constrained for that species by its specific habitat. Plants hold isotope values related to their photosynthetic pathway (C3 or C4), and/or the aridity of an area. Animals, fish and shellfish have enriched carbon and/or nitrogen according to their position within the food chain (their tropic levels), so that carnivores are enriched (more positive isotope values) compared to herbivores. If we analyse the stable isotopes of both carbon and nitrogen from a single species and present this data as a bi-variate plot, we can observe species-specific inter-regional patterning; for instance, kangaroos' nitrogen values become more positive in relation to increasing aridity (Anson 1997). A baseline dataset for an environmental provenance can thus be established by analysing a range of plant and/or animal species within the whole food web (herbivores, omnivores and carnivores).

The modern-day food web of South Australia's southern bioregions has been isotopically characterised, and the geographic distributions of species have been related to climatic zones (Owen 2004; Owen and Pate 2014). An analysis of the pollen record from wetlands and stable isotopes from kangaroo bones excavated from stratified rock shelters (Roberts et al. 1999) has shown that over the last 5,000 years, South Australia's long-term climate was relatively stable. With this understanding, the baseline dataset (the bioregion's characterisation) can be used to interpret stable isotopes retained in human bone collagen. For humans, the stable carbon and nitrogen isotope ratios reflect the food protein groups consumed over approximately a 10-year period. For instance, a long-term vegetarian would present distinct isotope values contrasted against a person who primarily ate seafood. Investigations into long-term diet have been undertaken for both South Australian Aboriginal (Owen 2004; Owen and Pate 2014; Pate and Owen 2014) and non-Aboriginal diets (Pate and Anson 2012), and patterns of migration (Adams et al. 2022; Pate et al. 2002).

In South Australia, collaborative research between Aboriginal groups (broad regions for these groups is shown in Figure 1.1), including the Kaurna People (the Traditional Owners of the Adelaide Plains) and the Ngarrindjeri Nation (the Traditional Owners of the western end of the Murray, eastern Fleurieu Peninsula, and the Coorong), has provided insight into long-term connections between Country and each Aboriginal group's ancient food system(s). The work was undertaken with the permission of the Aboriginal Traditional Owners, and involved analysis of ancestral remains that were either curated in a museum or were unintentionally disturbed through excavation works. Multiple individuals from each community group have been assessed for carbon and nitrogen stable isotopes (Table 1.1). The results are as distinct as each community – the diet consumed by each group reflected their Country and their bioregion (Owen and Pate 2014; Pate et al. 2002; Pate and Owen 2014). The distribution of groups as reflected by their diets is shown in Figure 1.2, and can be described thus:

- Coastal groups from the southern parts of South Australia ate large quantities of marine foods, to the extent that it formed the majority (>80 per cent) of their diet. These include peoples living on the Coorong.
- A very similar high percentage marine food diet was eaten by coastal peoples from the mid-north and Yorke Peninsula.

Figure 1.1 Approximate locations of South Australian Aboriginal groups investigated for stable isotopes. Source: Owen and Pate 2014, Figure 1.

- Peoples living in a coastal setting at the Murray River's mouth ate a diet with around 30 per cent seafood and 30 per cent meat, with the remaining 40 per cent terrestrial plant-based foods.
- Across the Adelaide region, there is a difference between diets north to south. The peoples in the south had a very similar diet to those at the Murray River's mouth, which has a similar environment and resources. However, peoples living on the plains in north Adelaide moved inland away from the coast during winter, meaning they ate less seafood, replacing this food with terrestrial meat.

Table 1.1 Summary of human bone collagen stable carbon and nitrogen isotope results from archaeological sites in the lower Murray River valley and Adelaide Plains (after Owen and Pate 2014, Table 1).

Environment	Site/Location	Rainfall (mm)	n	δ13C (‰) X ± SD	Range	δ15N (‰) X ± SD	Range
Coastal Marine	Coorong	500	27	-11.7 ± 1.2	-13.2, -9.6	14.7 ± 2.6	11.2, 22.2
	Salt Creek Coorong	500	3	-12.3 ± 0.8	-13.2, -11.8	14.6 ± 2.0	13.3, 16.9
Coastal River Mouth	Murray Mouth Lake Alexandrina	400	11	-16.1 ± 1.3	-17.9, -14.4	12.5 ± 0.9	11.0, 13.7
	Narrung	469	1	-16.4		11.2	
Inland Riverine	Swanport	346	110	-20.0 ± 0.8	-21.6, -18.1	10.1 ± 1.1	6.6, 12.3
	Roonka Flat	263	32	-20.1 ± 1.2	-22.9, -18.4	13.4 ± 1.2	10.9, 16.0
	Blanchetown Bridge	263	7	-19.1 ± 0.7	-20.4, -18.3	11.2 ± 0.3	10.9, 11.7
	Swan Reach	272	2	-19.7	-20.4, -19.0	11.8	11.2, 12.3
Coastal Plain	Salisbury	475	1	-18.6		7.4	
	Historical European St Marys cemetery	475	20	-18.6 ± 0.8	-20.1, -17.3	12 ± 1.1	9.8, 13.7
	Hypothetical Adelaide Mound Diet			-18.9		10.9	

- Inland on the Murray, away from the coast, but not within the arid interior, the Aboriginal populations had a high dependence on foods from the riverine system. Around 50 per cent of their food originated from the river, or species that lived on the waters of the river, 20–35 per cent was terrestrial meat, and the total diet included 50 per cent plant-based foods (Owen 2004, Table 6-14, 266).
- Groups living inland in semi-arid areas, but near the Murray River, also had a greater dependency on foods from the riverine system, up to 70 per cent derived from the water catchment, with less terrestrial plant-based food being consumed.
- Finally, pre-colonial Aboriginal diets differed from the historical non-Aboriginal early (post 1836) population of Adelaide. The non-Aboriginal population consumed a diet of 60 per cent meat (e.g. beef or mutton), 32 per cent seafood and 8 per cent terrestrial vegetation (e.g. wheat and barley) (Adams et al. 2022, 4).

The studies have also identified individuals within an Aboriginal group who do not "fit" the broader diet of their group. Within one of the semi-arid Murray River groups there were 11 individuals (four female, seven male) who ate a diet comparable to the coastal Coorong region but had been buried inland (Owen 2004). The antiquity of these individuals (two were subject to radiocarbon dating) was the last 1,000 years. The reason for their burial away from the Coorong is not currently understood based on available evidence but could be connected with visiting the inland area for a social activity such as trade or ceremony.

A second example was the burial of a Kaurna "medicine man" or "sorcerer". This individual consumed a distinct diet based on terrestrial foods, with an absence of marine protein (refer to Figure 1.2, "Adelaide Plain – special individual"). The location, mode and stratigraphic context of the burial, coupled with the stable isotope results, suggest this individual had a different diet to other Kaurna men, which was confirmed through knowledge held by Traditional Owners (Owen and Pate 2014).

The studies show that regional diets reflect bioregional food availability. This understanding is important because it describes a system from the mid to the late Holocene where both territories and diets were relatively fixed. Successive generations of each cultural group remained within the same bioregion, reinforcing and continuing their connection to a specific area. Individuals did not move sufficient distances for their long-term diets to become a blend of resources from multiple bioregions – they practised a form of semi-sedentism. Within their bioregion each successive generation continued to consume the same food resources as their ancestors.

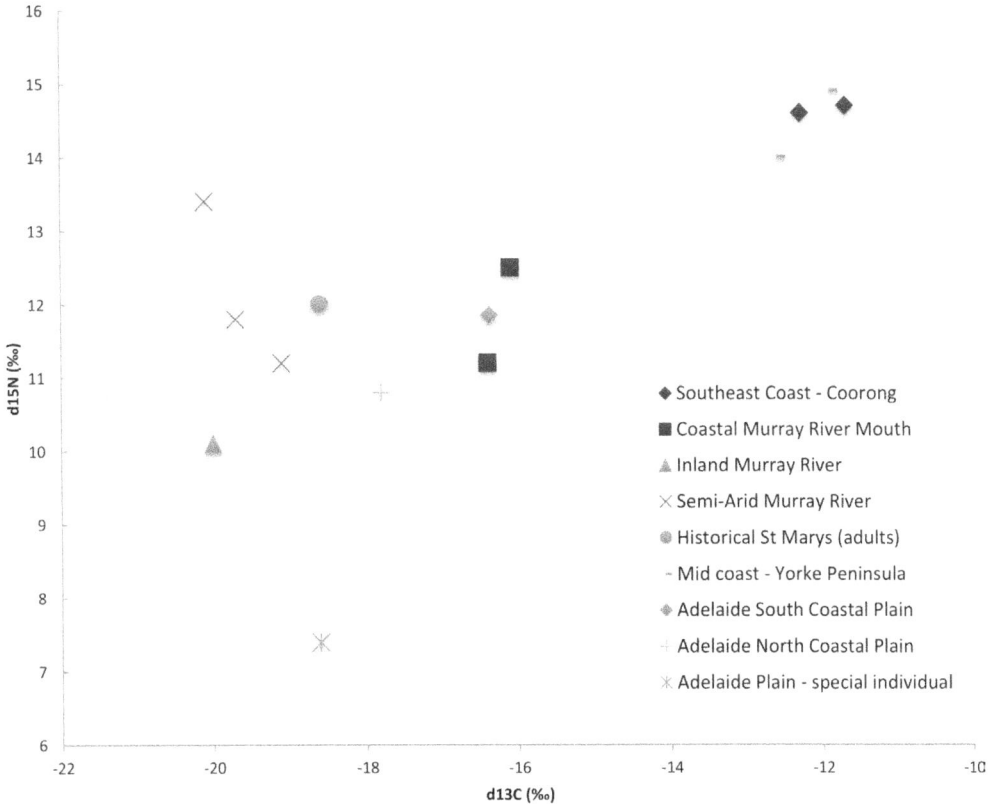

Figure 1.2 Long-term dietary differences in South Australian Aboriginal groups (and a non-Aboriginal group), expressed through the stable isotopes of nitrogen and carbon.

However, we know that as the Holocene progressed, social complexity increased, as did demographic pressures. This means that in the late Holocene (the last 2,000 years) greater numbers of peoples were living within a smaller area but still needing and seeking the same food resources. For food systems, this means an increase in economic output and/or to seek alternative food sources. Alternative foods could have lower energy values and require greater search and processing time. We understand from the stable isotope studies that Aboriginal groups did not alter the proportions of food proteins consumed, meaning that people continued to eat the same foods. We also understand from the complexity of Aboriginal societies that procurement of foodstuffs was not the defining characteristic of Aboriginal societies; Aboriginal peoples did not undertake "agricultural" activities that required the majority of their time and energy (unlike agrarian systems).

This means that the economic output and management of food sources must have changed, evolved and become more complex in the late Holocene. New or changed technologies must have been implemented to obtain higher energy dense foods in greater quantities. Social systems must have evolved to define how food sources were treated and accessed. The remainder of this chapter examines these systems and changes through the four stages of the food cycle: procurement, processing, consumption and disposal.

The economy of food

Foodstuffs hold many levels of importance, from basic metabolic purpose, through to complex symbolic and ritual function. Recent academic debate has focused on the degree of agrarian capability that Aboriginal peoples may have held (refer to the terminology and debate section above and the forum in Australian Archaeology 2021; Pascoe 2014; Sutton and Walsh 2021). This debate focuses on Aboriginal societies around the point of colonial invasion (post 1788), and is generally absent of substance related to long-term changes through time (temporality), regionality (in that different groups had distinct diets, as described above), and does not delve into complexities associated with Aboriginal food economies (as will be consequentially described).

Outside of the terminological discourse, with reference to this topic, it can be stated that later Holocene changes within Aboriginal social and economic systems allowed the development of complex food extraction methods (e.g. Burrawang (*Macrozamia*) extraction), new technologies and methods for food procurement (e.g. Asmussen 2010; Attenbrow 2010, 76– and underpinned a *form* of intensification that provided the basis for new subsistence strategies such as habitation on mound sites in wetland and flood prone areas (Coutts et al. 1979; Westell and Wood 2014). However, the outcomes from the stable isotope studies show that over the last 4,000 years, the baseline composition of Aboriginal diets in southern South Australia did not vary – that is, Aboriginal peoples continued eating the same foodstuffs, in approximately the same baseline protein proportions. Through the mid to late Holocene, significant changes to the environment and Aboriginal societies did occur. Agents that influenced change included climate alterations (precipitation and temperature) and changes to landmasses, vegetation communities and shorelines.

The "farming" debate, along with several academic projects, have identified patterning within Holocene Aboriginal subsistence strategies. The stable isotope investigations identify that the changing strategies relied on a consistent and stable source of food – groups did not switch from consuming marine to land-based protein. The identification of changed subsistence strategies, which maintain the same food consumption pattern, is an important distinction. It means that Aboriginal peoples needed to alter aspects of their food procurement strategies. This could include the commencement of practices that led to improvements in wild food yields, management of land areas, and soils, so that foods would consistently be

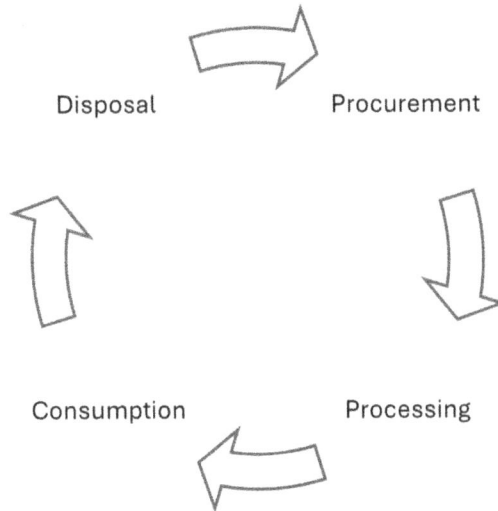

Figure 1.3 The Aboriginal food system with four interconnected aspects. Each aspect changes over time and by social group.

(seasonally) available (Cahir et al. 2018, 59). Methods for obtaining large quantities of a foodstuff were developed, along with techniques for food preservation, storage and accumulation of food surpluses (Berndt and Berndt 1974, 46, 1993, 74–96).

In itself, the retention of food surpluses allows for the development of social systems with large gatherings of people. Non-Aboriginal accounts (following invasion) record many lengthy gatherings with up to 2,000 Aboriginal peoples. Food can be seen to support the social and spiritual aspects of life, which often took precedence over the food system. For many Aboriginal peoples, it was often not the *primary* factor underpinning the system of economy, it was subservient to other facets of life. It can be viewed as both essential and non-essential; essential in that one must eat to survive, but non-essential in that sufficient food could be quickly obtained within most environments. Maintaining these systems therefore required complex (group-specific) frameworks that function on several levels. There needed to be systems and law which prevented over-exploitation, created understanding of yearly food cycles and availability, connected peoples to their Country, and facilitated the long-term intensification of food economies.

The economy surrounding Aboriginal food systems can be described in four parts: procurement, processing, consumption and disposal (Figure 1.3). Each of these parts may hold significant complexity, underpinned by a variety of local traditions and the regional environments. These systems changed and evolved over time; therefore, when describing any part of the food system, consideration to a temporal framework must be given. The remainder of this section will examine the four parts, outlining some of the complexities.

Procurement

The initial part in the food system is procurement, or the systems, mechanisms, methods, rules, laws and considerations which underpin obtaining food prior to its processing and consumption. Systems connected with procuring (obtaining) food were complex and varied from clan to clan. The rights to access food, strategies engaged to obtain food, methods and techniques of food collection (separate to processing, which is the next stage in the food system), and technologies associated with food procurement all evolved and changed through time.

Within hierarchical Aboriginal societies, access to food could vary by social position, and food restrictions were often linked with totems and/or periods of initiation. Totems could be associated with creation mythology, where animals, etc., came about as a consequence of land formation, events or division of other larger animals. At birth, many Aboriginal peoples are connected to or assigned a totem, which was frequently intertwined with social systems such as hereditary rights or future marriage systems. Totems are frequently land fauna (from kangaroos to lizards), birds (such as eagles) or sea creatures (from fish to turtles), attributed with special powers for the person given the totem. Most societies had restrictions on hunting or eating totems, resulting in a special and symbolic relationship (refer to comments in Berndt and Berndt 1993; Clarke 2012).

Outside the totemic system, there were also social, gender and age restrictions on certain foods, such as the descriptions of the Ngarrindjeri people (South Australia) by Berndt and Berndt (1993, 122–30). For instance, in some groups following initiation (novice) males had a list of taboo foods, which if consumed, would lead to punishment through a supernatural force, resulting in effects ranging between grey hair, ugliness, disease, hiccupping, stomach upset, sores and ulcers, to the growth of a large tusk-like appendage from the mouth! Pregnant women could also be subject to food taboos, notably food thought to affect the foetus. Restricted foods could include those high in fat, certain roots and vegetables and foods such as crabs and crustaceans thought to lacerate the foetus. There could also be restrictions on consuming food collected by novices during their initiation period. The extent of taboos and restrictions demonstrates the extensive range of foods readily available and indicates that many alternatives could be obtained. In the instance of the novice, the restriction likely had a practical purpose, making the novices expand their repertoire of skills – perhaps restricting them to "difficult" to obtain foods encouraged proficiency in collection.

In some places, the right to access food could be "owned" by an individual, a family or groups within a clan. This could include restrictions on access to land areas such as yam beds, wetlands, parts of rivers or coastal zones with high biotic quotas. These restrictions could be maintained through systems of privileged and hierarchical control with hereditary intergenerational transfer of ownership. It is likely that ownership restrictions changed over time, notably as the environment and landmasses changed through the Pleistocene and Holocene. Patterns in access and ownership can be examined archaeologically through stratified archaeological sequences and/or analysis of data from across many archaeological sites (e.g. Owen et al. 2022).

Strategies for obtaining food must be considered from a point of temporality. This is because through the Pleistocene and Holocene the environment changed greatly, as did the location of Australia's coastline. Intra-region there were significant changes to procurement strategies through time, and at a single time point there could be large differences between adjacent clan groups. If one considers Australia's coastal capital cities (Adelaide, Brisbane, Darwin, Hobart, Melbourne, Perth, Sydney), the traditional subsistence base through the Holocene would be considered coastal or salt water, likely with a high percentage of seafoods. However, prior to late Pleistocene sea level changes, each of these locations would have been 20 km or more inland (e.g. Lewis et al. 2013), meaning these places were not on the coast, and coastal foods were not accessible. Temporal considerations must therefore determine the period and landmass location for any description of the subsistence base such as Pleistocene versus Holocene, and coastal, riverine or inland.

The examination of strategies through the Holocene requires large quantities of archaeological data, which can reveal changes in social and demographic patterns (e.g. Attenbrow 2006). Within these systems it becomes apparent that regional or clan specific strategies have start and end points. One widely known aspect of Aboriginal land management practices is "fire stick farming", with low intensity bush-burning used to control vegetation understories for many different purposes. These purposes could include: the need for certain flora species seeds to be fire germinated – resulting in new vegetation growth, which created both new plant resources and also attracted fauna to graze on new shoots; management of land for habitation purposes – clearing a campground prior to occupation (Clarke 2012); and, hunting methods – where game animals could be driven by fire towards waiting hunters or traps. It is thought that the maintenance of small-scale habitat mosaics increased small-animal hunting productivity, and could be linked with more sedentary Aboriginal societies, which had focused subsistence economies (Bird et al. 2008).

Food subsistence strategies were frequently based on resource availability by season (seasonality). Specific details connected with seasonality are often held through local traditions and provide a basis for understanding and interpreting late Holocene modes of subsistence. Aboriginal calendars described between six and 12 seasons.

Traditions that described the seasons vary between groups, and are distinguished by many aspects, such as the movement of the stars and other celestial bodies, the growth of particular plants, the appearance of various creatures (e.g. fish species or the migration of whales) and alterations to weather patterns. The Kaurna people (South Australia) describe several seasons (after Hayes 1999), including a hot season (Woltatti) or hot north winds that blow in summer (Bokarra), time for building huts against fallen trees (Wadlworngatti) or when the Parna star appears in autumn (Parnatti), icy-cold winds from the south west (Kudlilla), and when the Wilto-willo star appears in spring (Wullutti). Kaurna people responded to these seasons with localised movement between coastal and inland places, described through oral evidence and distinguished through stable isotope studies (Owen and Pate 2014). Understanding the traditions and influence of seasonality on Aboriginal subsistence strategies across the Holocene and Pleistocene would require an understanding of localised changes to ecological communities, weather patterns (including rainfall) and landmass alterations.

The east–central Australia exchange and trade network concerns a diversity of items, raw materials, symbolic items (songs, dances, stories) and manufactured goods (McBryde 1997). Trade strategies involving processed foodstuff (bone and shell items), more local movement of processed foods and the extensive movement of the tobacco/narcotic pituri, demonstrates that "food" could be a valuable commodity and a part of regional networks. The growth, processing and consequent trade of pituri has been charted through the centre of Australia, covering thousands of kilometres. Trade of food resources also occurred over shorter distances and was linked to methods of food preservation. Food rationing could also be used as a method of conserving limited supplies of certain higher value foods, for instance honey would be collected from native beehives, but only part of the honeycomb would be removed, retaining enough for the bees' consumption. Rationing was also linked with "propagation" of foods such as yams, which, when sufficient, were left for new growth to occur thereby ensuring a future crop.

The methods and techniques used to procure food altered by region, the dietary base, and temporality. Archaeological studies have identified many significant developments in methods and techniques through the Holocene. The methods evolved in complexity, allowing either for an intensification in collection of food, or gender specific modes of gathering. At the end of the Holocene, within the alluvial wetland areas of South Australia, NSW and Victoria, Aboriginal groups started living on raised mound sites (e.g. Westell and Wood 2014 review mound sites across the Adelaide region). These artificial mounds raised people above wetland areas, providing dry platforms for habitation activities in otherwise flood prone landscapes. Mounds likely served a range of economic and social functions, as locations for habitation, deliberate markers in the landscape, places where specific plants could be grown, locations used for human burials and by allowing the occupation of previously marginal landscapes during period of inundation. The mounds could be clustered in small groups, providing spatial separation between individuals, families and activity areas. Most landscapes with mound sites have a high biotic quota, and the mounds were frequently built up from cooked organic materials, including major food source plants such as *Typha* (e.g. Coutts et al. 1979). The occupation of the mounds may have been seasonal, responding to seasonality and the growth and presence of major food resources at certain points of the year. The production of mounds and their occupation appears to be restricted to the late Holocene (the last 2,000 years), demonstrating a significant shift at this time in terms of economic land use strategies, perhaps responding to other social factors such as population increases and territorial boundary closure.

Through the late Holocene, we know that some food collection techniques changed. For instance, in the coastal Sydney region, women manufactured small fishhooks, used to fish on a line from bark canoes on the harbours (Attenbrow 2010b). These activities only commenced in the last 1,000 years and demonstrate a significant localised shift in gendered subsistence patterns. Increasing complexity in the methods and techniques used to "hunt" animals often focused on passive techniques, or techniques that guaranteed food in a short period of time. Development of complex fish traps and fishing nets, eel traps, and bird and animal traps allowed land, riverine and sea animals to be caught, without the need for direct human involvement in the process. Some techniques became so sophisticated that an industry around the manufacture of large bird catching and fishing nets developed within groups such as the Ngarrindjeri (in South Australia, Berndt and Berndt 1993, 92–103). For instance, Ngarrindjeri hunts deployed nets over 10 m long to capture large flocks of small birds from wetland areas. These were consequentially processed and could be stored for future consumption.

This short review provides an overview of complexities connected to the procurement of food. It demonstrates how social lore, law and tradition governed how food could be collected. Food seasonal availability and an understanding of resource scarcity were equally important.

Processing

Once a food was obtained, the food systems connected with processing commenced. Many foods could be eaten raw, particularly plants and berries, and the only processing required was to remove adhering vegetation, or cracking kernels to access nuts. However, as for systems of procurement, there could be a complexity connected with processing, and these changed considerably through deep time. Continent-wide research into the process of Pleistocene colonisation has identified that a general set of plant processing techniques was holistically adopted. As Aboriginal peoples moved over the Australian landmass, the generalist practices were tailored to different regions and biotic resources. During the mid Holocene, multiple new behaviours were adopted in different places, allowing for specific regional adaptation and increased local complexity (Denham et al. 2009).

Levels of complexity could range from needing to properly cook a food, to specific processing and treatment of the food to render it edible, removing toxins before cooking. Further complexity could be introduced through gendered roles in processing, to permissions to process food governed by hierarchical systems. Temporality also needs to be considered, as modes of cooking evolved and advanced over the Holocene, with new techniques allowing complex starches in tubers to be broken down into edible carbohydrates. Descriptions of processing can be divided into preparation and cooking.

Preparation of plant resources was undertaken to break down plant material and/or render it safe for consumption. The methods of preparation included heating, placing plants in solutions (such as salt water, or running fresh water), fermentation, adsorption (by clay and charcoal), curing (changing pH by the addition of ashes or acids) and drying (Clarke 2012). Physical processing included grating, grinding, pounding and (in very cold climates) freezing (Rowland 2002). Discussion here focuses on some of the more commonly known methods that were used across large parts of Australia for long periods of time.

From the mid Holocene on, Aboriginal peoples across the drier and hotter parts of Australia practised seed collection, followed by a process of winnowing and grinding. Evidence for seed grinding is frequently identified within an archaeological context; handheld grinding stones, and grinding patches and hollows in bed rock, or portable sandstone grinding stones provide evidence for these practices. Many different plants (and animals) were ground to produce flour or pastes, which would be cooked before consumption.

Obtaining sufficient grain (seeds) to manufacture damper required an understanding of seasonality associated with grass ripening. In some parts of South Australia, New South Wales and Victoria, Aboriginal peoples practised both deliberate spreading of wild grass seeds (for future crops) and collection of surplus grain, with methods of dry storage used to save grain for periods of the year when it would not otherwise be available (including storage in modified tree hollows and woven baskets). During seasons of abundance the surplus provided a means of increased sociality, with evidence for human movement between territories facilitated because of the surplus (Macdonald 2017, 82). Evidence of movement of foodstuff can be detected archaeologically. For instance, the process of grinding seeds and plants on grinding platforms with stones leaves behind spores, pollen and starches. Careful sampling from the surface of the stone can recover these food remains, which may be identified through microscopic analysis. This provides the basis for understanding plant use (not just for food but also medicinal use) and the movement of plants through a landscape – where plants can be moved long distances before being processed (e.g. Owen et al. 2019).

Many nuts consumed in large quantities are toxic or noxious. Knowledge of nut preparation techniques to make these edible has built up regionally across Australia. Processing systems for toxic and noxious nuts including collection, removal of flesh, cooking (in an oven), cracking shells to remove kernels, leeching, drying and grinding or pulverising, followed by preparation into an edible item. The period required to produce an edible product could be days. However, experimental archaeology has shown that each stage was relatively quick and, most importantly, the outcome was a food resource high in energy (Tuechler and Cosgrove 2014).

Importantly, the effort and time expended to obtain high energy source foods like nuts and seeds was relatively low compared against the effort required to collect and process these foods. This is the case for cycad seeds (Macrozamia), which is an example of an important food that required traditional processing knowledge. *Macrozamia* are one of 11 genera of Cycadales and are endemic to Australia. *Macrozamia's* starchy kernels (mega-gametophyte) are eaten, but require the removal of toxins to render them safe. Aboriginal peoples have a long history of *Macrozamia* processing; archaeological sites containing the processed remains of the internal hard stony shell (sclerotesta) have been dated back to the Pleistocene, and archaeological research has demonstrated increased consumption of *Macrozamia* through the early to mid Holocene (Asmussen 2010).

A riverine to semi-arid inland food which required processing before consumption is nardoo (*Marsilea drummondii*). Nardoo is a perennial aquatic fern, with underground stems (rhizomes). The plant produces a hard fruit called a sporocarp, which can be collected but must be roasted before being ground. It produces a yellow flour that can be made into a dough. If the fruit is eaten raw, the thiaminases (an enzyme) present causes vitamin B1 deficiency (beri-beri) – untreated, beri-beri can result in death. This was the downfall of European "explorers" Burke and Wills, who in 1861 died in the South Australian outback after eating large amounts of unprocessed nardoo (National Museum of Australia 2023).

The preparation and cooking of foods was specific to the actual food. Species-specific techniques rendered the food more appetising if prepared and cooked in a particular way. It also allowed for personal and culturally defined taste preferences. Food preparation considered not just the food, but the secondary products which came from the animals, fish and birds. Animal skins needed specific treatment if they were to be used for consequent clothing production. Likewise, bone, tendons and sinew from animals needed to be prepared and removed in specific ways if intended to be used once the meal was consumed. For certain Aboriginal groups, particular species may have gender or "magical" restrictions that necessitated very careful preparation and disposal of particular parts of the creature.

Each species would have a unique way of being prepared and cooked. For instance, the Ngarrindjeri's technique for preparing a Murray cod was elaborate and resulted in 10 separate portions which would be shared within a family; the person who caught the fish rarely took the best part for themselves (Berndt and Berndt 1993, 105).

The methods of cooking were varied and could be tailored to each species. Sydney's Pleistocene Aboriginal populations used small flat pieces of sandstone as heating or cooking plates, presumably placed over the fire to heat the stone. The prevalence of these sandstone items within the archaeological record varies through the Pleistocene, with increased use either side of the Last Glacial Maximum (LGM), disappearing altogether in the Holocene (White 2018).

In the later Holocene (the last 1,500 years), Aboriginal peoples in south-east and southern Australia developed cooking methods using ground ovens. This specialisation allowed for slower and longer cooking periods, thereby providing a means to cook larger animals. A by-product of the cooking process itself was a large amount of organic plant material and cooked clay, which was used to form mound sites (Coutts et al. 1979; Westell and Wood 2014). To cook in a ground oven, fires were made within an excavated depression (the size and shape of the item to be cooked). Cooking stones or specifically manufactured clay cooking/heating balls were heaped onto the coals within these depressions. Further fires adjacent to the depression heated further clay/stone balls. Once the fires had died down, grasses (and edible plant material, such as Typha) were placed over the coals, food was placed on the grass, and further cooking stones/clay balls packed over the top. The oven was sealed with the excavated spoil of soil or sand. Over one or more hours the oven would cook the food at a temperature controlled by the quantity of cooking clays/stones. A steam method could be introduced, with a hole poked into the side of the oven and water poured into the centre. Once cooked and cooled the oven would be broken open and the food removed for consumption.

The manufacture of the clay cooking balls appears to reflect a specialised industry. To make these items suitable, clay needs to be obtained and then tempered with a grit/gravel/sand or plant chaff. The balls must be air dried before being cooked themselves at a defined temperature for several hours. Simple lumps of dry clay cannot be used in a ground oven because these explode or disintegrate, contaminating the food. Use of ground ovens represents an economic production system with three steps: firstly, the manufacture of cooking balls; secondly, the development of methods to obtain the animals, fish, birds and vegetables; and finally, development of specialised cooking techniques.

The food production economy in the late Holocene focused on processing methods and the creation of food surplus. This surplus was generated through the preservation of vegetables, smoke-drying of animals and fish, and the preparation of oils (Berndt and Berndt 1993, 109–16). Food surplus was important for three reasons. Firstly, during the colder and wetter winter months half the number of food items were available (to groups such as the Ngarrindjeri or Kaurna, across South Australia) compared to the summer months. Food surpluses could be used to even out the availability of wild foods over the year (Owen 2004, 89–91) and provide reliable long-term food sources. Secondly, food surplus allowed for increased population numbers and provided a context for social closure with firmer boundaries between groups (Lourandos 1997) – it provided one means to change subsistence and economic activities. Food surplus became a part of the trade network, and the necessity for traditional trading expeditions. Thirdly, the movement of people across Country and between groups throughout the southern parts of Australia is well known for purposes of trade, exchange and ceremony. Having food to take on these journeys would have been vital and could only be achieved through a food surplus.

Consumption

Once prepared, whether that be simple preparation of raw food, cooking, elaborate processing or preservation, food would be consumed. Consumption systems depended on both the type of food and whether the food was to be consumed by an individual or group of people.

Individuals consumed raw, simply processed or preserved food throughout the day, often collecting and eating fruits and berries, or foods carried from the camp, such as smoked fish. This type of simple consumption did not require much consideration or post-consumption disposal of waste.

Individuals could also consume larger meals, which necessitated consideration of consumption systems. For instance, it was recorded by colonists that the Cadigal women (the people on the southern side of Sydney Harbour) fished on the harbour from small canoes using a line (Tench 1789). The canoe would hold a small clay pad, on which a fire could be built. Women would catch, process, cook and then eat fish whilst fishing. However, the purpose of fishing was to collect food for more than one individual. During periods of the year when fish were less plentiful, or adverse weather conditions made fishing became a difficult task, women needed to balance the quantity of fish caught against their own consumption. During larger social gatherings, with over 1,000 people, perhaps from multiple clan groups, the systems of food gathering, cooking and sharing could become very complex.

This example introduces the main consideration underpinning consumption systems – how food was divided and shared. The intricacies of this system mean they were socially based and probably varied between clan groups across Australia. Consideration of food division depended on the type of food, for instance different rules existed for certain fish, kangaroo and birds. Some simple hierarchical principles existed, where elder males (and in some cases females) would hold rights to the highest protein or fat portions of a meal. Conversely, for some food items, the "best" portions were reserved for the youngest members of the clan.

Division of food commenced with preparation (as described above) and, once cooked, the person responsible for preparation and cooking would divide and distribute the food. For instance, bandicoots, possums or quolls would be dismembered after cooking. A cut on the back was made either side of the tail, which was given a sharp pull to remove it. This meat was regarded as the sweetest and given to the children. The spine was then cut along its length and bent until it broke. Three cuts either side of the spine divided the meat into seven portions, one being the head (Berndt and Berndt 1993, 100 and 102). Portion size was controlled so each person received an equal and fair amount. Portion allocation also considered disposal requirements, with certain parts of animals subject to strict taboos and superstition.

Finally, Aboriginal peoples occasionally consumed items with no nutritional value, but as items for medicine, digestion or superstition. Certain types of clay or carbon could be eaten to aid digestion or to settle an upset stomach. Consumption of small stones (gastroliths) could occur for purposes connected with magic or ceremony, with certain items thought to possess properties that imparted special powers or values. One commonly known non-food item that formed an important part of ritualistic life was the tobacco/narcotic pituri. Providing a hallucinogen effect, this plant is known to form an important part of higher men's business for certain Aboriginal groups.

Disposal

The final part of the food system is disposal – the process of removing the food wastes once consumption is complete. There were multiple ways to dispose of food waste, some of which were linked to specific production economies. Archaeologically, some of these disposal systems can be identified and form deposits which are the focus of research. Discard was either intentional or unintentional. Unintentional discard may be described as random and unpremeditated. This could include discard whilst walking, or actions where discard would not hold implications for waste management, such as throwing scraps to camp dogs, thereby entirely disposing of any food wastes.

Intentional discard is a process where discard becomes a deliberate action, in some instances governed by rules and traditions. Intentional discard could include collection and replanting to generate new/additional food sources, collection and re-use of materials for future manufacture into secondary products, deliberate disposal such as burning in a fire to avoid issues connected with superstition or magic, and deliberate waste management strategies, such as accumulating waste in a specific location to form a waste dump, mound, heap or pile. The final consideration for disposal of "food" were processes connected to human waste management (notably faeces), generally in more permanent camping locations or during large gatherings.

Replanting and redistribution of foods (uncooked but sometimes processed) was a noted method for deliberate propagation of plants, especially seeds and tubers. In parts of NSW where seeds were a food staple used to produce a flour for pastes and dampers, Aboriginal Elders describe the (continuing) practice of slowly dropping grass seeds from their hand as they walk through specific parts of Country. This aids the distribution and next season's growth of the plant, and expands the area with food sources. Locations chosen for seed distribution could be specific, connected with shallow slopes above creek systems, where it was known that the seeds would grow, and can still be collected.

The food cycle associated with wetland and dryland plants was deliberately managed to generate ongoing growth. The production economy could be associated with digging soil beds, turning over nutrient-rich alluvial soil, splitting and replanting tubers. Stands of dense plants were thinned out, reducing the competition for light and nutrients among the remaining plants, thereby improving their growth (Gott 1982). In some places during the late Holocene, wetland plants formed a staple as a carbohydrate source. Important food species included cumbungi or bulrush (*Typha domingensis* and *T. orientalis*), marsh club-rush (*Scirpus medianus*), and water-ribbons (*Triglochin procera*), that grow abundantly in waterways. Wiradjuri (NSW) traditions describe how specific parts of each important waterway was cared for by an individual who would have responsibility for the resources and maintaining water flow through a certain portion of the creek (Macdonald 2017, 76). The responsibilities included management of reeds, grass, trees and other plants. These systems are frequently connected with "caring for Country", the ecological management of land with a symbiotic relationship between the land and Aboriginal peoples. These practices are linked to disposal because they represent Aboriginal peoples returning plant material to regrow or generate new growth.

The process of caring for Country extended into waste management. Some strategies involved a deliberate process of collecting waste products in a predefined area. Collation of waste could be both functional (such as allowing food remains to decay and rot in specific locations, thereby containing vermin or flies) and also symbolic (creating landscape markers or preventing misuse of food remains).

The accumulation of waste in a dump or mound could result in the formation of a raised platform. For many Aboriginal groups, these platforms or mounds were both functional and held symbolic meanings. The functionality of a mound is associated with the raised nature of the platform and the flat upper surface of the mound. Across Kaurna Country (now called Adelaide), mounds were most frequently constructed in clusters within wetland or flood zones. The mound's height above any flood waters allowed habitation and other cultural activities to occur in a dry setting. Clusters of mounds were grouped together, each mound holding a specific function, akin to the layout of a traditional camp on an open plain. The mounds were typically quite large, oval to circular, and could measure 50 metres in diameter. Some mounds on Kaurna Country were over one metre in height. Landscape patterning is evident within the distribution of Kaurna mounds, and the mounds functioned as visible markers in the cultural landscape. They were identifiable locations which designated boundaries, movement corridors and specific places. In some instances, they represented "hold points" which visitors from other clans could not pass until provided with permission or a taken by a guide.

Mounds are archaeologically rich, composed primarily from decayed organic materials – fibrous plant remains, and inorganic materials – clay cooking balls and carbon (Coutts et al. 1979; Westell and Wood 2014). Mounds frequently contain the remains of ground ovens, and some served as burial locations, occasionally containing multiple interments. Radiocarbon dating of materials from mounds suggests that most were constructed in the late Holocene (the last 1,500 years). Functionally, the mound site can be attributed to the need to extract more resources from a small territory, or an area that was perhaps previously marginal in terms of resource extraction. Notably found within wetland areas or on alluvial flood plains, the mounds are connected with locations that have a high biotic quota and year-round food resources. Mounds provided a dry space within the wetland zone and therefore increased the habitable portion of Country. They provided a location to collect and process food from wetland areas, reducing the time required for hunting and gathering activities.

1 Aboriginal traditions of food

Another archaeologically common type of waste disposal rubbish dump is the shell midden. Frequently found along the foreshores of Australia's current coast and inland waters, a midden is an accumulation of consumed shellfish, coupled with animal bones, fish ear bones (otoliths), carbon from fires and hearths, and perhaps discarded stone artefacts. Middens are archaeologically important because, if stratigraphically excavated, the shellfish remains can provide all manner of information on consumption patterns over time. Midden composition allows us to understand the type of shellfish that Aboriginal peoples consumed and, when coupled with stable isotope analysis of the shell's calcium carbonate, the period during the year of consumption. Middens can be deep deposits; sometimes metres of shell have accumulated. Analysis of species composition with depth and time control can identify changing local environmental conditions, such as a change from a sandy beach environment to an anerobic mangrove environment. Middens could also be markers in a landscape, defining where certain social and economic activities occurred, although their ubiquitous nature means interpretation of such function needs to be connected to local traditions.

Many Aboriginal societies also practised different forms of sorcery and magic and held numerous superstitions – including in the manner of food disposal. Each group could have its own traditions, often connected with hierarchy within the society, and notably, higher initiated people. Sorcery has been described as an ever-present phenomenon, and individuals practiced certain traditions connected with food disposal in an effort to avoid magic and the possible dangers from its effects. For instance, for the Ngarrindjeri peoples (South Australia) it was an established practice to dispose of certain food remains following consumption:

> Every adult blackfellow is constantly on the look-out for bones of duck, swans, or other birds, or of the fish called *ponde* (Murray cod), the flesh of which has been eaten by anybody. Of these he constructs his charms. All the natives [sic] therefore, are careful to burn the bones of animals which they eat, so as to prevent their enemies from getting hold of them; but in spite of this precaution, such bones are commonly obtained by disease-makers who want them. When a man has obtained a bone – for instance, the leg bone of a duck – he supposes that he possesses the power of life and death over the man, woman, or child who ate its flesh (Taplin 1879, 24).

One type of Ngarrindjeri sorcery, called *Ngadungi*, involved obtaining leftover food from the intended victim. The aim was to inflict an ailment on the victim, and the nature of the ailment depended on the type of food remains obtained. Predominantly for the Ngarrindjeri, food remains used in sorcery were often from

43

birds or fish, rather than land-based animals (which could reflect the basis of their diets inland on the Murray River or coastal on the Coorong). Collecting a splinter of bone from a duck's head could be used to cause headaches; skin from the duck's wing caused a diseased arm; or skin from its body could result in internal diseases. The process of magic was long and involved engaging a sorcerer, who would take the food remains and prepare a sorcery object. This object was then placed under the intended victim's hut or in their belongings, eventually making them ill (Berndt and Berndt 1993, 258–9).

Beyond magic and sorcery, the products from plants and animals were vital commodities, essential within many Aboriginal production economies. Many parts of animals, from the skins, bones, fats, sinews and tendons were used as secondary products. Plant material not consumed was manufactured into twine, ropes and strings – and in turn manufactured into ropes, nets, baskets and ornaments. The skins and pelts for many land-based animals were carefully collected prior to cooking the animal, and those without blemishes or tears selected for further processing.

The Ngarrindjeri processed skins to make them soft and pliant. The process involved drying by pinning the skin fur side down and driving the moisture from the skin by covering with hot ashes. Once dry, the skin was scraped clean and then softened through scoring with a stone blade. The resultant skin could be folded for storage (or trade) and was eventually sewn into a cloak of other clothing or rug using sinews from kangaroo tails (Berndt and Berndt 1993, 113).

Longer animal bones, such as kangaroo tibia, were worked into bone points (tools), pointing bones (associated with magic) and other useful tools (Walshe 2008). In coastal locations, the shells from larger shellfish were broken and used as small cutting knives. In the Sydney region, shells were manufactured by grinding to form shellfish hooks – an entire gendered industry was connected with this practice (Attenbrow 2010b).

The final act of disposal is connected with human waste management, including faeces, urine and phlegm. Archaeologically, little consideration is given to human waste disposal, but it would have been a major consideration in camp establishment and management. For some groups, such as the Ngarrindjeri, these human bodily products could also be collected by unscrupulous individuals and consequently used in sorcery – "a little of the substance obtained was mixed with dead person's fat: the result of urine sorcery was bladder trouble; with phlegm and saliva, a severe cold with chest pains that could lead to death" (Berndt and Berndt 1993, 258).

Discussion

This chapter has provided an overview of long-term diets relating to Aboriginal peoples in temperate Southern Australia. Current analysis of diet directly measurable from stable isotopes in human skeletal remains suggests that from the mid Holocene to the point of invasion, Aboriginal diets had regional specificity but remained unchanged. The long-term stability in Aboriginal diet is an important factor when considering known changes to the regional environments of southern Australia (such as changes in climate, the environment, precipitation, temperature and sea levels). When coupled with the perceived changes to Aboriginal societies, such as social closure limiting unrestricted movement of people, demographic changes or increasing population densities in the late Holocene, stability in long-term diet must have implications for concepts associated with intensification models (e.g. Morgan 2015).

We know through archaeological studies of individual sites (e.g. Attenbrow 2006), or large-scale material and tool technologies (e.g. Hiscock and Attenbrow 2005) that significant changes to Aboriginal technologies and societies occurred through the Pleistocene into the Holocene. However, it is the bioarchaeological studies which can present data that informs debate around specialisation, diversification and innovation in the food systems.

The food systems described above are complex and intertwined with changing and evolving Aboriginal social traditions. It is clear that many regional specialisations exist, and that the systems themselves would change through time. Understanding a local food system is an important part of describing any Aboriginal clan or group but knowing that basic models of protein food group consumption remained stable for long periods of time is important when investigating aspects such as land use intensification, changing productivity or alterations in efficiency (in food collection and processing).

These complex and evolving social traditions around food can lead to many different regional specialisations, diversifications and innovations (after Morgan 2015, 199). Specialisation could include systems such as the Eastern Regional System for stone artefacts, or creation of local food production economies with the collection of large amounts of food through new innovative techniques (such as net manufacture) – coupled with means of preserving foods for long-term storage and later consumption or trade. Diversification in terms of food could mean accessing more food but from the same resources – but not necessarily an increase in dietary breadth outside the base protein group. For example, if freshwater fish was the main source of protein in a diet, then diversification saw new techniques that allowed more and different species of fish to be caught, not a change to hunting land-based animals. Such diversification can be linked to innovation that allowed access to previously restricted environments, for example the commencement of mound construction allowed long term access and habitation in wetland and flood prone landscapes. Innovation can be seen within many food procurement and processing systems, including the development of means to detoxify foods. It is also apparent in methods of cooking, with the advent of the common use of the ground oven, making food taste better, and also more hygienic (killing bacteria through cooking).

These food systems can variously describe both increases and decreases in efficiency, that is the time required at each stage of the food system. Food is an essential part of life, but also essential to the function of a society. Some of the innovations and adaptations, such as fishing from a canoe using a line and a bara (shell fishhook), may not have increased the economic productivity (in terms of quantity) of an Aboriginal society. However, the advent of this mode of fishing by women did hold social importance, potentially increasing the social richness and diversity of daily life for women within their communities.

Conversely, many of the changes described allowed for significant increases in economic and social complexity. Methods used to obtain large quantities of food allowed for mass gatherings of Aboriginal peoples, for long periods of time. Regular gatherings of large groups for trade, ceremony and other activities again suggests increased social complexity through the Holocene. Understanding the food systems is important because it provides context for agents of change, such as social closure or increased spirituality, which could have influenced Aboriginal peoples' mobility, access to food, trade and territoriality.

References

Adams, C., T. Owen, D. Pate, D. Bruce, K. Nielson, R. Klaebe, M. Henneberg and I. Moffat (2022). "Do dead men tell no tales?" The geographic origin of a colonial period Anglican cemetery population in Adelaide, South Australia, determined by isotope analyses. *Australian Archaeology* 88(2): 144–58. DOI: 10.1080/03122417.2022.2086200.

Anson, T. (1997). The effect of climate on stable nitrogen isotope enrichment in modern South Australian mammals. Master's thesis, Flinders University, Adelaide, SA.

Asmussen, B. (2010). In a nutshell: the identification and archaeological application of experimentally defined correlates of *Macrozamia* seed processing. *Journal of Archaeological Science* 37: 2117–25.

Australian Archaeology (2021). *Forum* 87(3): 300–25.

Attenbrow, V. (2010a). *Sydney's Aboriginal past: investigating the archaeological and historical records.* Sydney: University of New South Wales Press.

Attenbrow, V. (2010b). Aboriginal fishing on Port Jackson, and the introduction of shell fish-hooks to coastal New South Wales, Australia. In P. Hutching, D. Lunney and D. Hochuli, eds. *The natural history of Sydney*, 16–34. Mosman: Royal Zoological Society of New South Wales.

Attenbrow, V. (2006). *What's changing: population size or land-use patterns? The archaeology of Upper Mangrove Creek, Sydney Basin. Terra Australis 21.* Canberra: ANU Press.

Berndt, C. and R. Berndt (1993). *A world that was. The Yaraldi of the Murry River and the lakes, South Australia.* Carlton: Melbourne University Press.

Berndt, C. and R. Berndt (1974). *The First Australians,* 3rd edn. Sydney: Ure Smith.

Bird, R., D. Bird, B. Codding, C. Parker and J. Jones (2008). The "fire stick farming" hypothesis: Australian Aboriginal foraging strategies, biodiversity, and anthropogenic fire mosaics. *PNAS* 105(39): 14796–801.

Brockwell, S., B. Ó Foghlú, J. Fenner, J. Stevenson, U. Proske and J. Shiner (2017). New dates for earth mounds at Weipa, North Queensland, Australia. *Archaeology in Oceania* 52: 127–34.

Cahir, F., I. Clark and P. Clarke (2018). *Aboriginal biocultural knowledge in south-eastern Australia. Perspectives of the early colonists.* Clayton South: CSIRO Publishing.

Clarke, P. (2012). *Australian plants as Aboriginal tools.* Dural: Rosenberg Publishing.

Coutts, P., P. Henderson and R. Fullagar (1979). *A preliminary investigation of Aboriginal mounds in north western Victoria.* Records of the Victorian Archaeological Survey 9: Ministry for Conservation.

Denham, T., R. Fullagar and L. Head (2009). Plant exploitation on Sahul: From colonisation to the emergence of regional specialisation during the Holocene. *Quaternary International* 202: 29–40.

Hayes, S. (1999). The Kaurna calendar: seasons of the Adelaide Plains. Honours thesis, the University of Adelaide, SA.

Hiscock, P. and V. Attenbrow (2005). *Australia's Eastern Regional Sequence revisited: technology and change at Capertee 3.* BAR International Series 1397. Oxford: Archaeopress.

Gott, B. (1982). Ecology of root use by the Aborigines of southern Australia. *Archaeology of Oceania* 17: 59–67.

Lewis, S., C. Sloss, C. Murray-Wallace, C. Woodroffe and S. Smithers (2013). Post-glacial sea-level changes around the Australian margin: a review. *Quaternary Science Reviews* 74: 115–38.

Littleton J., K. Walshe and J. Hodges (2013). Burials and time at Gillman Mound, northern Adelaide, South Australia. *Australian Archaeology* 77: 38–51.

Lourandos, H. (1997). *Continent of hunter-gatherers: new perspectives in Australian prehistory*. Cambridge: Cambridge University Press.

McBryde, I. (1997). The cultural landscapes of Aboriginal long distance exchange systems: can they be confined within our heritage registers? *Historic environment* 13: 6–14.

Macdonald, G. (2017). Focussing on creeks: Wiradjuri ecology, sociality and cosmology. *Journal of the Anthropological Society of South Australia* 41: 63–92.

Morgan, C. (2015). Is it intensification yet? Current archaeological perspectives on the evolution of hunter-gatherer economies. *Journal of Archaeological Research* 23: 163–213.

National Museum of Australia (NMA) (2023). *Burke and Wills*, NMA website, accessed 28 May 2023. https://www.nma.gov.au/defining-moments/resources/burke-and-wills.

Ó Foghlú, B. (2021). Mounds of the north: discerning the nature of earth mounds in north Australia. Doctoral thesis, Australian National University, Canberra, ACT.

Owen, T. (2004). "Of more than usual interest": a bioarchaeological analysis of ancient Aboriginal skeletal material from southeastern South Australia. Doctoral thesis, Flinders University, Adelaide, SA.

Owen, T. and Pate D. (2014). A Kaurna burial, Salisbury, South Australia: further evidence for complex late Holocene Aboriginal social systems in the Adelaide region. *Australian Archaeology* 79: 45–53.

Owen, T., J. Field, S. Luu, Kokatha Aboriginal People, B. Stephenson and A. Coster (2019). Ancient starch analysis of grinding stones from Kokatha Country, South Australia. *Journal of Archaeological Science* 23: 178–88.

Owen, T.D., J. Jones-Webb, L. Watson and C. Norman (2022). Parramatta, NSW: A deep time Aboriginal cultural landscape. *Journal of the Australian Association of Consulting Archaeologists* 9: 10–29.

Pascoe, B. (2014). *Dark emu: black seeds: agriculture or accident?* Broome: Magabala Books.

Pate, F.D., R. Brodie and T. Owen (2002). Determination of geographic origin of unprovenanced Aboriginal skeletal remains in South Australia employing carbon and nitrogen isotope analysis. *Australian Archaeology* 55: 1–7.

Pate, F.D. and T. Anson (2012). Stable isotopes and dietary composition in the mid-late 19th century Anglican population, Adelaide, South Australia. *Journal of the Anthropological Society of South Australia* 35: 1–16.

Pate, F.D. and T. Owen (2014). Stable carbon and nitrogen isotopes as indicators of sedentism and territoriality in late Holocene South Australia. *Archaeology in Oceania* 49(1): 56–65.

Roberts, A., D. Pate and R. Hunter (1999). Late Holocene climatic changes recorded in macropod bone collagen stable carbon and nitrogen isotopes at Fromm's Landing, South Australia. *Australian Archaeology* 49: 48–9.

Rowland, M. (2002). Geophagy: an assessment of implications for the development of Australian Indigenous plant processing technologies. *Australian Aboriginal Studies* 2002(1): 50–65.

Sutton P. and K. Walsh (2021). *Farmers or hunter-gather? The Dark Emu debate.* Carlton: Melbourne University Press.

Taplin, G. (1879). The Narrinyeri. In J. Woods, ed. *The native tribes of South Australia.* Adelaide: ES Wigg & Son.

Tench, W. (1789). *1788: a narrative of the expedition to Botany Bay and a complete account of the settlement at Port Jackson* (T. Flannery, ed). Melbourne: The Text Publishing Company.

Tuechler, A., A. Ferrier and R. Cosgrove (2014). Transforming the inedible to the edible: an analysis of the nutritional returns from Aboriginal nut processing in Queensland's Wet Tropics. *Australian Archaeology* 79: 26–33.

Walshe, K. (2008). Pointing bones and bone points in the Australian Aboriginal collection of the South Australia Museum. *Journal of the Anthropological Society of South Australia* 33: 167–203.

Westell, C. and V. Wood (2014). An introduction to earthen mound sites in South Australia. *Journal of the Anthropological Society of South Australia* 38: 30–65.

White, B. (2018). Time matters on shallow open sites: an example from Western Sydney, Australia. Doctoral thesis, the University of Sydney, Sydney, NSW.

White, B. (2017). Analysis with confidence: distinguishing Pre-Bondaian and Bondaian IMSTC artefact assemblages from the Cumberland Plain of Western Sydney, New South Wales. *Australian Archaeology* 83(3): 143–61.

Williams, A. (2013). A new population curve for prehistoric Australia. Proceedings of the Royal Society B 280: 20130486. DOI: 10.1098/rspb.2013.0486.

Williams, A., S. Ulm, T. Sapienza, S. Lewis and C. Turney (2018). Sea-level change and demography during the last glacial termination and early Holocene across the Australian continent. *Quaternary Science Reviews* 182: 144–54.

2

Aboriginal plant use and ecological knowledge
47,000 years of monsoon rainforest connections in the Kimberley, north-west Australia

India Ella Dilkes-Hall, June Davis† and Helen Malo

Introduction

Archaeobotany – the recovery and analysis of plant remains excavated from stratified archaeological contexts – provides insights into people's diets and ecological relationships in the past. Taxonomic information obtained from archaeobotanical assemblages contributes greatly to reconstructions of diet, subsistence, landscape use, environmental conditions and palaeoclimate. A significant proportion of Australian Aboriginal diets and nutrition is met using food obtained from plants. However, the application of archaeobotany in Australian archaeology has been infrequent and the focus of archaeological discourse on lithic technologies and hunting strategies has largely neglected the role of plant foods and plant-related activities in Aboriginal societies, creating an incomplete picture of the past. This chapter begins with a brief overview of global archaeobotanical themes and Australian archaeobotany. It then focuses on the Kimberley region of Western Australia, where archaeobotanical research has revealed a rich and complex record of Aboriginal plant uses spanning 47,000 years of occupation.

Plants in the archaeological record

The visibility/invisibility of plants in the archaeological record has been a subject of ongoing inquiry since the first studies of plant remains derived from European archaeological contexts in the mid-nineteenth century (Hastorf 1999, 55). Visibility

51

of plant remains is far less when compared to more robust cultural materials, such as stone tools (Hastorf 1999) from which it is only possible to infer plant use (e.g. Hayes et al. 2018; Hiscock et al. 2016; Maloney and Dilkes-Hall 2020; Wallis and O'Connor 1998). Direct evidence for food plants can be elusive and, in archaeological sites where plants do preserve, botanical remains represent only a fraction of what was originally used and deposited by humans; their occurrence in the archaeological record is often accidental (Yen 1988).

When preservation allows, archaeobotanical research can provide considerable information on people-plant relationships in the past and human interaction with the surrounding environment by answering questions about plant-based economies, subsistence strategies, cultural preferences, resource scheduling, seasonality, ecological targeting, habitat modification, mobility, land management strategies, domestication processes, agriculture, horticulture, arboriculture, environmental and climatic conditions, and, by extension, social ornamentation, identity, maritime capabilities and other plant-based perishable technologies (e.g. Antolín et al. 2016; Balme 2013; Balme and Morse 2006; Balme et al. 2022; Cappers and Neef 2012; Denham et al. 2009; Fuller 2018; Hastorf 1999; Hather 1994; Hather and Mason 2002; Pearsall 2010; Sayok and Teucher 2018).

Types of archaeobotanical remains

Plant remains enter archaeological sites via two main pathways: anthropogenic (direct and indirect) and non-anthropogenic introduction (Gallagher 2014, 29). It is important that culturally and naturally introduced archaeobotanical remains are differentiated as the two provide different types of information – the former reflective of diet, subsistence and human agency, the latter reflecting the environmental setting (Minnis 1981). Microbotanical remains include pollen, phytoliths and starch grains, while macrobotanical remains include wood charcoal, uncharred wood, bark, stems, leaves, flowers, fruits, seeds, nuts and modified botanical materials such as string, wooden tools and other plant-based technologies (Pearsall 2010).

This chapter is primarily concerned with macrobotanical remains and, more specifically, seed/fruit/nut remains, which – when shown to be introduced anthropogenically – offer information directly related to plants chosen for food by societies in the past.

Preservation of macrobotanical remains

All types of macrobotanical remains have the best potential to preserve in extreme environmental conditions, which prevent physical and chemical decay of organic plant materials and inhibit destructive biological processes (e.g. dry/wet/cold), or through exposure to fire, which transforms organic material to carbon (Miksicek

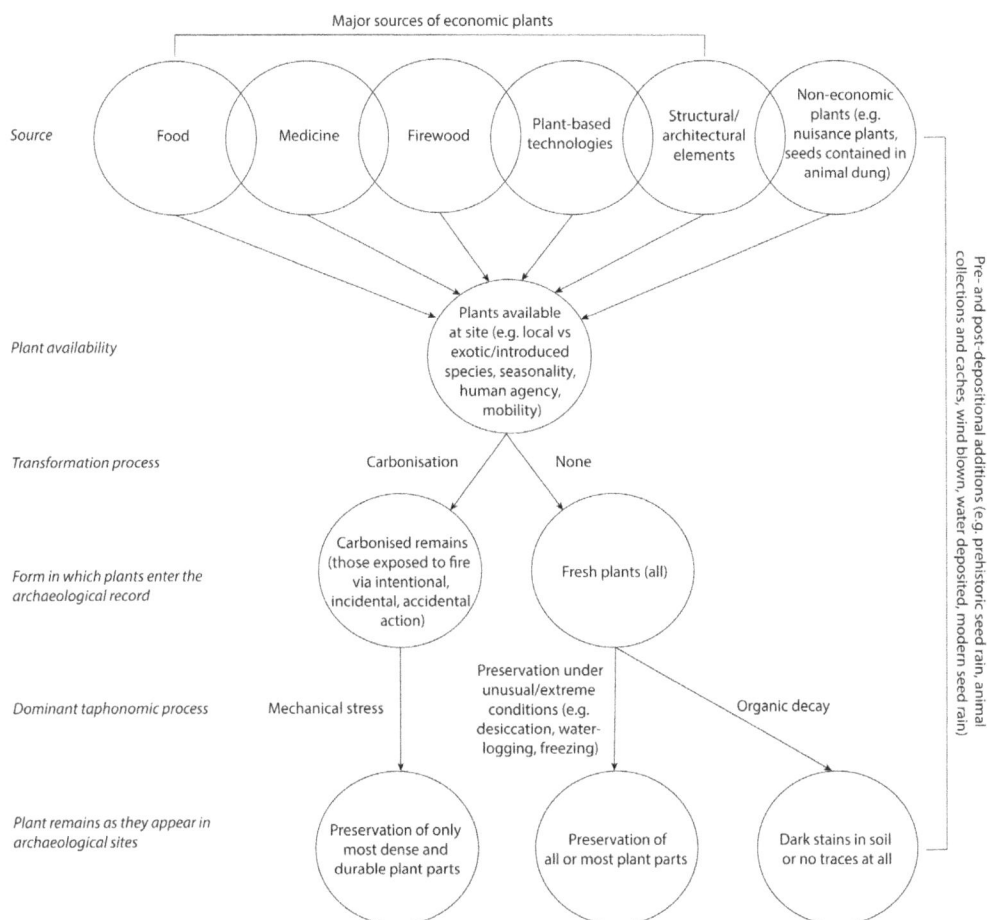

Figure 2.1 Anthropogenic and non-anthropogenic sources of macrobotanical remains and pre-depositional, depositional and post-depositional processes (adapted from Bush 2004, Figure 2.1, 19).

1987, 213–19). In Australian contexts, the two most common modes of preservation of macrobotanical remains are carbonisation and desiccation.

As with all organic archaeological remains, preservation and/or decomposition of plant material over time is complicated by several pre-depositional, depositional and post-depositional processes. Consequently, the quality, quantity and type of botanical material preserved can vary enormously within and across archaeological sites, producing intra- and inter-site difference/s (Clarke 1989; Hather 1994). Figure 2.1 traces various sources of botanical materials and how these enter archaeological sites alongside taphonomic processes that influence the probability of preservation.

Global archaeobotanical themes

Globally, archaeobotanical investigation concentrates on origin centres of plant domestication and the rise and spread of agricultural societies (e.g. Denham 2018; Heiser 1990; Piperno 2018; Reed 1977; Ucko and Dimbleby 1969). Preoccupation of archaeobotanical studies with agriculture is underpinned by the fact that long-term human exploitation of botanical resources can have significant effects on plant morphology and genetics (Fuller and Allaby 2009), and morphological changes in plant structures associated with human manipulation can usually be identified and observed in the archaeobotanical record (Hancock 2004).

Changes to people-plant relationships in foraging societies are less visible because different plant propagation mechanisms (i.e. short-lived annuals versus long-lived perennials and vegetatively propagated crops) mean domestication of some plants is not always possible or morphologically distinguishable. In terms of morphological change in macrobotanical remains, domestication of perennial fruiting trees, shrubs and vines, and, to a lesser extent, underground storage organs, is not as well understood as it is for annual cereal crops (Denham et al. 2020; Fuller 2018).

Recent research has aimed to address the role of plants in foraging societies (e.g. Antolín et al. 2016; Hardy and Kubiak-Martens 2016; Mooney and Martín-Seijo 2021). However, the focus of archaeobotanical research on the origins of plant domestication and agricultural societies has perpetuated the notion that transitions from foraging to farming represent the only significant change in people-plant relationships in the past, presenting agriculture as an inevitable end on a linear trajectory (e.g. Ford 1985, 6; Harris 1990, 39). An example of the pervasiveness of the farming/foraging dichotomy can be observed in the traditional division of the Pleistocene continent Sahul (Australia, Tasmania, New Guinea and Aru Islands) into the Melanesian agricultural north and the Australian Aboriginal hunter-gatherer-fisher south (Figure 2.2).

Although efforts have been made to shake the divide (e.g. Florin and Carah 2018) and terms more inclusive of Australian Aboriginal plant uses and landscape management have been created and recreated over time, e.g. plant husbandry (Higgs and Jarman 1972), domiculture (Hynes and Chase 1982), incipient agriculture (Ford 1985), plant mothering (Hastorf 1998), low-level food production (Smith 2001), vegeculture (Barton and Denham 2018) and ecoscaping (Ouzman et al. 2019), archaeobotanical research in the region continues to concentrate on New Guinea as one of the global centres of plant domestication and agriculture (e.g. Denham 2018; Golson et al. 2017; Piperno 2018; Spengler III 2020). In contrast, less attention has been paid to archaeobotanical evidence from Australian contexts that can help to shed light on people-plant relationships and changes in plant use over time.

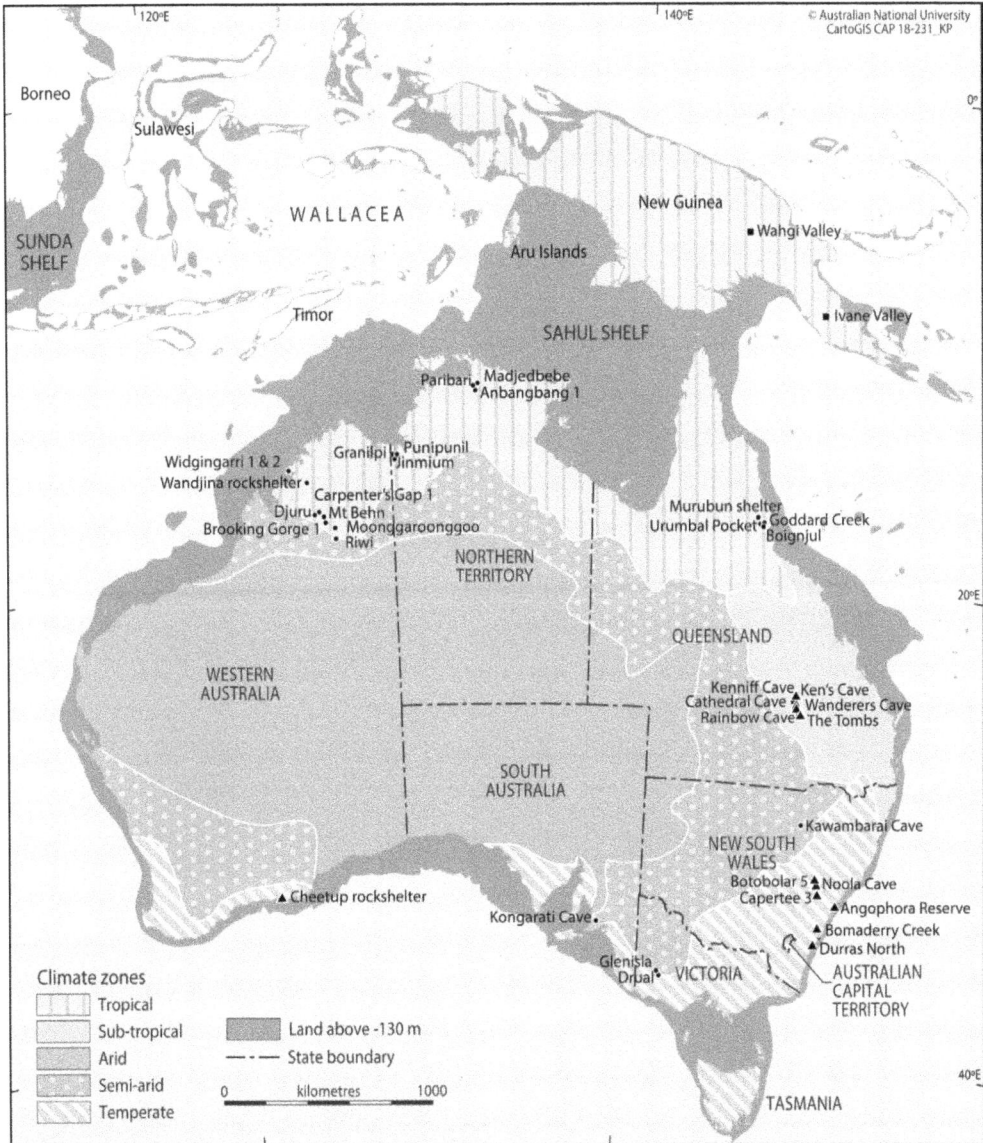

Figure 2.2 Australia with climatic zones, Last Glacial Maximum (LGM) coastline, and archaeological sites with non-woody seed/fruit macrobotanical investigation. Archaeological sites associated with plant domestication and agriculture display ■ icon. Archaeological sites associated with toxic plants display ▲ icon (adapted from Whitau 2018, Figure 2.4, 46; CAD: CartoGIS, Australian National University).

Australian archaeobotany

The late 1970s and 80s saw increased interest in archaeobotany by Australian researchers (e.g. Beaton 1977; Beck 1980; Clarke 1987; Head 1984) culminating in the seminal and unique monograph *Plants in Australian Archaeology* (Beck et al. 1989; see Brockwell et al. 2016 for a comprehensive overview of research on plants in Australian archaeology). Despite calls to shift Australian archaeobotanical research from the periphery to the core of archaeological pursuits (Denham et al. 2009), studies have remained sporadic. Overall, macrobotanical (here and hereafter excluding wood charcoal) research across the Australian continent is fragmentary, mainly targeting the eastern seaboard, and has largely centred on the use of toxic plants (e.g. *Macrozamia*). Figure 2.2 demonstrates macrobotanical remains preserved in different environments and site types across Australia. Despite this, "lack of preservation" is consistently cited by archaeologists who commonly draw upon this blanket statement to support their lack of engagement with archaeobotanical theory, method, fieldwork technique/s and research. This is especially astounding given that a considerable proportion (>50 per cent) of the dietary needs of Aboriginal peoples are met using plant foods (e.g. Kaberry 1935; McArthur 1960; Meehan 1989; Meggitt 1964; O'Dea et al. 1991; Russell-Smith et al. 1997), and the fact that plants are known to maintain important cultural connections to identity, language and Country (e.g. Blythe and Wightman 2003; Hercus 2012).

The publication of *Dark Emu: Black Seeds: Agriculture or Accident?* (Pascoe 2014) has been integral in drawing the attention of the Australian public and global readers to consider the complexities of Aboriginal plant use and resource management in the past. However, this has not taken place without significant conservative furore (O'Brien 2019, 2021a) and academic criticism (Keen 2021; Porr and Vivian-Williams 2021; Sutton and Walsh 2021). While it is not the purpose of this chapter to enter the debate surrounding *Dark Emu*, it is nonetheless important to highlight here that both Pascoe and critics alike fail entirely to consider and/or engage with available Australian archaeobotanical data (Australian examples include but are not limited to: Asmussen 2008, 2010; Asmussen and McInnes 2013; Atchison 2009; Atchison et al. 2005; Beck 1992; Byrne et al. 2021, 2019; Carah 2017; Clarke 1989, 1985; Cosgrove et al. 2007; Dotte-Sarout et al. 2015; Field et al. 2016; Ferrier and Cosgrove 2012; Florin et al. 2021, 2020; Hayes et al. 2018; King and Dotte-Sarout 2019; McConnell 1998; McConnell and O'Connor 1997; Owen et al. 2019; Roberts et al. 2021; Smith 1982; Walsh 2021; Walsh et al. 2024; Whitau et al. 2018a, 2018b, 2017).

Aboriginal ecological knowledge and monsoon rainforest connections spanning 47,000 years in the Kimberley

Study area

Recently, analyses of macrobotanical data from nine limestone cave and rock-shelter sites in the Kimberley region of north-west Australia have provided a detailed history of Aboriginal ecological knowledge relating to plant use spanning 47,000 years of occupation (Dilkes-Hall 2019; Dilkes-Hall et al. 2019a, 2019b, 2019c; Dilkes-Hall et al. 2020a, 2020b). The archaeological sites (Brooking Gorge 1, Carpenter's Gap 1, Djuru, Moonggaroonggoo, Mount Behn, Riwi, Wandjina rock-shelter, and Widgingarri 1 and 2) are distributed from the north-east Kimberley coast to the south-central interior, across some 370 km; their locations positioning them across four Native Title determined lands: Dambimangari, Wilinggin, Bunuba, and the southernmost Gooniyandi (Figure 2.3).

Monsoon rainforest

In the Kimberley, four major phytogeographic botanical districts – Dampier, Hall, Gardner and Fitzgerald after Beard (1979) – are overlapped by patches of monsoon rainforest (Figure 2.4). Monsoon rainforest occurs in coastal areas and persists further inland in fire protected gorges and limestone ranges and outcrops where water seepage maintains these sensitive vegetative communities (Beard 1976).

The monsoonal climate of northern Western Australia strongly influences the seasonal availability of plant resources. Monsoon rainforests are floristically rich in plant species that – being physiologically adapted to monsoonal climatic conditions – rely on seasonal rainfall (November–April) for fruit development (Kenneally 2018). Plant species associated with monsoon rainforest are rare if not entirely absent from the surrounding open woodlands and include *Celtis strychnoides* (hackberry), *Ficus* spp. (fig), *Flueggea virosa* (white currant), *Grewia* spp. (currant bush), *Terminalia* spp. (terminalia) and *Vitex* spp. (black plum) (Kenneally 2018).

Preservation

At all nine of these Kimberley archaeological sites, macrobotanical materials were preserved primarily by desiccation. Generally, European convention favours analysis of only carbonised macrobotanical remains – fire as an inference for cultural association – discounting desiccated materials as modern in origin (Diestch 1996; Keepax 1997; Minnis 1981). Cultural aversion to burning particular taxa and/or specific plant parts in camp fires is not uncommon among Aboriginal groups in relation to food plants (Dilkes-Hall et al. 2019b); findings that are consistent with

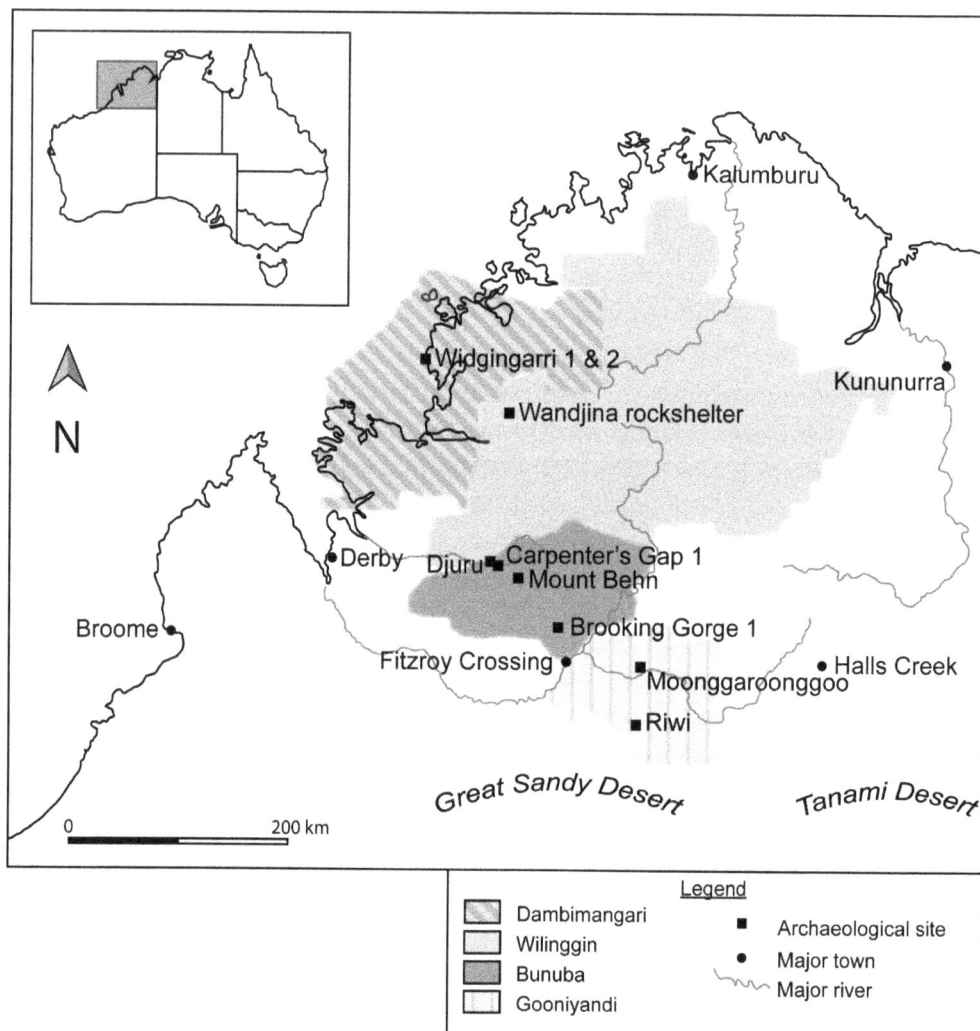

Figure 2.3 Map of the Kimberley showing locations of the archaeological sites with well-preserved macrobotanical sequences analysed for this research. Native Title determined lands after Kimberley Land Council (2022).

customs documented elsewhere in Australia concerning plants used for fuel (Byrne et al. 2019, 2013; Whitau et al. 2018a). Consequently, it is important to note here that carbonisation as a reliable analytical tool to separate anthropogenic from non-anthropogenic macrobotanical remains in Australian archaeological contexts is inconsistent with Aboriginal cultural practices and experiences. Therefore, the importance of dedicated analysis of desiccated components of macrobotanical assemblages cannot be overstated. As a result, this research analysed both desiccated and carbonised remains.

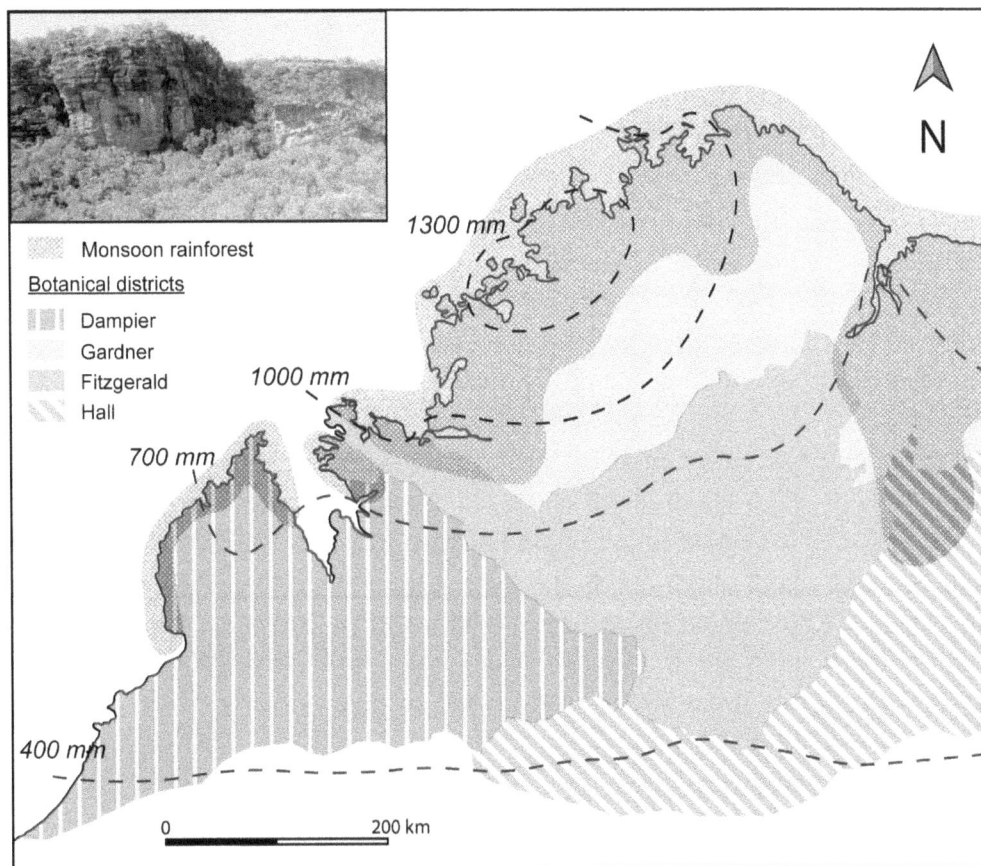

Figure 2.4 Map of the Kimberley region of north-west Western Australia. Botanical districts after Beard (1979). Present day monsoon rainforest distribution after Kenneally (2018). Rainfall isohyets after Bureau of Meteorology (1996).

Methodology

Recovery techniques

Excavation and recovery techniques for each site have been described in detail elsewhere; Brooking Gorge 1, Djuru, Wandjina rock-shelter, and Widgingarri 1 and 2 (Dilkes-Hall et al. 2020b), Carpenter's Gap 1 (Dilkes-Hall et al. 2019a), Moonggaroonggoo (Dilkes-Hall 2019), Mount Behn (Whitau et al. 2018) and Riwi (Dilkes-Hall et al. 2020a). For this research, working with previously excavated materials (legacy collections), difficulties accessing water during fieldwork in remote semi-arid/arid areas, and the fact that most macrobotanical materials are preserved by desiccation and so would be harmed by water exposure (Pearsall 2010, 80–1), meant flotation, which separates charred botanical material from sediment and recovers small botanical remains (Fairbairn 2005; Pearsall 2010), was not carried out for the majority of sites.

All analysed material derive from dry sieving, except in the case of Mount Behn where flotation was used in conjunction with dry sieving (see Whitau et al. 2018).

Taxonomic identification

The first stages of taxonomic identification see macrobotanical remains grouped into analytical units based on morphological similarities, such as shape, dimension, length, width, surface and texture (see Fritz and Nesbitt 2014). Other attributes, such as dispersal mechanisms and rodent gnaw marks, were recorded to help determine non-anthropogenic taxa (Dilkes-Hall et al. 2019a, 37).

Grouped according to morphological attributes, taxonomic identifications are made by referring to one or more comparative reference collections of modern vouchered botanical specimens. Unavailability of comparative reference material can result in taxonomic misidentification generating misinterpretation (see Dilkes-Hall et al. 2019a). Development of collections is time-consuming, costly, often developed by individual researchers and/or for specific projects and are rarely readily accessible or made available digitally. Access to and development of reference collections is the single largest obstacle facing Australian archaeobotanical research today.

For this research, it was necessary to visit and document existing archaeobotanical and botanical collections housed in universities, museums and herbaria, and, in order to fill remaining gaps in the comparative reference collection, conduct botanical collection in the Kimberley region. The physical collection is housed in the archaeology laboratory at the University of Western Australia and is available to researchers. In conjunction, a database (FileMaker Pro) collates images and morphological descriptions of identified archaeobotanical remains alongside botanical information and examples of modern specimens, and is available on request.

Quantification

Quantification of macrobotanical remains included absolute counts (number of identified specimens [NISP]), mass, presence/absence and relative frequencies (these and other quantitative methods outlined in Popper 1988, 53–71).

To account for degrees of fragmentation disregarded by NISP, attempts were made to quantify minimum number of individuals (MNI). For this research, MNI was calculated by determining a single common characteristic distinct to each taxon. Although not generally accepted for publication, MNI is worthy of consideration to highlight variable patterns of fragmentation within and across taxa. For example, analysis of natural patterns of fragmentation of *Vitex glabrata* (Figure 2.5) allowed for the identification of accurate diagnostic elements with which to calculate MNI (e.g. the calyx, the whole fruit or a whole endocarp) and provided direct evidence to compare processed fruits against (discussed further below).

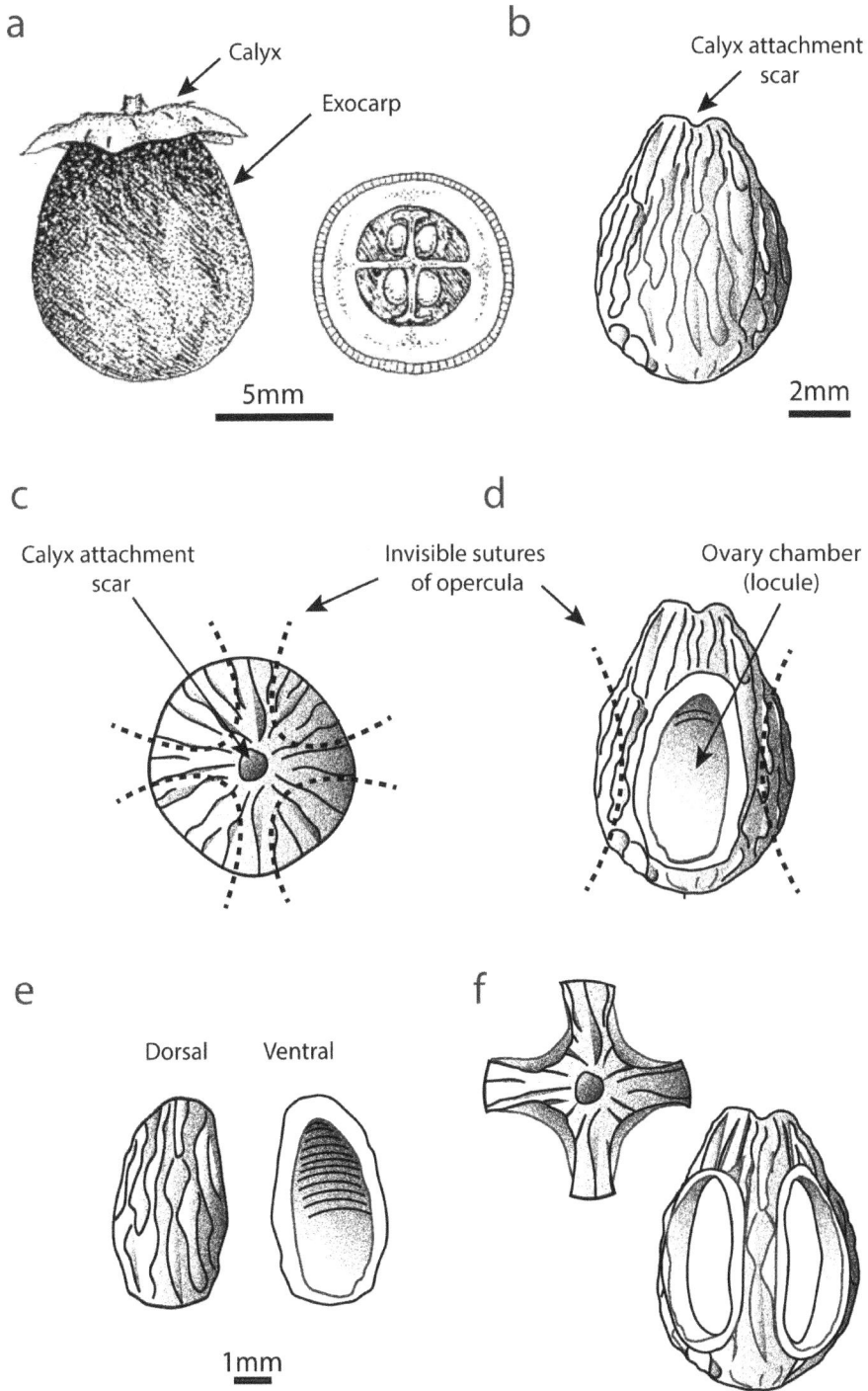

Figure 2.5 *Vitex glabrata* natural pattern of fragmentation: a) *V. glabrata* whole fruit profile and cross section (modified from Munir 1987, 45); b) Endocarp profile; c) Endocarp apex; d) Endocarp profile with operculum removed; e) Operculum; f) Endocarp structure with four opercula removed shown from the apex and profile.

Table 2.1 Total NISP and mass of macrobotanical remains recovered from archaeological sites.

Archaeological site	NISP	Mass (g)
Brooking Gorge 1	4,138	151.39
Carpenter's Gap 1	7,846	185.56
Djuru	96	8.08
Moonggaroonggoo	604	22.14
Mount Behn	203	6.67
Riwi	7,609	61.18
Wandjina rock-shelter	487	5.82
Widgingarri Shelter 1	739	74.79
Widgingarri Shelter 2	111	14.34
Total	**21,833**	**592.97**

Results

From the nine archaeological sites examined, a total of 21,833 macrobotanical remains were analysed (Table 2.1).

Fifty-seven taxa were identified to varying taxonomic levels (Dilkes-Hall et al. 2020b, 1735). Forty-five of these are recognised as economically important plants by Aboriginal groups in the Kimberley today, contributing significantly to our understanding of the different economic, social and technological roles that plants played in Aboriginal lifeways in the past. Overall, taxonomic identification of macrobotanical remains demonstrates – consistently across time and space – one vegetation unit was primarily targeted for the collection of food plants in the Kimberley, monsoon rainforest.

Discussion

Seasonality, mobility and women

Seasonal movements of Aboriginal groups are evidenced in the macrobotanical archives because fruiting times of monsoon rainforest taxa correspond directly to periods of rainfall. As documented in recent history (Scarlett 1985), macrobotanical evidence shows the spatial location of Aboriginal campsites in the past is linked to the tempo of wet/dry climatic cycles of the monsoonal tropics (Dilkes-Hall et al. 2020b, 322).

People's movements to caves and rock-shelters during periods of rainfall have less to do with evading inclement weather and far more to do with ecological knowledge pertaining to resource availability, with people moving to locations where economic botanical resources are known to be coming into abundance (Dilkes-Hall et al. 2019b, 11).

A strong association exists between flora and fauna and, unsurprisingly, monsoon rainforest fruit production coincides with the collection of a number of important seasonal faunal resources (e.g. catfish, stingray, turtles, turtle eggs and goanna) because they too have reached their highest fat and nutritional content during this time of year (Crawford 1982; Davis et al. 2011; Smith and Kalotas 1985). Interestingly, these specific types of faunal resources are, as with plants, most often collected by women (Crawford 1982, 18; Davis, personal communication, 2016; O'Dea et al. 1991, 234). In this way, macrobotanical data available for the Kimberley region shows intimate connections between plants, animals, women, seasonality, landscape use and food traditions, which together strongly influence the configuration of social identity and group membership in Aboriginal societies by showing "that you belong to the country, that you are a product of the country" (Blythe and Wightman 2003, 69).

Plant processing and foodways

When discernible in macrobotanical archives, plant processing activities can provide important insights into processing techniques, cultural preferences and foodways in the past. At Riwi, numerous macrobotanical remains were documented as economic plants by Gooniyandi Traditional Owners (Figure 2.6) and food plants are dominated by monsoon rainforest species, in particular *Vitex* cf. *glabrata* (Gooniyandi name: girndi). Careful analysis of desiccated girndi remains, as opposed to discounting them altogether (e.g. Keepax 1977; Minnis 1981), provided extraordinary evidence of fruit processing (Dilkes-Hall et al. 2019b).

Preservation of girndi calyces by desiccation is important to note here, not only acting as an accurate diagnostic element with which to calculate MNI (n=720), but providing evidence for stage one processing where whole fruits are dehydrated by the camp fire – a process that detaches calyces from fruits and makes robust endocarps brittle and easier to process during stage two (Dilkes-Hall et al. 2019b, 6). Fragmentation patterns produced by stage two processing were discernible from natural breakage patterns, with fragmentation as a result of processing, thereby producing jagged pieces that do not follow natural sutures (Figure 2.5) and cut across the strongest part of the endocarp, the operculum (Figure 2.7). At Riwi, fruit processing, food conservation and associated storage techniques dating to the mid Holocene indicate innovative socio-economic technological

Figure 2.6 Macrobotanical remains recovered from Riwi documented as economic plants by Gooniyandi Traditional Owners: a) *Acacia* sp. Type A pod; b) *Celtis strychnoides* endocarps; c) *Eucalyptus-Corymbia* gall; d) *Eucalyptus-Corymbia* capsule; e) *Ficus* spp. fruits; f) *Flueggea virosa* seeds; g) *Melaleuca* spp. paperbark; h) *Premna acuminata* endocarp; i) *Senna* sp. seed; j) *Terminalia* sp. Type A (cf. *ferdinandiana*) endocarp; k) *Triodia* cf. *pungens* spikelets; l) *Vitex* cf. *glabrata* endocarps (from Dilkes-Hall et al. 2019c, Figure 7, 19).

change to incorporate, manage and conserve seasonally abundant girndi fruits (Dilkes-Hall et al. 2019b).

Here, macrobotanical evidence coupled with documentation of traditional ecological knowledge, plant collection and experimental archaeology worked together to shed light on women's activities, introducing women into an archaeological narrative that they have largely been excluded from (e.g. Bowdler and Balme 2010; Hastorf 1998; Watson and Kennedy 1991). Most importantly, this aspect of the

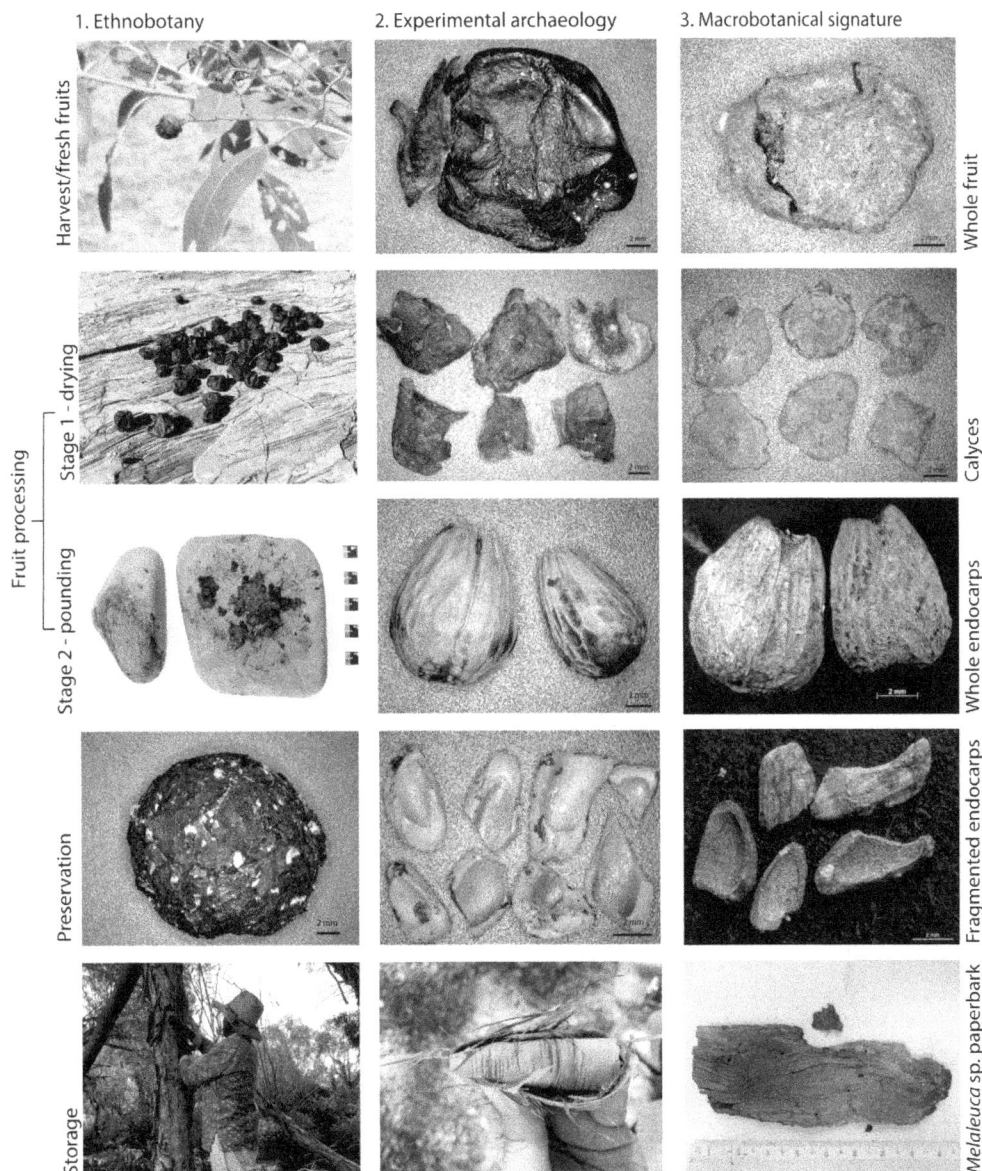

Figure 2.7 Girndi (*Vitex glabrata*) from harvest to storage. Results shown across the three lines of evidence documented 1) ethnobotany 2) experimental archaeology 3) macrobotanical signature. Images produced by Dilkes-Hall using a Canon IXUS 180 digital camera and Dino-Lite Edge digital microscope (from Dilkes-Hall et al. 2019b, Figures 4, 9).

research highlights and strengthens the cultural links between Gooniyandi women today, who maintain the tradition of collection and processing activities, and their ancestors who performed similarly crucial tasks and societal roles several thousand years ago.

Human responses to climate/environmental change

Macrobotanical research offers a unique opportunity to investigate questions around human responses to major palaeoclimatic and palaeoenvironmental changes recorded for the Kimberley since human occupation. Specifically, structural changes in vegetation are indicated by periods of peak aridity, such as the LGM (~18,000 years ago) and late Holocene El Niño–Southern Oscillation (ENSO) driven climate change (~4,200 years ago onwards) (Denniston et al. 2013; Lambeck et al. 2002). Surprisingly, during these sustained periods of aridity – when significant reorganisation of diet and subsistence in response to environmental change might be expected – continued use of monsoon rainforest taxa was observed in the macrobotanical archives with little evidence of dramatic changes to diet and subsistence (Dilkes-Hall et al. 2020b, 1736).

These findings are in contrast to changes indicated by other archaeological materials from some of the same sites under investigation, such as lithic and faunal records at Carpenter's Gap 1 (Maloney et al. 2018), which provide evidence for adjustments coincident to climate and environmental changes. Ultimately, the results demonstrate that changes in people's subsistence strategies and responses to environmental change vary across different economic resources (e.g. stone, fauna and flora), suggesting differences in women's and men's responses to climate change that may have affected the activities and roles of these gendered groups differently, and/or that monsoon rainforest – especially escarpment forests – remained steady as a resource zone despite climate change (Russell-Smith 1985, 243).

A common botanical heritage, colonisation and ecological knowledge

Overall, macrobotanical evidence from the Kimberley indicates a botanical heritage shared by Indigenous peoples across the Indo-Pacific region and other parts of the world. For example, *Terminalia* species have also been recovered from archaeological sites in Papua New Guinea (Gorecki et al. 1991) and Timor-Leste (Oliveria 2008). *Adansonia*, *Grewia* and *Vitex* species have been identified in African macrobotanical records (Kahlheber et al. 2009; Neumann et al. 1998; Sievers 2006). *Celtis* species have been recovered from archaeological sites located in Africa (Kahlheber et al. 2009; Sievers 2006), Georgia (Messager et al. 2010), Israel (Simchoni et al. 2011), New Ireland (Rosenfeld 1997), Papua New Guinea (Fredericksen et al. 1993) and Turkey (Fairbairn et al. 2002). *Canarium* species are present in macrobotanical records from sites in Africa (Kahlheber et al. 2009), Sri Lanka (Perera et al. 2011; Wedage et al. 2020), Borneo (Barton et al. 2016; Dilkes-Hall et al. forthcoming), the Philippines (Pawlik et al. 2014) and New Guinea and Near and Remote Oceania

(Fairbairn and Florin 2022). This interconnectedness indicates a common botanical heritage with foundations along migration pathways to Sahul.

Golson (1971, 209) hypothesised that continental colonisation by Aboriginal groups was assisted by familiarity with Indo-Malaysian plants found in monsoon rainforests across northern Australia. The presence of important Indo-Malaysian botanical elements, *Terminalia* and *Vitex* species, in the earliest cultural unit at Carpenter's Gap 1, dating to 51–39 ka (Dilkes-Hall et al. 2019a, 34), is testimony to this. Early colonising groups likely encountered *Terminalia* and *Vitex* species throughout Sunda and Island Southeast Asia and entered northern Sahul equipped with ecological knowledge of nutritious fruit-bearing trees of these genera, successfully applying this taxonomy to monsoon rainforest environments as observed at Carpenter's Gap 1 (Dilkes-Hall et al. 2019a) and earlier still in the Northern Territory at Madjedbebe by 65–53 ka (Florin et al. 2020).

Transmission of ecological knowledge onto new landscapes likely facilitated expedient identification of nutritious monsoon rainforest plants, easing the process of having to adapt to otherwise totally unknown environments. Available macrobotanical data for the Kimberley indicates monsoon rainforests represented secure and familiar environments to Aboriginal groups, demonstrating their importance in Aboriginal foodways and subsistence systems over 47,000 years of occupation.

Despite dramatic alteration to Aboriginal lifeways since European invasion, monsoon rainforest ecosystems remain a vital resource for Aboriginal groups today. Monsoon rainforests are often associated with important cultural sites and are actively protected from wildfires using traditional land management practices, particularly controlled fire, to maintain boundaries between rainforest and savannah (Vigilante et al. 2017). Maintenance of these ecosystems goes far beyond the simple protection of important economic plant species with these deeply socio-cultural activities encompassing affirmations of group identity, kinship systems, language and cultural connections to Country.

Conclusions
First Nations engagement and archaeobotanical research

To explore Aboriginal plant uses successfully using archaeobotanical evidence, it is fundamental that researchers work closely with Traditional Owners – the local experts in both contemporary and traditional ecological knowledge. Partnership and collaboration with Traditional Owners is essential to understanding plant use in the past and, through two-way learning, mutual benefits can be gained. For example, plant use can be documented with Traditional Owners on botanical surveys and collection, and researchers can demonstrate analytical techniques, return archaeological information pertaining to past plant use, develop interpretations with Traditional Owners and support First Nations authorship.

Engagement between researchers and Traditional Owners has great benefits for knowledge and understanding of plant use, plant resource management, women's activities, landscape use, changing subsistence strategies and responses to environmental change. Collaboration and engagement at the earliest stages of planning shapes research projects for the better (e.g. Maloney et al. 2017) and educates researchers on how archaeological and archaeobotanical records might be better observed and interpreted in a way that has meaningful outcomes for local Aboriginal groups (Davis et al. 2021; Dilkes-Hall et al. 2019c).

Resilience through continuity

Overall, from the macrobotanical evidence available for the Kimberley region, a broad picture of continuity emerges. Here, the notion of continuity should not be taken to suggest a static continuum of botanical knowledge. Instead, macrobotanical evidence suggests that complex socio-economic strategies, such as seasonal scheduling, fruit processing technologies, and landscape management practices (e.g. fire regimes and translocation of economic botanical species), were likely to have been employed by Aboriginal groups to ensure the future availability of important botanical resources (fruit-bearing monsoon rainforest trees) across not only time – as evidenced in the macrobotanical archives by the continued use of these food plants – but also geographical space – as evidenced by the spatial locations of archaeological sites analysed.

Continuity in plants targeted for food through time demonstrates the importance of resilience in both monsoon rainforest vegetation and the subsistence systems employed by Aboriginal groups that target this specific type of vegetation. Simultaneously, this research draws archaeological attention to the significant role of women in Aboriginal economies. Further, collection of plant foods, often carried out as a group activity, encompasses intangible aspects of social life, such as reinforcing identity and group cohesion and fulfilling the vital role of passing on important ecological knowledge to younger generations.

Since colonisation of Sahul ~65,000 years ago (Clarkson et al. 2017), persistent use of monsoon rainforest fruits through to the present demonstrates botanical knowledge carried by early Aboriginal populations was passed down intergenerationally. In the Kimberley, macrobotanical evidence shows transmission of ecological knowledge over 47,000 years highlighting the important role of Aboriginal oral traditions and the essential function/s that these perform in culture, society and economy while informing our understanding of vulnerability and resilience to climate change in the past.

Acknowledgements

The author India Ella Dilkes-Hall (IEDH) thanks the Dambimangari, Wilinggin, Bunuba and Gooniyandi Aboriginal communities of the lands where archaeological excavations took place. Specifically, IEDH acknowledges support from Gooniyandi Traditional Owners, Muludja community members and Gooniyandi Rangers. A special thanks to Rosemary Nuggett and the Mimbi Community. To record ethnobotanical knowledge with Gooniyandi Traditional Owners, ethics approval was granted by the Human Ethics Office at the University of Western Australia (RA/4/1/8255). The Girndi Project, undertaken with senior Gooniyandi Traditional Owners June Davis and Helen Malo, was supported by Graduate Women (WA) Jillian Bradshaw Scholarship 2017 and the Australian Archaeological Association Student Research Grant Scheme 2017 received by IEDH. Thank you to Matthew David Barrett, Russell Lindsey Barrett and Kevin Kenneally for assistance with taxonomic identifications over the course of my doctoral research. At time of writing, IEDH was a Forrest Foundation Prospect Fellow supported by the Forrest Research Foundation. In August 2018, June Davis† passed away. Her laughter sings out across Gooniyandi Country for eternity. Her family and community have asked that her name and photos continue to be used in recognition of her great contributions to the research. A special mention to Dr Tim Ryan Maloney†, without whom crucial parts of this research would not have been possible. Simply the best.

References

Antolín, F., M.B. Azorin and O. López-Bultó (2016). Archaeobotany of wild plant use: approaches to the exploitation of wild plant resources in the past and its social implications. *Quaternary International* 404: 1–3.

Asmussen, B. (2010). In a nutshell: the identification and archaeological application of experimentally defined correlates of *Macrozamia* seed processing. *Journal of Archaeological Science* 37(9): 2117–25.

Asmussen, B. (2008). Anything more than a picnic? Re-considering arguments for ceremonial *Macrozamia* use in mid-Holocene Australia. *Archaeology in Oceania* 43(3): 93–103.

Asmussen, B. and P. McInnes (2013). Assessing the impact of mid-to-late Holocene ENSO-driven climate change on toxic *Macrozamia* seed use: a 5,000 year record from eastern Australia. *Journal of Archaeological Science* 40(1): 471–80.

Atchison, J. (2009). Human impacts on *Persoonia falcata*. Perspectives on post-contact vegetation change in the Keep River region, Australia, from contemporary vegetation surveys. *Vegetation History and Archaeobotany* 18(2): 147–57.

Atchison, J., L. Head and R. Fullagar (2005). Archaeobotany of fruit seed processing in a monsoon savanna environment: evidence from the Keep River region, Northern Territory, Australia. *Journal of Archaeological Science* 32(2): 167–81.

Balme, J. (2013). Of boats and string: the maritime colonisation of Australia. *Quaternary International* 285: 68–75.

Balme, J. and K. Morse (2006). Shell beads and social behaviour in Pleistocene Australia. *Antiquity* 80(310): 799–811.

Balme, J., S. O'Connor, T.R. Maloney, K. Akerman, B. Keaney and I.E. Dilkes-Hall (2022). Fibre technologies in Indigenous Australia: evidence from archaeological excavations in the Kimberley region. *Australian Archaeology* 88(2): 115–28. DOI: 10.1080/03122417.2022.2054510.

Barton, H. and T. Denham (2018). Vegecultures and the social-biological transformations of plants and people. *Quaternary International* 489: 17–25.

Barton, H., V. Paz and A.J. Carlos (2016). Plant food remains from the Niah caves: macroscopic and microscopic approaches. In G. Barker and L. Farr, eds. *Archaeological investigations in the Niah caves, Sarawak, The Archaeology of the Niah Caves, Sarawak, vol. 2*, 455–68. Cambridge: McDonald Institute for Archaeological Research.

Beard, J.S. (1979). *The vegetation of the Kimberley area: explanatory notes to sheet 1*. Perth: University of Western Australia Press.

Beard, J.S. (1976). The monsoon forests of the Admiralty Gulf, Western Australia. *Vegetatio* 31(3): 177–92.

Beaton, J.M. (1977). Dangerous harvest: investigations in late pre-historic occupation of upland south-east central Queensland. Doctoral thesis, Australian National University, Canberra, ACT.

Beck, W. (1992). Aboriginal preparation of *Cycas* seeds in Australia. *Economic Botany* 46(2): 133–47.

Beck, W. (1980). Aspects of plant taphonomy in Australian archaeology. Master's thesis, La Trobe University, Melbourne, Vic.

Beck, W., A. Clarke and L. Head, eds (1989). *Plants in Australian archaeology*. TEMPUS, Series No. 1. St Lucia: Anthropology Museum, University of Queensland.

Blythe, J. and G. Wightman (2003). The role of animals and plants in maintaining links. In J. Blythe and R.M. Brown, eds. *Maintaining the links: language, identity and the land. Proceedings of the seventh conference presented by the Foundation for Endangered Languages*, 69–77. Bath: Foundation for Endangered Languages.

Bowdler, S. and J. Balme (2010). Gatherers and grannies: further thoughts on the origins of gender. *Australian Feminist Studies* 25(66): 391–405.

Brockwell, S., J. Stevenson and A. Clarke (2016). Plants and archaeology in Australia. In K. Hardy and L. Kubiak-Martens, eds. *Wild harvest: plants in the hominin and pre-agrarian human worlds*, 273–99. Oxford: Oxbow Books.

Bureau of Meteorology (1996). *Kimberley, Western Australia: climatic survey*. Canberra: Australian Government Publishing Service.

Byrne, C., E. Dotte-Sarout and V. Winton (2013). Charcoals as indicators of ancient tree and fuel strategies: an application of anthracology in the Australian midwest. *Australian Archaeology* 77(1): 94–106.

Byrne, C., T. Dooley, T. Manne, A. Paterson and E. Dotte-Sarout (2019). Island survival: the anthracological and archaeofaunal evidence for colonial-era events on Barrow Island, north-west Australia. *Archaeology in Oceania* 55(1): 15–32.

Byrne, C., E. Dotte-Sarout, S. van Leeuwen, J. McDonald and P. Veth (2021). The dependable deep time *Acacia*: anthracological analysis from Australia's oldest Western Desert site. *Journal of Archaeological Science: Reports* 40: 103–87.

Bush, L.L. (2004). *Boundary conditions: macrobotanical remains and the Oliver Phase of central Indiana, A.D. 1200–1450*. Tuscaloosa: University of Alabama Press.

Cappers, R.T.J. and R. Neef (2012). *Handbook of plant palaeoecology*. Groningen: Barkhuis.

Carah, X.A. (2017). Regime change: an anthracological assessment of fuel selection and management at Madjedbebe (Malakunanja II), Mirarr country, Australia. Doctoral thesis, University of Queensland, Brisbane, Qld.

Clarke, A. (1989). Macroscopic plant remains. In W. Beck, A. Clarke and L. Head, eds. *Plants in Australian archaeology*, 54–89. Tempus, Series No. 1. St Lucia: Anthropology Museum, University of Queensland.

Clarke, A. (1987). An analysis of archaeobotanical data from two sites in Kakadu National Park, Northern Territory. Master's thesis, University of Western Australia, Crawley, WA.

Clarke, A. (1985). A preliminary archaeobotanical analysis of the Anbangbang I site. In R. Jones, ed. *Archaeological research in Kakadu National Park*, 77–96. Australian National Parks and Wildlife Service, Special Publication 13. Canberra: Australian National University.

Clarkson, C., Z. Jacobs, B. Marwick, R. Fullagar, L.A. Wallis, M. Smith et al. (2017). Human occupation of northern Australia by 65,000 years ago. *Nature* 547(7663): 306–13.

Cosgrove, R., J. Field and A. Ferrier (2007). The archaeology of Australia's tropical rainforests. *Palaeogeography, Palaeoclimatology, Palaeoecology* 251(1): 150–73.

Crawford, I.M. (1982). *Traditional Aboriginal plant resources in the Kalumburu area: aspects in ethno-economics*. Perth: Western Australian Museum.

Davis, J., M. Street, H. Malo, I. Cherel and E. Woodward (2011). *Mingayooroo – Manyi Waranggiri Yarrangi. Gooniyandi seasons (calendar) Margaret River, Fitzroy Valley, Western Australia*. Darwin: CSIRO Ecosystem Sciences.

Davis, J., H. Malo, E. Cherel, M. Street, W. Cherrabun, B. Cherel and I.E. Dilkes-Hall (2021). *Gooniyandi Binarri*. Crawley: The Author.

Denham, T.P. (2018). *Tracing early agriculture in the highlands of New Guinea: plot, mound and ditch*. Oxford: Routledge.

Denham, T., J. Atchison, J. Austin, S. Bestel, D. Bowdery, A. Crowther, N. Dolby, A. Fairbairn, J. Field and A. Kennedy (2009). Archaeobotany in Australia and New Guinea: practice, potential and prospects. *Australian Archaeology* 68(1): 1–10.

Denham, T., H. Barton, C.C. Castillo, A. Crowther, E. Dotte-Sarout, S.A. Florin, J. Pritchard, A. Barron, Y. Zhang and D.Q. Fuller (2020). The domestication syndrome in vegetatively propagated field crops. *Annals of Botany* 125: 581–97.

Denniston, R.F., K.H. Wyrwoll, V.J. Polyak, J.R. Brown, Y. Asmerom, A.D. Wanamaker Jr et al. (2013). A stalagmite record for Holocene Indonesian-Australian summer monsoon variability from the Australian tropics. *Quaternary Science Reviews* 78: 155–68.

Dietsch, M-F. (1996). Gathered fruits and cultivated plants at Bercy (Paris), a Neolithic village in a fluvial context. *Vegetation History and Archaeobotany* 5(1/2): 89–97.

Dilkes-Hall, I.E. (2019). Macrobotanical remains and preservational bias: an example from Moonggaroonggoo, Gooniyandi Country, Western Australia. *Australian Archaeology* 85(2): 210–14.

Dilkes-Hall, I.E., S. O'Connor and J. Balme (2019a). People-plant interaction and economic botany over 47,000 years of occupation at Carpenter's Gap 1, south central Kimberley. *Australian Archaeology* 85(1): 30–47.

Dilkes-Hall, I.E., J. Davis and H. Malo (2019b). "*Doog girndi*". Using experimental archaeology to understand the archaeobotanical record: an investigation of mid-Holocene *Vitex glabrata* fruit processing in Gooniyandi Country, northwest Australia. *The Artefact* 42: 3–16.

Dilkes-Hall, I.E., T.R. Maloney, J. Davis, H. Malo, E. Cherel, M. Street, W. Cherrabun and B. Cherel (2019c). Understanding archaeobotany through ethnobotany: an example from Gooniyandi Country, northwest, Western Australia. *Journal of Anthropological Society of South Australia* 43: 5–33.

Dilkes-Hall, I.E., J. Balme, S. O'Connor and E. Dotte-Sarout (2020a). Archaeobotany of Aboriginal plant foods during the Holocene at Riwi, south central Kimberley, Western Australia. *Vegetation History and Archaeobotany* 29(3): 309–25.

Dilkes-Hall I.E., J. Balme, S. O'Connor and E. Dotte-Sarout (2020b). Evaluating people's responses to ENSO driven climate change during the Holocene in northwest Australia through macrobotanical analyses. *The Holocene* 30 (12): 1728–40.

Dilkes-Hall, I.E., T.R. Maloney, E. Sriputri, A. Priyatno, Febryanto, M. Effendy et al. (forthcoming). Planting the seeds: an overview of archaeobotany in Borneo and new directions for East Kalimantan. *KALPATARU*.

Dotte-Sarout, E., X. Carah and C. Byrne (2015). Not just carbon: assessment and prospects for the application of anthracology in Oceania. *Archaeology in Oceania* 50(1): 1–22.

Fairbairn, A.S. and S.A. Florin (2022). Archaeological identification of fragmented nuts and fruits from key Asia-Pacific economic tree species using anatomical criteria: comparative analysis of *Canarium, Pandanus* and *Terminalia. Archaeology in Oceania* 57: 160–88.

Fairbairn, A., E. Asouti, J. Near and D. Martinoli (2002). Macro-botanical evidence for plant use at neolithic Çatalhöyük, south-central Anatolia. Turkey. *Vegetation History and Archaeobotany* 11(1): 41–54.

Ferrier, A. and R. Cosgrove (2012). Aboriginal exploitation of toxic nuts as a late-Holocene subsistence strategy in Australia's tropical rainforests. In S. Haberle and B. David, eds. *Peopled landscapes: archaeological and biogeographical approaches to landscapes*, 103–20. Terra Australis 34. Acton: Australian National University E Press.

Field, J.H., L. Kealhofer, R. Cosgrove and A.C.F. Coster (2016). Human-environment dynamics during the Holocene in the Australian wet tropics of NE Queensland: a starch and phytolith study. *Journal of Anthropological Archaeology* 44: 216–34.

Florin, S.A. and X. Carah (2018). Moving past the "Neolithic problem": the development and interaction of subsistence systems across northern Sahul. *Quaternary International* 489: 46–62.

Florin, S.A., A.S. Fairbairn, M. Nango, D. Djandjomerr, B. Marwick, R. Fullagar et al. (2020). The first Australian plant foods at Madjedbebe, 65,000–53,000 years ago. *Nature Communications* 11(924). DOI: 10.1038/s41467-020-14723-0.

Florin, S.A., P. Roberts, B. Marwick, N.R. Patton, J. Shulmeister, C.E. Lovelock et al. (2021). Pandanus nutshell generates a palaeoprecipitation record for human occupation at Madjedbebe, northern Australia. *Nature Ecology and Evolution* 5(3): 295–303.

Ford, R.I. (1985). Patterns of prehistoric food production in North America. In R.I. Ford, ed. *Prehistoric food production in North America*, 341–64. Michigan: University of Michigan, Museum of Anthropology.

Fredericksen, C., M. Spriggs and W. Ambrose (1993). Pamwak rockshelter: a Pleistocene site on Manus Island, Papua New Guinea. In M.A. Smith, M. Spriggs and B. Frankhauser, eds. *Sahul in review: Pleistocene archaeology in Australia, New Guinea and Island Melanesia. Occasional papers in prehistory, No. 24,* 144–52. Canberra: Australian National University.

Fritz, G. and M. Nesbitt (2014). Laboratory analysis and identification of plant macroremains. In J.M. Marston, J. D'alpoim Guedes and C. Warinner, eds. *Method and theory in paleoethnobotany,* 115–45. Boulder: University Press of Colorado.

Fuller, D.Q. (2018). Long and attenuated: comparative trends in the domestication of tree fruits. *Vegetation History and Archaeobotany* 27(1): 165–76.

Fuller, D.Q. and R. Allaby (2009). Seed dispersal and crop domestication: shattering, germination, and seasonality in evolution under cultivation. In L. Østergaard, ed. *Fruit development and seed dispersal,* 238–95. Annual Plant Reviews Volume 38. Chichester: Blackwell Publishing.

Gallagher, D.E. (2014). Formation processes of the macrobotanical record. In J.M. Marston, J. D'alpoim Guedes and C. Warinner, eds. *Method and theory in paleoethnobotany,* 19–34. Boulder: University Press of Colorado.

Golson, J. (1971). Australian Aboriginal food plants: some ecological and culture-historical implications. In D.J. Mulvaney and J. Golson, eds. *Aboriginal man and environment in Australia,* 196–238. Canberra: Australian National University.

Golson, J., T.P. Denham, P.J. Hughes, P. Swadling and J. Muke, eds (2017). *Ten thousand years of cultivation at Kuk Swamp in the highlands of Papua New Guinea.* Terra Australis 46. Canberra: Australian National University E Press.

Gorecki, P., M. Mabin and J. Campbell (1991). Archaeology and geomorphology of the Vanimo coast, Papua New Guinea: preliminary results. *Archaeology in Oceania* 26(3): 119–22.

Hancock, J.F. (2004). *Plant evolution and the origin of crop species.* Wallingford: CABI Publishing.

Hardy, K. and L. Kubiak-Martens, eds (2016). *Wild harvest: plants in the hominin and pre-agrarian human worlds.* Oxford: Oxbow Books.

Harris, D.R. (1990). *Settling down and breaking ground: rethinking the Neolithic revolution.* Amsterdam: Stichting Nederlands Museum voor Anthropologie en Prehistorie, Twaalfde Kroon-Voordracht.

Hastorf, C.A. (1999). Recent research in paleothnobotany. *Journal of Archaeological Research* 7(1): 55–103.

Hastorf, C.A. (1998). The cultural life of early domestic plant use. *Antiquity* 72(278): 773–82.

Hather, J.G. (1994). *Tropical archaeobotany: applications and new developments.* London: Routledge.

Hather, J.G. and S.L.R. Mason, eds (2002). *Hunter-gatherer archaeobotany: perspectives from the northern temperate zone.* London: Institute of Archaeology, University College London.

Hayes, E., R. Fullagar, K. Mulvaney and K. Connell (2018). Food or fibercraft? Grinding stones and Aboriginal use of *Triodia* grass (spinifex). *Quaternary International* 468(Part B): 271–83.

Head, L. (1984). Environment as artefact: a palaeoecological contribution to the prehistory of southwestern Victoria. Doctoral thesis, Monash University, Melbourne, Vic.

Heiser, C.B. (1990). *Seed to civilization.* Cambridge: Harvard University Press.

Hercus, L. (2012). Trees from the Dreaming. *The Artefact* 35: 40–9.

Higgs, E. and M.R. Jarman (1972). The origins of animal and plant husbandry. In E. Higgs, ed. *Papers in economic prehistory*, 3–13. Cambridge: Cambridge University Press.

Hiscock, P., S. O'Connor, J. Balme and T. Maloney (2016). World's earliest ground-edge axe production coincides with human colonisation of Australia. *Australian Archaeology* 82(1): 2–11.

Hynes, R.A. and A.K. Chase (1982). Plants, sites and domiculture: Aboriginal influence upon plant communities in Cape York Peninsula. *Archaeology in Oceania* 17(1): 38–50.

Kaberry, P. (1935). The Forrest River and Lyne River tribes of north-west Australia: a report on field work. *Oceania* 5(4): 408–36.

Kahlheber, S., A. Höhn and N. Rupp (2009). Archaeobotanical studies at Nok sites: an interim report. *Nyame Akuma* 71: 2–17.

Kenneally, K.F. (2018). Kimberley tropical monsoon rainforest of Western Australia: perspectives on biological diversity. *Journal of the Botanical Research Institute of Texas* 12(1): 149–228.

Keen, I. (2021). Foragers or farmers: dark emu and the controversy over Aboriginal agriculture. *Anthropological Forum* 31(1): 106–28.

Keepax, C. (1977). Contamination of archaeological deposits by seeds of modern origin with particular reference to the use of flotation machines. *Journal of Archaeological Science* 4(3): 221–9.

King, F. and E. Dotte-Sarout (2019). Wood charcoal analysis in tropical rainforest: a pilot study identifying firewood used at toxic nut processing sites in northeast Queensland, Australia. *Vegetation History and Archaeobotany* 28(2): 163–85.

Kimberley Land Council (2022). *Native title map,* KLC website, accessed 13 January 2022. https://www.klc.org.au/native-title-map.

Lambeck, K., Y. Yokoyama and T. Purcell (2002). Into and out of the Last Glacial Maximum: sea-level change during Oxygen Isotope Stages 3 and 2. *Quaternary Science Reviews* 21: 343–360.

Maloney, T.R. and I.E. Dilkes-Hall (2020). Assessing the spread and uptake of tula adze technology in the late Holocene across the southern Kimberley of Western Australia. *Australian Archaeology* 86(3): 264–83.

Maloney, T., I.E. Dilkes-Hall and J. Davis (2017). Indigenous led archaeological excavation at Moonggaroonggoo, Gooniyandi country, Western Australia, reveals late Holocene occupation. *Australian Archaeology* 83(3): 178–84.

Maloney, T., S. O'Connor, R. Wood and J. Balme (2018). Carpenters Gap 1: A 47,000 year old record of Indigenous adaption and innovation. *Quaternary Science Reviews* 191: 204–28.

McArthur, M. (1960). Food consumption and dietary levels of groups of Aborigines living on naturally occuring foods. In C.P. Mountford, ed. *Record of the American-Australian expedition in Arnhem Land, Vol II, Anthropology and Nutrition,* 90–135. Melbourne: University of Melbourne.

McConnell, K. (1998). The prehistoric use of Chenopodiaceae in Australia: evidence from Carpenter's Gap Shelter 1 in the Kimberley, Australia. *Vegetation History and Archaeobotany* 7(3): 179–88.

McConnell, K. and S. O'Connor (1997). 40,000 year record of food plants in the southern Kimberley ranges, Western Australia. *Australian Archaeology* 45(1): 20–31.

Meehan, B. (1989). Plant use in a contemporary Aboriginal community and prehistoric implications. In W. Beck, A. Clarke and L. Head, eds. *Plants in Australian Archaeology,* 14–30. Tempus, Series No. 1. St Lucia: Anthropology Museum, University of Queensland.

Meggitt, M.J. (1964). Aboriginal food-gatherers of tropical Australia. In *The Ecology of Man in the tropical Environment,* 30–37. International Union for Conservation of Native and Natural Resources, Ninth Technical Meeting, Publication Series 4. Morges, Switzerland: International Union for Conservation of Native and Natural Resources.

Messager, E., A. Badou, F. Fröhlich, B. Deniaux, D. Lordkipanidze and P. Voinchet (2010). Fruit and seed biomineralization and its effect on preservation. *Archaeological and Anthropological Sciences* 2(1): 25–34.

Miksicek, C.H. (1987). Formation processes of the archaeobotanical record. *Advances in Archaeological Method and Theory* 10: 211–47.

Minnis, P.E. (1981). Seeds in archaeological sites: sources and some interpretive problems. *American Antiquity* 46(1): 143–52.

Mooney, D.E. and M. Martín-Seijo (2021). Editorial: archaeobotany in the wider landscape. *Environmental Archaeology* 26(2): 115–21.

Munir, A.A. (1987). A taxonomic revision of the genus *Vitex* L. (Verbenaceae) in Australia *Journal of the Adelaide Botanic Gardens* 10(1): 31–79.

O'Brien, P. (2019). The bogus Aboriginal world of Bruce Pascoe. *Quandrant online.* https://quadrant.org.au/magazine/2019/12/the-bogus-aboriginal-world-of-brucepascoe/.

O'Brien, P. (2021a). A left-flank dismissal of "Dark Emu". *Quadrant online.* quadrant.org.au/opinion/review/2021/07/a-left-flank-dismissal-of-dark-emu/.

Neumann, K., S. Kahlheber and D. Uebel (1998). Remains of woody plants from Saouga, a medieval west African village. *Vegetation History and Archaeobotany* 7(2): 57–77.

O'Dea, K., P.A. Jewell, A. Whiten, S.A. Altmann, S.S. Strickland and O.T. Oftedal (1991). Traditional diet and food preferences of Australian Aboriginal hunter-gatherers. *Philosophical Transactions: Biological Sciences* 334(1270): 233–41.

Oliveira, N.V. (2008). Subsistence archaeobotany: food production and the agricultural transition in East Timor. Doctoral thesis, Australian National University, Canberra, ACT.

Ouzman, S., P. Veth, C. Myers, P. Heaney and K.F. Kenneally (2019). Plants before animals?: Aboriginal rock art as evidence of ecoscaping in Australia's Kimberley. In B. David and I.J. McNiven, eds. *The Oxford handbook of the archaeology and anthropology of rock art*, 1–13. Oxford: Oxford University Press.

Owen, T., J. Field, S. Luu, P. Kokatha Aboriginal, B. Stephenson and A.C.F. Coster (2019). Ancient starch analysis of grinding stones from Kokatha Country, South Australia. *Journal of Archaeological Science: Reports* 23: 178–88.

Pascoe, B. (2014). *Dark emu: black seeds: agriculture or accident?* Broome: Magabala Books.

Pawlik, A.F., P.J. Piper, M.G.P.G. Faylona, S.B. Padilla, J. Carlos, A.S.B. Mijares et al. (2014). Adaptation and foraging from the terminal Pleistocene to the early Holocene: excavation at Bubog on Ilin Island, Philippines. *Journal of Field Archaeology* 39(3): 230–47.

Pearsall, D.M. (2010). *Paleoethnobotany: a handbook of procedures.* California: Left Coast Press.

Perera, N., N. Kourampas, I.A. Simpson, S.U. Deraniyagala, D. Bulbeck, J. Kamminga et al. (2011). People of the ancient rainforest: Late Pleistocene foragers at the Batadomba-lena rockshelter, Sri Lanka. *Journal of Human Evolution* 61(3): 254–69.

Piperno, D.R. (2018). A model of agricultural origins. *Nature Human Behaviour* 2(7): 446–7.

Porr, M. and E. Vivian-Williams (2021). The tragedy of Bruce Pascoe's *Dark Emu*. *Australian Archaeology* 87(3): 300–4.

Popper, V.S. (1988). Selecting quantitative measurements in paleoethnobotany. In C.A. Hastorf and V.S. Popper, eds. *Current paleoethnobotany: analytical methods and cultural interpretations of archeological plant remains*, 53–71. Prehistoric Archeology and Ecology Series. Chicago: University of Chicago Press.

Reed, C.A., ed (1977). *Origins of agriculture*. The Hague: Mouton Publishers.

Roberts, P., A. Buhrich, V. Caetano-Andrade, R. Cosgrove, A. Fairbairn, S.A. Florin et al. (2021). Reimagining the relationship between Gondwanan forests and Aboriginal land management in Australia's "wet tropics" *iScience* 24(3): 102190.

Rosenfeld, A. (1997). Excavation at Buang Merabak, central New Ireland. *Bulletin of the Indo-Pacific Prehistory Association* 16: 213–24.

Russell-Smith, J. (1985). Studies in the jungle: people, fire, and monsoon forest. In R. Jones, ed. *Archaeological research in Kakadu National Park*, 241–67. Canberra: Australian National University.

Russell-Smith, J., D. Lucas, M. Gapindi, B. Gunbunuka, N. Kapirigi, G. Namingum, K. Lucas, P. Giuliani and G. Chaloupka (1997). Aboriginal resource utilization and fire management practice in western Arnhem Land, monsoonal northern Australia: notes for prehistory, lessons for the future. *Human Ecology* 25(2): 159–95.

Sayok, A.K. and U. Teucher (2018). Loss of food plants knowledge and identity among Indigenous peoples in Malaysia. *Journal of Advanced Research in Social and Behavioural Sciences* 11(1): 174–88.

Scarlett, N.H. (1985). *A preliminary account of the ethnobotany of the Kija people of Bungle Bungle outcamp*. East Kimberley Working Paper 6. Canberra: Center for Resource and Environmental Studies.

Sievers, C. (2006). Seeds from the Middle Stone Age layers at Sibudu Cave. *Southern African Humanities* 18(1): 203–22.

Simchoni, O. and M.E. Kislev (2011). Early finds of *Celtis australis* in the southern Levant. *Vegetation History and Archaeobotany* 20(4): 267–71.

Smith, B.D. (2001). Low-level food production. *Journal of Archaeological Research* 9(1): 1–43.

Smith, M. (1982). Late Pleistocene *Zamia* exploitation in southern Western Australia. *Archaeology in Oceania* 17(3): 117–21.

Smith, M. and A.C. Kalotas (1985). Bardi plants: an annotated list of plants and their use by the Bardi Aborigines of Dampierland, northwestern Australia. *Records of the Western Australian Museum* 12(3): 317–59.

Spengler III, R.N. (2020). Anthropogenic seed dispersal: rethinking the origins of plant domestication. *Trends in Plant Science* 25(4): 340–48.

Sutton, P. and K. Walshe (2021). *Farmers or hunter-gatherers? The Dark Emu debate.* Melbourne: Melbourne University Press.

Ucko, P.J. and G.W. Dimbleby, eds (1969). *The domestication and exploitation of plants and animals.* London: Gerald Duckworth & Co. Ltd.

Vigilante, T., S. Ondei, C. Goonack, D. Williams, P. Young and D.M.J.S. Bowman (2017). Collaborative research on the ecology and management of the "Wulo" monsoon rainforest in Wunambal Gaambera Country, north Kimberley, Australia. *Land* 6(4): 68–88.

Wallis, L.A. and S. O'Connor (1998). Residues on a sample of stone points from the west Kimberley. In R. Fullager, ed. *A closer look: recent Australian studies of stone tools*, 149–78. Sydney: Archaeological Computing Laboratory, School of Archaeology, the University of Sydney.

Walsh, M. (2021). There's something about *marnunggurrun*: wood charcoal as an indicator of earth ovens and anthropogenic fire regimes at Walanjiwurru 1, Marra Country. Honours thesis, University of Western Australia, Crawley, WA.

Walsh, M., E. Dotte-Sarout, L.M. Brady, J. Bradley, J. Ash, D. Wesley, S. Evans and D. Barrett (2024). Collaborative anthracology and cultural understandings of wood charcoal in Marra Country (northern Australia). *Archaeological and Anthropological Sciences* 16(9): 148. DOI: 10.1007/s12520-024-02052-y.

Watson, P.J. and M. Kennedy (1991). The development of horticulture in the eastern woodlands of North America: women's role. In J. Gero and M. Conkey, eds. *Engendering archaeology*, 255–75. Oxford: Basil Blackwell.

Wedage, O., P. Roberts, P. Faulkner, A. Crowther, K. Douka, A. Picin et al. (2020). Late Pleistocene to early-Holocene rainforest foraging in Sri Lanka: Multidisciplinary analysis at Kitulgala Beli-lena. *Quaternary Science Reviews* 231: 106200. DOI: 10.1016/j.quascirev.2020.106200.

Whitau, R. (2018). Late Quaternary human-environment interaction in Bunuba and Gooniyandi country, Western Australia. Doctoral thesis, Australian National University, Canberra, ACT.

Whitau, R., J. Balme, S. O'Connor and R. Wood (2017). Wood charcoal analysis at Riwi cave, Gooniyandi country, Western Australia. *Quaternary International* 457: 140–54.

Whitau, R., I.E. Dilkes-Hall, D. Vannieuwenhuyse, S. O'Connor and J. Balme (2018a). The curious case of Proteaceae: macrobotanical investigations at Mount Behn rockshelter, Bunuba Country, Western Australia. *Australian Archaeology* 84(1): 19–36.

Whitau, R., D. Vannieuwenhuyse, E. Dotte-Sarout, J. Balme and S. O'Connor (2018b). Home is where the hearth is: anthracological and microstratigraphic analyses of Pleistocene and Holocene combustion features, Riwi Cave (Kimberley, Western Australia). *Journal of Archaeological Method and Theory* 25(3): 739–76.

Yen, D.E. (1988). Introduction to group of papers about plants. In B. Meehan and R. Jones, eds. *Archaeology with ethnography: an Australian perspective.* Canberra: Australian National University.

3

There were plenty of fish in the sea
The archaeology of fish consumption in Australia

Morgan C.F. Disspain[1], Tiina Manne[2]
and Ariana B.J. Lambrides[3]

Introduction

Settlement of the Australian continent occurred 60,000–65,000 years ago (Clarkson, et al. 2017). At that time, global sea levels were considerably lower, and Australia was part of a vast landmass, called Sahul, joined with Papua New Guinea to the north and Tasmania to the south. We know that people must have made water-crossings to reach Sahul, either from the north into New Guinea, or south along the Lesser Sunda Islands into Australia. Did people eat fish and other marine resources thousands of years ago when they crossed into Australia? This question is difficult to answer, as today the coastline of most of this supercontinent lies submerged, creating challenges for understanding how people may have used these earlier coastlines.

The history of fishing in Australia has been dynamic; from the earliest evidence of First Nations fisheries to colonial encounters, the nineteenth and twentieth century industrialisation of fisheries, and widescale uptake of recreational fishing over the past 50 years. Beginning with evidence of fishing just to the north of Australia at 42,000 years ago and continuing through to early nineteenth century British colonisation, we examine what we know about the role of fish in Australia's past.

1   Niche Environment and Heritage Pty Ltd, North Parramatta, New South Wales
2   School of Social Science, The University of Queensland, Brisbane
3   ARC Centre of Excellence for Indigenous and Environmental Histories and Futures, College of Arts, Society and Education, James Cook University, Queensland

We look at the numerous ways that archaeologists study fish remains (a specialist field termed "ichthyoarchaeology"), from simple taxonomic identifications to highly specialised scientific methods like isotope analysis, and discuss case studies from archaeological sites across Australia. These archaeological assemblages are of vital importance, and we discuss how they can contribute unique information about the social and cultural significance of fish as food for the inhabitants of Australia in the past and through to the present-day.

Where do archaeologists find fish remains and what do they find?

Shell middens and mounds

Archaeological fish remains can be found in an assortment of different site types in Australia, and the preservation of these remains is largely dependent on the individual site formation processes and depositional conditions. The kinds of fish remains that can be found include bones, otoliths (ear bones), teeth and scales; however, evidence of fish consumption can also be gleaned from the presence of fishing tools and technologies such as fishhooks, nets and traps (McNiven and Lambrides 2021; Rowland and Ulm 2011).

One of the most common site types in coastal, estuarine or riverine environments in Australia is shell middens. These are accumulations of animal remains including shell (or mollusc), fish and other marine and terrestrial fauna, artefacts, charcoal and hearth stones from fires, and other floral remains, which were constructed by Aboriginal and Torres Strait Islander people. These sites were often culturally important meeting or gathering places, where people would come together and prepare food and use the shells and other raw materials, such as stone, to manufacture tools and ornaments like fishhooks, shell beads and flaked stone tools. Over hundreds, or even thousands of years of use, these sites continue to grow in height and surface area and become what archaeologists would characterise as a shell midden or mound. Ages of middens along the present coastline in Australia typically range from the time of the most recent sea level stabilisation, from ~7,000 years ago (Manne and Veth 2015; McNiven 2006), but most date to the past 4,000 years (Faulkner 2013; Lambrides et al. 2020). Some much earlier middens have also been recorded (Barker 2004; Richards 2012). Riverine/freshwater middens along some of the country's ancient inland systems have been dated to approximately 29,000 years ago (Westell et al. 2020). Middens can also contain historic material, dating from after British colonisation.

Shell middens provide valuable information about Aboriginal and Torres Strait Islander Peoples' subsistence regimes, food preferences, species availability, and the impacts of natural and human-induced environmental changes. The dates of middens, their location and their contents indicate that different areas of the coast were used at different times, which is likely a result of a diverse range of cultural and environmental factors, such as sea level stabilisation, marine productivity, and population and sociocultural changes. While shell middens are frequently dominated by mollusc remains, fish remains and other fauna within them can provide valuable and often unique information.

Fish bones and teeth

Fish bones are made up of organic (primarily collagen) and inorganic (bioapatite) components, along with lipids and water. Fish bone can vary in its inorganic composition, and this can make it prone to degradation (Nicholson 1996; Szpak 2011). Bone survives in conditions with a relatively neutral pH, because if sediments are too acidic, the bones will leach away and if they are too alkaline, they can crumble and disintegrate. Bones also degrade when conditions alternate between wet and dry, and if they are left exposed to the elements for extended time periods rather than buried relatively quickly. It is because of this that, in many parts of Australia, bone only survives in protected environments like rock-shelters and caves, or within a shell midden. Shell middens are ideal places to preserve bone because the shells create an environment with a neutral pH.

Fish skeletons are composed of spines, vertebrae and distinctive cranial bones. Traditionally, archaeologists use a set of five paired cranial bones (dentary, premaxilla, maxilla, articular and quadrate) (Figures 3.1a to 3.1c) and "special" bones (such as unusual vertebrae or spines) to identify different fish taxa, although more recently, it has been convincingly demonstrated that fish may also be identified using all of their vertebrae (Figure 3.1d) (Lambrides and Weisler 2016 Figures 3 and 4). Fish come in all shapes and sizes, with some species having more delicate and fragile bones (i.e. mullet, surgeonfish, flying fish) and others having relatively robust skeletons (i.e. tuna, parrotfish, grouper, catfish). What is preserved at an archaeological site is therefore a result of soil chemistry (pH), the robusticity of skeletal elements and how bones are treated prior to, during and after consumption.

Fish otoliths

Otoliths are hard, calcium carbonate structures that assist with a fish's balance and hearing. They are located in the head of all bony fish, directly behind the brain (Figure 3.2). They form in the embryonic stages of a fish's development, grow continuously throughout its life, and possess unique characteristics that set them apart from all other skeletal structures. Different fish species have otoliths of different shapes and sizes, and an otolith's internal structure has seasonal growth rings, similar

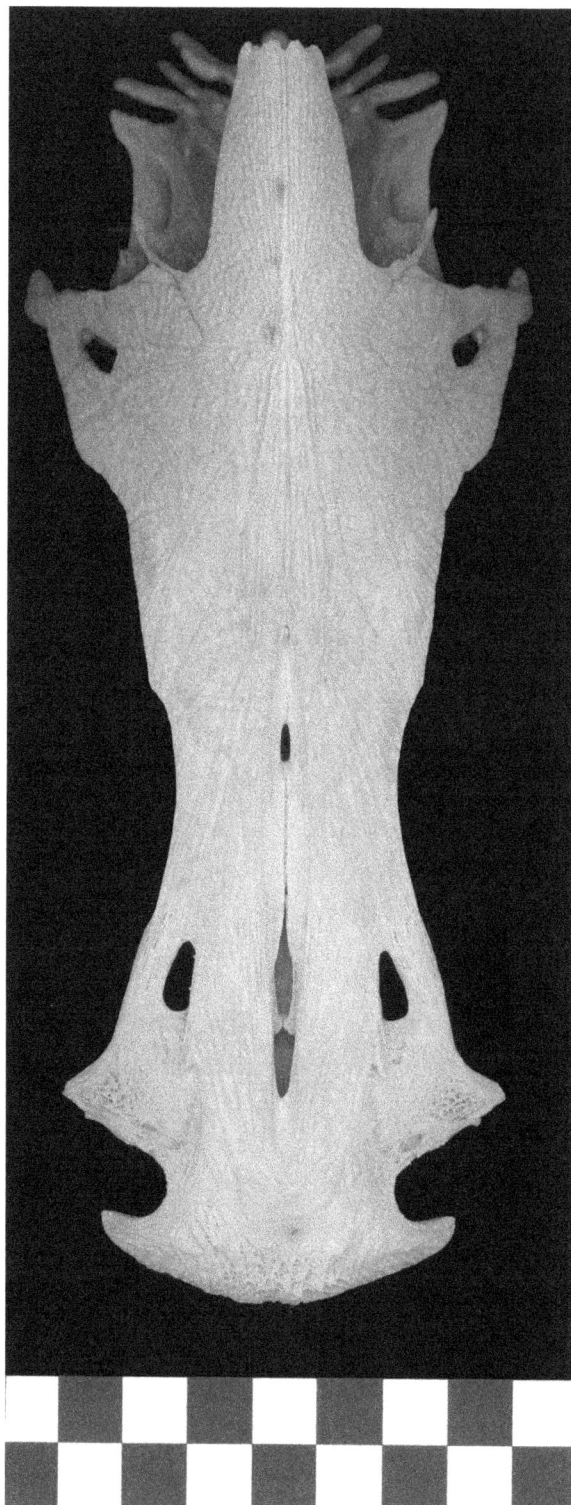

Figure 3.1a Warrior catfish (*Hemiarius dioctes*) neurocranium (part of the skull). © Tiina Manne.

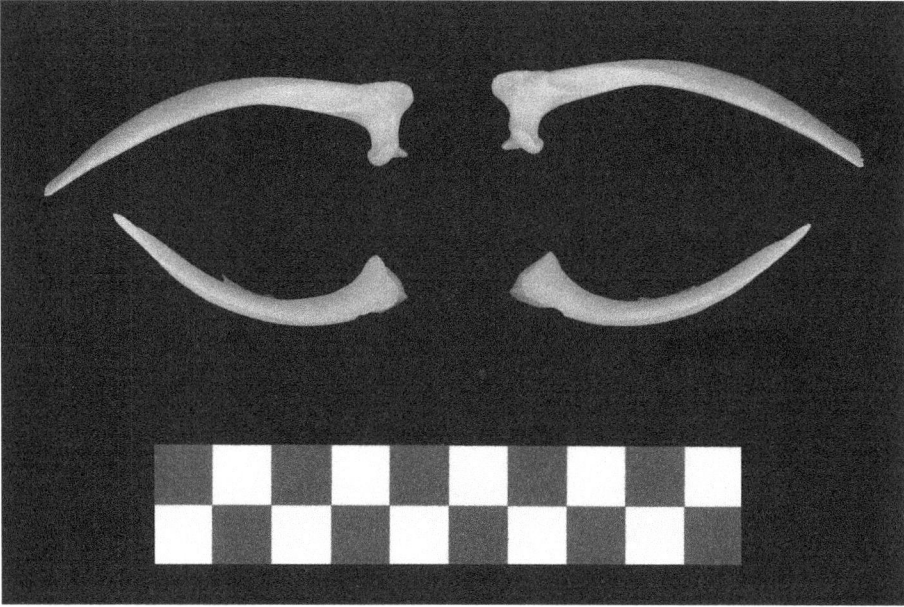

Figure 3.1b Barramundi (*Lates calcarifer*) premaxilla and maxilla (part of the craniumskull, associated with the mouth). © Tiina Manne.

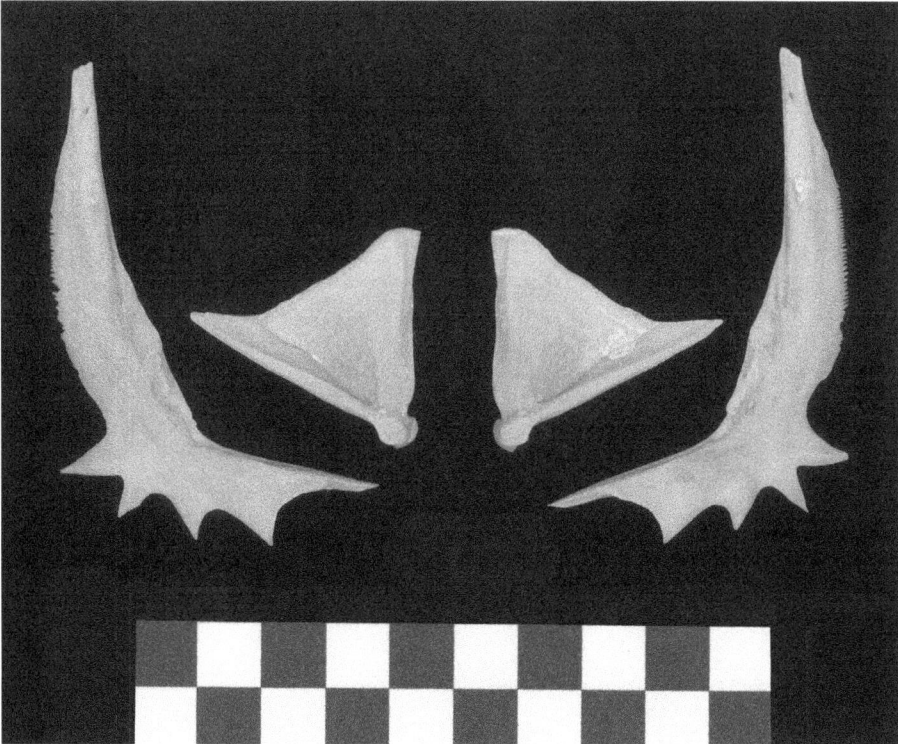

Figure 3.1c Barramundi (*Lates calcarifer*) quadrate and preopercle (part of the craniumskull). © Tiina Manne.

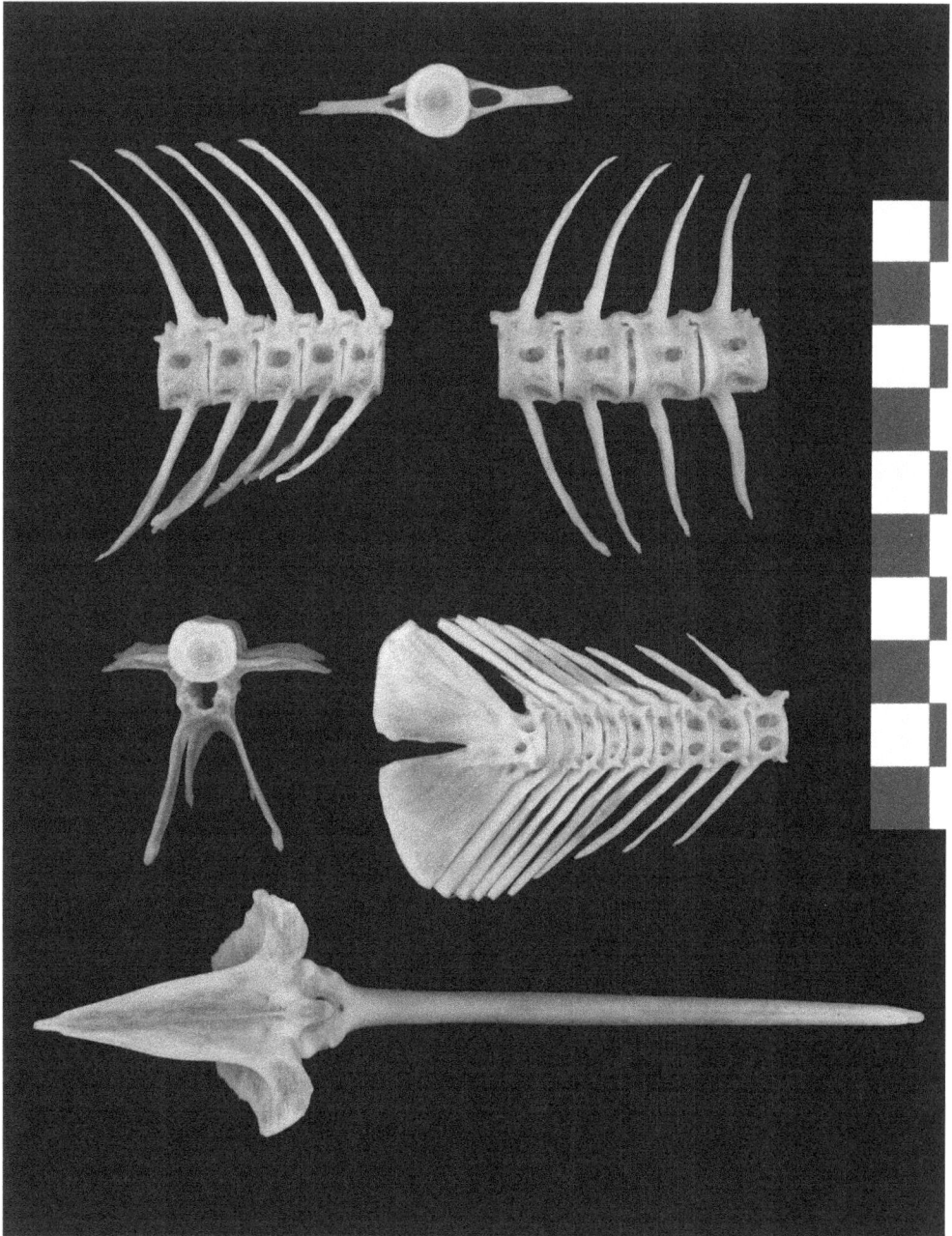

Figure 3.1d Salmon catfish (*Netuma thalassina*) vertebrae. © Tiina Manne.

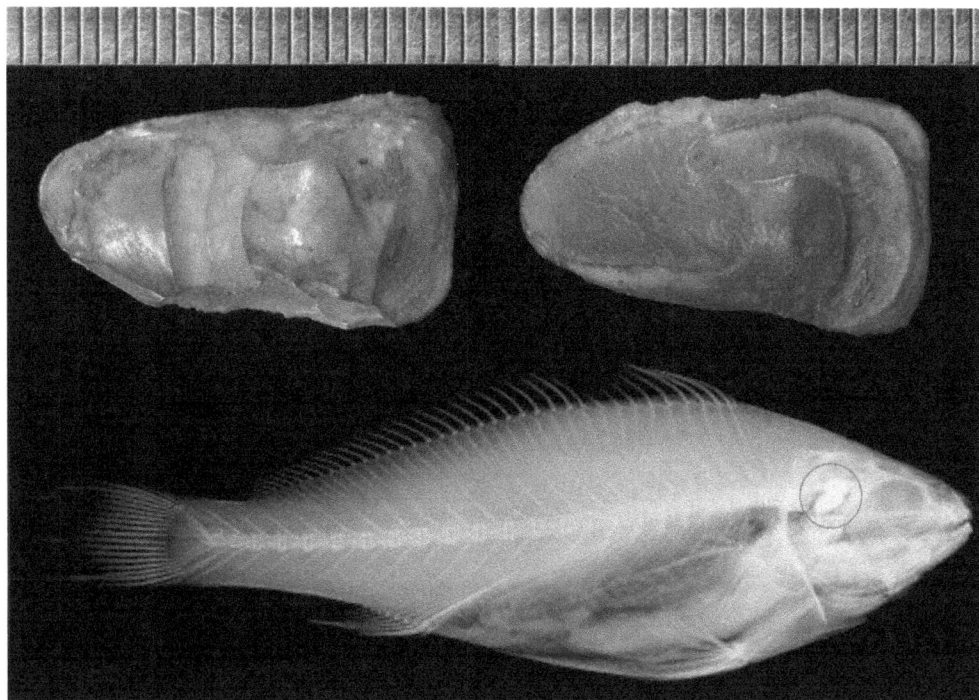

Figure 3.2 Close-up X-ray of otoliths © Morgan Disspain. Mulloway skeleton with otolith circled: James King © Australian Museum.

to those of a tree. Features of otoliths can be used to identify the species, size, age, growth rate and season of death of an individual fish (Disspain et al. 2016).

Fish scales

Most bony fishes have scales covering their bodies in a sheet of flexible, overlapping plates. Structurally, there are two types of bony fish scales: ganoid or rhombic, which are found in some early fishes; and, round or bony-ridge scales, which are found in most bony fishes. While both types of scales can be used to identify fish to family, and sometimes to even species level, they are rarely found in archaeological sites owing to their fragility. There are exceptions to this however, such as the plate-like scales of triggerfish and boxfish, which preserve well and are readily recovered from Australasian coastal archaeological sites. The continued growth of fish throughout their lives results in sustained growth of bony-ridge scales, and the addition of material to the edges of each scale results in low ridges and depressions, called circuli. As a result of these growth records, fish scales can be used in studies of seasonality and aging (Guillaud et al. 2017; Robson et al. 2018).

How do archaeologists study fish remains?

Some archaeologists spend a considerable proportion of their time in a laboratory, and for those that study animals remains, such as ichthyoarchaeologists, many hundreds of hours are spent sorting, quantifying and identifying fish remains assemblages. The first stage of archaeological fish remains analysis involves the detailed examination of all recovered remains to determine the fish bone elements that have preserved in the site. The morphology, or shape, of an individual element is variable between families, genera and often species. Through comparisons with modern reference collections, archaeologists can identify ancient bones, otoliths or scales to taxon. It then becomes possible to determine the range of fish species that people targeted in the past and whether this changes through time (Lambrides et al. 2019).

Increasingly, biomolecular techniques are being used in conjunction with traditional identification protocols that rely on morphological differences between elements to facilitate identifications. These biomolecular techniques, such as aDNA (ancient DNA) and ZooMS (Zooarchaeology by Mass Spectrometry) facilitate more specific (i.e. to genus or species-level) identifications and quality assurance (i.e. testing whether morphological identifications are accurate) (Richter et al. 2011).

Significantly, because fish remains are organic, they can be dated using radiocarbon dating techniques, which allows archaeologists to assign timeframes to the fish's death, and by association, the activities of the peoples that captured and ate the fish (Disspain et al. 2017).

Fish generally grow larger the longer they live, and as a result, the size of some individual elements (specifically otoliths and vertebrae) can be used to estimate the size of a fish. In order to do this, ichthyoarchaeologists first need to establish the relationship between fish body size and individual element size. This is accomplished through the development of reference collections. Fish are captured, weighed and measured, and their remains are then processed, weighed and measured. Once adequate sample sizes are obtained, the relationships between the weight or length of an element such as an otolith and the overall weight or length of a fish can be established. Subsequently, once an otolith from that same species is found within an archaeological site, it can be used to estimate the size of the fish it originated from.

The morphology of fish remains can also be used to determine the age a fish was when it died. Elements – scales and otoliths, in particular – contain growth rings, which can be attributed to growth fluctuations in response to seasonal variations in environmental conditions. Therefore, counting the growth rings can provide an estimate of the age of the fish at the time of its death. In addition to providing an estimate of the age of death of the fish, the annuli/circuli can also provide information

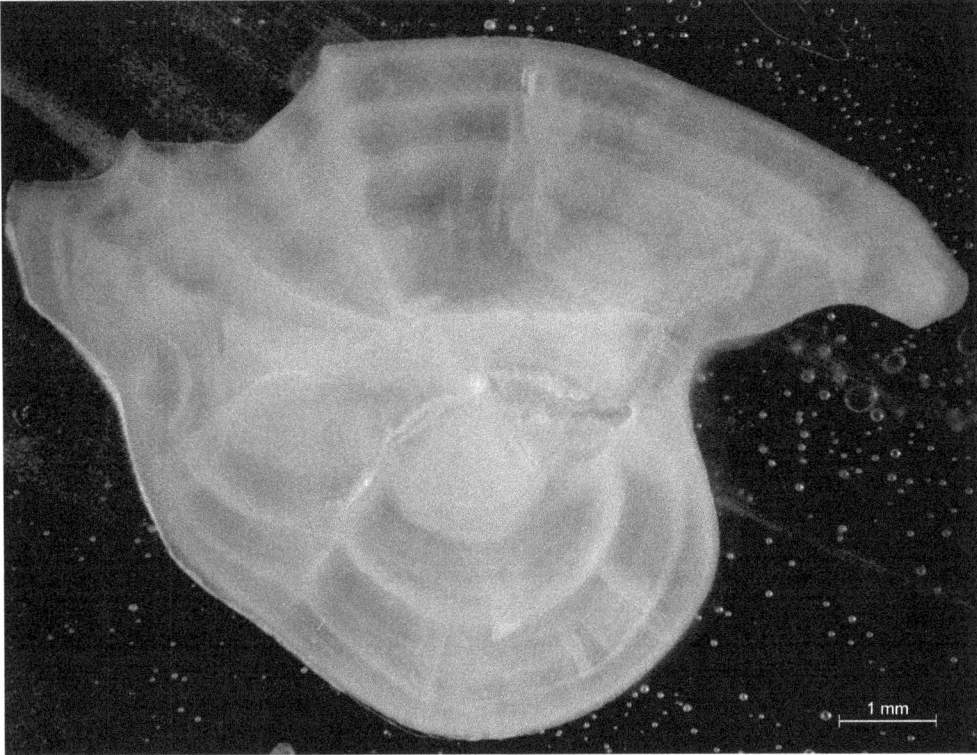

Figure 3.3 Mulloway otolith section showing annuli (Disspain et al. 2016).

about the season of death. By recording the nature of the edge increment, and whether it was laid down in a warm (fast growth) or cool (slow growth) season, the season of fish capture can be determined (Figure 3.3) (Disspain et al. 2016).

Stable isotopic analysis looks at the isotopes – atoms with extra or missing neutrons – of different elements. The ratios of isotopes of the same elements vary between different substances (e.g. different types of food) and ecosystems (e.g. freshwater and sea, or between different climate zones). As fish grow and continually renew their tissues, the isotopes that are in the food they eat and the water they live in are constantly being incorporated into their body tissues, including their skeleton, scales and otoliths. Analysis of the oxygen isotope values of fish otoliths can provide information on the temperature of the water in which the fish lived (Rowell et al. 2008; West et al. 2012), while strontium isotopes can be used to investigate where the fish were being caught (Dufour et al. 2007). Studying concentrations of trace elements (chemical elements whose concentration is very low) in fish remains such as barium, through techniques such as inductively coupled plasma mass spectrometry (ICP-MS), can indicate the salinity levels of the water that the fish lived in throughout its life (Disspain et al. 2011).

Historical records can be used to bridge ichthyoarchaeological data with contemporary fisheries records. Historical data sources include archival fisheries reports, early fishing publications, newspaper articles, menus, artworks (Thurstan et al. 2015, 2016), archived fish remains (Schaerlaekens et al. 2011; Selleslagh et al. 2016) and early fisheries datasets (Fowler and Ling 2010). Oral histories are also particularly useful, and contain information relating to fish abundance, location of catch, fish size, catch rates, fishing methods and technologies, and which fish were (or were not) popular.

Why do archaeologists study fish remains?

Ancient fish remains are a key source of evidence to help archaeologists and palaeoecologists reconstruct past fishing practices, capture technologies, cultural preferences for certain fish species, past environments and fish habitats through deep time (Balme 1995; Lambrides et al. 2019). This information can then be used to investigate people's behaviours and how they used their environment, as well as any environmental change caused by their activities (Casteel 1976; Disspain et al. 2016; Izzo et al. 2016).

To find out about people

Through the study of past Aboriginal and Torres Strait Islander fish use and management, and changes in fishing strategies over time, we can gain an understanding of pre-colonial social-ecological marine and freshwater systems. Fishing remained an important source of subsistence throughout the post-contact period and beyond. Aboriginal and Torres Strait Islander peoples' interactions with water bodies are an integral facet of contemporary cultural knowledge and practice, and waterways have provided (and continue to provide) a vital continuous connection to Country. Ancient information obtained from archaeological fish assemblages provides valuable snapshots into the subsistence activities of peoples in the past, as well as social dimensions of these fisheries – such as types and numbers of fish captured, and the time of year fish were caught. Furthermore, fish assemblages may provide understandings of whether people used specific techniques to enhance fish habitats and populations, and whether there may have been a gendered division of labour.

A variety of fishing techniques or capture technologies were employed by Aboriginal and Torres Strait Islander people across the continent, including spear fishing, line fishing, harpooning, poison and the use of stone, coral, wooden and fibre fish traps (e.g. basket traps, stake fence weirs, coral/stone-walled fish traps) (McNiven and Lambrides 2021, Tables 2 and 4). The Gunditjmara people of western

Victoria constructed elaborate stone-walled fish traps to harvest short-finned eels. McNiven and Bell (2010) estimate that Gunditjmara eel catches during the eeling season (late summer and autumn) weighed many tonnes and likely numbered in the tens of thousands of eels. Careful excavation and comprehensive radiocarbon analyses demonstrated that the sediment infill of a channel dated to 6,600 cal. BP (McNiven et al. 2012), which makes this the oldest known fish trap in the world. In 2019, these aquaculture systems were recognised on the UNESCO World Heritage List, with the Budj Bim Cultural Landscape being one of the first sites in Australia to be listed for its Aboriginal cultural values alone. Some fish traps, such as the nationally significant network of extensive stone fish traps at Brewarrina in the Murray Darling Basin, are still in use by Aboriginal people today (Black 1947; Hope and Vines 1994). Past fishing methods can inform our understanding of the technological skills and ecological knowledge of a community and may indicate the relative importance of fish within wider subsistence activities as a function of the time and energy invested in fishing.

The identification of archaeological fish remains to taxon can usefully inform our understanding of peoples' interactions with seasonally available species. The presence or absence of these seasonally available species in an assemblage may convey information about the way people moved around the landscape throughout the year to target these potentially culturally important or preferred fish species (Colley 1990; O'Connor 2000). Examples of these sorts of studies are common (e.g. Bowler, et al. 1970; Hale and Tindale 1930; Ulm 2006).

Some studies have attempted to link archaeological fish remains to possible capture techniques by examining the relationship between fish feeding behaviour, fish size and likely procurement strategy (Balme 1995; Butler 1994; Colley 1987). For example, Colley (1987) identified archaeological fish bones from two sites, dating to approximately 8,000 BP at Rocky Cape (north-west Tasmania), and determined the samples were dominated by rocky reef fish including wrasse, conger eel, porcupine fish and leatherjacket. The site also included species commonly found in association with bays and estuaries, such as freshwater eel, barracouta, whiting and mullet. Based on local knowledge concerning the environment and fishing methods, it was suggested that the rocky reef fish were most likely to have been caught using a baited box trap, while the fish from the bays and estuaries were most likely harvested using a constructed tidal trap.

Additionally, the size of fish present in the archaeological record may be indicative of the fishing techniques that were employed by Aboriginal and Torres Strait Islander people (Disspain et al. 2016; O'Connor and Veth 2000). For example, spearing in shallow water usually results in the capture of larger prey, as larger individuals are easier to hit. On the other hand, gill nets capture a narrow size range of fish dependent on the net's mesh size, while fish traps constructed of netting or wickerwork will catch all fish over a certain size (O'Connor 2000). Balme (1995) inferred from the spatial distribution and uniform size of >500 otoliths that nets were the most likely fishing technique used at the Casuarina North Ridge site, from the lower Darling River area of western NSW. Similarly, at the nearby Kaleenatha Loop site dating to the early to mid Holocene, the size and species of otoliths were interpreted as being from fish that were gathered from small pools or traps. It was concluded that people must have made string from vegetable fibre, had a social structure that allowed them sufficient time to make and maintain nets, and been aware of the conditions under which netting was effective (Balme 1995). Balme (1995) also discussed how net fishing was a cooperative venture, requiring two or more people, and that the fish meal provided by netting was an end product of a corporate investment of labour. Ultimately, the labour involved was costly, but the abundant food resulting from the use of the net was equally considerable. Hence, information about fish size enables researchers to deduce information concerning fish population dynamics, Aboriginal subsistence strategies and social structures.

In many cultures around the world, women are predominantly responsible for the collection of fish (Chapman 1987; Lahn 2006). In Australia today – and likely in the past, as evidenced by ethnographic and historic records – fishing was undertaken by both men and women, with recorded differences across the continent in male-only and female-only activities. For example, woven fishing baskets are made by the Gunditjmara women of south-west Victoria but are used by men to fish (Gunditjmara People and Wettenhall 2010). Weisler and McNiven (2016) argued that archaeological evidence for small-sized fish in Torres Strait middens most likely reflected capture of small fish in reef pools at low tide by women and children as recorded ethnographically. Along the Sydney coast, prior to and shortly after 1788, the predominance of women fishers was widely documented (Attenbrow 2002). Despite the widespread continuation of traditional fishing techniques post-contact, there is some suggestion that late nineteenth-century attempts by the Aborigines Protection Board to encourage Aboriginal men to pursue fishing as a commercial venture by giving them boats, fishing nets and fishing lines, led to a decline in the role of women as fishers in Aboriginal communities (Bennett 2007; Roberts 2010).

To find out about past fish populations and their environment

Fish stocks have experienced severe depletion since the industrialisation of fishing during the nineteenth and twentieth centuries, with changes over time in fish abundance, size and growth rates indicating the depopulation of key species. Having long-term age/size/growth structure data for a fish stock provides an opportunity to assess how population characteristics change as a consequence of fishery exploitation (Disspain et al. 2018; Fowler and Ling 2010). Fish populations generally experience some degree of size and age truncation that reflects the removal of the larger, older individuals from the population, even when relatively conservative fishing regimes are implemented (Longhurst 1998).

Attempting to return pre-colonial fish stocks to "baseline states" is difficult because of the shifting baseline syndrome (Hobday 2011; Izzo et al. 2016; Pauly 1995). The "shifting baseline syndrome" refers to the concept that fish populations are measured against baselines identified by each successive generation of researchers, baselines which themselves may represent significant changes from even earlier states.

The establishment of ancient fisheries baselines is advocated by contemporary fisheries experts as a means of understanding and potentially maintaining and restoring degraded and collapsing fisheries. There are problems associated with using only recent data when examining how fish populations have changed over time, as earlier changes will not be accounted for, resulting in the establishment of inappropriate reference points for evaluating losses from overfishing or decreased water flows due to modern water use for agricultural purposes, or for identifying rehabilitation targets (Pauly 1995).

Systematic collection of fisheries data in most parts of the world only covers a very shallow timeframe (often 1970s onwards), making assessment of long-term population dynamics beyond the industrialised fishing era problematic. Using fish remains from archaeological sites can circumvent this issue and extend the recent record of fish population data (see Disspain et al. 2018; Galik et al. 2015; Jones et al. 2016 for examples). When combined with historical archival information and/or modern fisheries data, changes in fish abundance, age and size over time can be examined, thereby addressing the shifting baseline issue (Haidvogl et al. 2015). Understanding the dynamics of fish populations prior to industrialised fishing can be challenging, but provides critical baseline data for fish conservation, rehabilitation and management.

A history of fishing in Australia

Deep time First Nations fisheries

The earliest record for fish remains in the Australasian region is found at the site of Asitau Kuru (formerly Jerimalai) in East Timor, where mackerel, tuna and bonito were caught and consumed 38,000 to 42,000 years ago (O'Connor et al. 2011). In addition to fish remains, early evidence for complex fishing technology (O'Connor et al. 2011) was recovered at Asitau Kuru, along with evidence for the manufacture of ornamental artefacts from the mollusc *Nautilus* (Langley et al. 2016; see also Langley and O'Connor 2018 for a review). Langley and colleagues (2016) argue that the *Nautilus* artefacts, in combination with the fishing technology, suggest that coastal landscapes were closely tied to cultural practices and were a significant part of the social lives of the people visiting the site. Other archaeological sites with early evidence of marine fish and mollusc consumption in Australasia include Laili Cave in East Timor (44,000 BP), Gua Makpan on Alor Island (40,000 to 38,000 BP), Buang Merabak in the Bismarck Archipelago (41,000 BP) and Kilu in the Solomon Islands (29,000 BP) (Hawkins et al. 2017; Kealy et al. 2020; Leavesley and Allen 1998; O'Connor and Chappell 2003; O'Connor et al. 2011; O'Connell et al. 2010; O'Connor et al. 2017; Wickler 2001 but see Anderson 2013a; Anderson 2013b; Bailey 2013; Erlandson 2013).

The earliest evidence for coastal exploitation in northern Australia comes from Barrow Island off the present-day coast of Western Australia (Veth et al. 2017). Here, evidence is in the form of marine molluscs at the site of Boodie Cave, which date to 42,000 years ago, when the coast was 30 to 40 km to its west. They included mudwhelks, a robust gastropod mollusc that could have been brought overland in clumps of mud. Fish are not recovered until after 10,000 years ago, when the coastline was much closer. Once the coastline is adjacent to the site, a diverse array of marine resources was brought up to the cave; wrasse, bream, surgeonfish, tangs, triggerfish and shark, along with turtles, crabs, sea urchin and over 40 species of mollusc (Veth et al. 2017). Nearby to the north, in the Montebello Islands, a similar pattern is found with a marked increase in marine foods at Haynes Cave, including fish, once the coastline reaches the rock-shelters approximately 7,000 years ago (Manne and Veth 2015; Veth et al. 2007).

Although there is limited evidence of coastal exploitation from approximately 10,000 years ago in other parts of Australia (e.g. Richards 2012), most archaeological evidence for the use of coastal resources occurs well after 7,000 years ago, usually the past few thousand years, once sea levels were close to their present levels (Lambrides et al. 2019; Monks 2021). This does not indicate that people only focused on marine resources following sea level stabilisation, but rather that older evidence is very likely to lie submerged (Benjamin et al. 2020; Ditchfield et al. 2022).

Along the eastern coast of Australia, there is evidence for an increase in reliance on marine fauna from 3,500 years ago, leading some archaeologists to suggest a significant and large-scale shift in the subsistence activities of coastal peoples, known as the emergence of *maritime specialist economies* (Lourandos 1997; McNiven 2004; Ulm 2011). To be a marine specialist is thought to go beyond a reliance on marine animals for protein needs, but rather, it is to be "spiritually embedded within seascapes rich in cosmological meaning" (McNiven 2004). A recent synthesis of archaeological fish data from 44 sites along the eastern Queensland coast supports this argument, suggesting that after 3000 BP, Aboriginal and Torres Strait Islander people began to have a much greater focus on fish and included an increasingly larger number of species into their subsistence regimes (Lambrides et al. 2019).

Colonial encounters and historic accounts of First Nations fisheries

The displacement of First Nations peoples throughout Australia reduced the capacity for Aboriginal communities to play a major role in waterway ecology; they were replaced by Europeans who related to, and managed, the rivers in a very different way (Humphries 2007). When the British arrived in Sydney in January 1788, they encountered communities of Aboriginal peoples who gained a substantial part of their diet from fish. Aboriginal fishing technologies (e.g. spears, shell fishhooks and small canoes) were well documented by colonial writers (Colley and Attenbrow 2012). Observations and accounts of fish in coastal waters form a small but continual part of the narrative of exploration and settlement (Pepperell 2018). Fish were obviously an important source of fresh food to the colonists, so it is not surprising that their supply was a subject of interest in early writings and records.

Examples of this are the ethnographic and ethnohistorical accounts that record details about Ngarrindjeri fishing practices in South Australia (e.g. Angas 1847; Krefft 1865; Taplin 1879) and, although such sources are inherently biased (Clarke 1994; Heider 1988), they can still provide useful information if used judiciously. From their observations, Krefft (1865) and Hawdon and Bonney (Hawdon and Bonney 1952) documented that Ngarrindjeri subsistence regimes traditionally consisted mainly of fish, a view supported today by community members (Ngarrindjeri Tendi et al. 2007; see also Chapter 1 in this volume). A variety of techniques were used by the Ngarrindjeri to harvest fish, including the use of fish nets made from *manangkeri* (bulrush *Typha* sp.); fishing weirs made from branches, stakes or woven rushes; spears and clubs; bark canoes, reed rafts and large floating fishing platforms; and woven baskets (Berndt et al. 1993; Clarke 1994; Ngarrindjeri Tendi et al. 2007). Interestingly, the fishhook and line were not used in the Lower Murray region until after the arrival of Europeans (Clarke 1994).

Angas' (1847; Angas cited in Tregenza 1980) illustrations of Aboriginal peoples and landscapes are also informative, with one image sketched at Second Valley, beside the mouth of the river Parananacooka (South Australia), showing people fishing with nets (Figure 3.4). Of the methods of fishing he observed, he noted:

Figure 3.4 Coast scene near Rapid Bay, sunset (Angas 1847).

> The mode adopted by the tribes inhabiting the vicinity of Rapid Bay, is nearly similar to that of Europeans; they use a net about twenty or thirty feet in length, stretched upon sticks placed crosswise at intervals; a couple of men will drag this net amongst the rocks and shallows where fish are most abundant, and, gradually getting it closer as they reach the shore, the fish are secured in the folds of the net, and but a few moments elapse before they are laid alive upon the embers of the native fires that are blazing ready before the adjoining huts. The nets are composed of chewed fibres of reeds, rolled up the thigh, and twisted into cord for the purpose (Angas cited in Tregenza 1980, 47).

Ethnographic and historical records also demonstrate that Aboriginal and Torres Strait Islander people actively managed aquatic and marine environments to enrich freshwater fish populations (see McNiven et al. 2012; McNiven and Lambrides 2021; McNiven et al. 2021 for detailed summaries). These methods included: constructing weirs to extend the duration of seasonally available freshwater; the creation of fish traps or pens from reeds, brush or stone arrangements to capture and keep fish alive until needed; the restocking of waterholes; and even the protected rearing of juvenile fish (Barber and Jackson 2011, 2015; Campbell 1965; Duncan-Kemp 1968; Gilmore 1934; Maclean 1978; Williams 1998).

Weirs, traps and pens were likely employed in many different regions of Australia to sequester freshwater and fish. In the Roper River region of the Northern Territory, Campbell (1965) describes how trees were cut down to create dams to capture water during the wet season. Water from streams was channelled toward the dams using structures made from stakes, paperbark and clay. By actively maintaining available freshwater, Aboriginal people created and extended the duration of available habitats for fish, water birds and other faunal and floral foods beyond the natural wet season (Gunn 1908; Jackson and Barber 2016). Fish traps and pens were also common in regions of Channel Country in south-western Queensland as well as along the interior waterways of New South Wales. Duncan-Kemp (1968) writes how Aboriginal people in Channel Country constructed pens using slabs of coolabah and woven reeds, along with large stone traps. Golden and silver perch, stickleback and bream, along with other fish could be kept "by the hundreds in good seasons, and here they were kept alive – and fat – until required for a feast … [and were] plentiful when other fish were scarce and shy of line and hook" (Duncan-Kemp 1968, 275). Gilmore (1934) reported the use of large log dams to trap fish between the upper Murray River and the Lachlan River during the 1870s and 1880s. In addition to these larger structures, Gilmore (1934) details numerous smaller fish traps placed in gullies along ephemeral water courses.

Gilmore (1934) also describes how Aboriginal people in New South Wales would both restock waterholes and protectively rear small fish. Waterholes without fish were restocked using fish eggs or small fish collected from elsewhere. This introduced stock would be transferred using "coolamons [large wooden dishes], water filled hollow logs or baskets" (Gilmore 1934, 196). Both male and female fish were introduced, presumably to create new generations of stock (Gilmore 1934). Along the Darling, Murrumbidgee and Lachlan Rivers, Aboriginal people created barriers from trees and stones to enhance fish stocks (Gilmore 1934). These barriers would allow small fish through, but prevent the larger ones, and, in doing so, would stop the large fish from consuming the small individuals and decimating the fish stocks.

Early European use of fish, nineteenth- and twentieth-century industry

Pepperall (2018) examines numerous early Dutch, English and French historical accounts of fishing in Australian waters to provide an understanding of what fishing was like during the seventeenth, eighteenth and early nineteenth centuries. Early accounts from the first few years of British settlement in Botany Bay describe seasonal shifts in fish abundance, with fish being scarce during the winter months

(Colley and Attenbrow 2012; Pepperell 2018). While summer fish stocks were more reliable and described as "tolerably plentiful" (Colley and Attenbrow 2012; Tench 1789, 128–9 [1979, 69]), fish catches even then only served to feed the population fresh fish, as there was never enough to preserve. Fish that were most commonly recorded as being caught in these early years included mullet, bream, mulloway, mackerel and multiple species of stingray.

Stingrays were happily consumed by the British colonists, which as Pepperall (2018) notes, were familiar as they were similar in shape to skates, a kind of ray that was caught and eaten in Britain. Sharks were also consumed seemingly regularly by early explorers and settlers, and they were likely also targeted for the oil that could be procured from their liver. Insight into how sharks may have been prepared may be gleaned from the writings of William Dampier, the English mariner and privateer. In May 1699, en-route to Australia from Brazil, Dampier notes:

> We caught 3 small Sharks, each 6 Foot 4 Inches long; and they were very good Food for us. The next Day we caught 3 more Sharks of the same Size, and we eat them also, esteeming them as good Fish boil'd and press'd, and then stew'd with Vinegar and Pepper (Pepperall 2018, 105).

While large numbers of fish were caught on occasion – such as during annual mullet runs along parts of the eastern coast – early European explorers frequently remarked on the inconsistent nature of fish catches. Pepperall (2018) argues that despite the diversity of marine fish species found in Australian waters (4800 species, with 520 being endemic), inconsistent fish catches were due to the overall low biological productivity of Australian waters. Alternatively, this inconsistency may very well indicate a lack of local ecological knowledge by early Europeans.

While ethnographic accounts provide a glimpse of the early historical period of Australia through the eyes of its newly arrived inhabitants, historical archaeological sites provide material evidence for fish use in the early colonial days. For example, Colley (2013) examined fish remains from the Quadrant Site in Sydney, which were mostly recovered from houses, tanneries and slaughterhouses dating between 1830 and 1860. Bones of native fish such as snapper, bream, garfish, mullets and flatheads dominated the assemblages, but there was also evidence for species that do not occur naturally in Australia, including ling and salmon. Many species of northern hemisphere salmons and trouts were introduced into Australian waters from the nineteenth century onward (Clements 1988), but ling was likely a preserved fish import, consistent with records documenting British settlers' preference for non-local fish species. Colley and Attenbrow (2012) also compared archaeological fish bones from Aboriginal sites in coastal Sydney with those from the Quadrant historical site. They determined that while technology – specifically imported nets for catching garfish and mullets – explains some fish bone assemblage variability, cultural attitudes, commercialisation and urbanism are also important factors (Colley and Attenbrow 2012).

Following European exploration and expansion, numerous industrial fisheries were developed throughout Australia, frequently in areas fished for millennia by Aboriginal and Torres Strait Islander peoples. One example of this is the fishery that grew within the Coorong and Lower Lakes region in South Australia. As discussed earlier, ichthyoarchaeological evidence from this region demonstrates that fish had provided significant food resources for the Ngarrindjeri people for thousands of years. Historical-era fishery continued to target various species in freshwater, estuarine and adjacent marine habitats in this region, with two fishers operating in the Coorong and Murray River mouth, even before 1846 (Ferguson et al. 2018; Olsen and Evans 1991). Further commercial fishing activities were stimulated by the development of the steamer-barge trade through the ports of Goolwa and Milang in 1853, and by completion of a rail link to Adelaide in 1885, with the number of fishers increasing to 30 in 1912 (Wallace-Carter 1987). To examine whether there had been any significant changes to mulloway populations in the waters of eastern South Australia over time, Disspain and colleagues (2018) compared archaeological fish size, age and growth data, as well as month of catch data, from archaeological fish otoliths, historical anecdotes and contemporary data sources. They found that the data corroborated each other in many aspects. The time of catch for all three datasets was seasonal, with increases evident during the summer months, and no evidence of significant change in fish length over the time span of the three data sources (1670–1308 cal. BP through to CE 2014). Given the impact that fishing in the region is regarded to have had, we suggest that while the maximum recorded size has remained stable over time, the abundance of these large specimens may have declined.

Looking forward to the future of Australia's fisheries

Ancient fish remains found in archaeological sites provide evidence that Australia's oceans, estuaries and inland waters have sustained its people for tens of thousands of years. For generations, fish and fishing have continued to occupy an important economic, cultural, social and spiritual role in the lives of many Australians.

In this chapter, we have presented ways that archaeologists study ancient fish remains and what they can tell us, and have discussed a sample of ichthyoarchaeological research in Australia. With the modern world's fisheries in a dire state, these archaeological records provide invaluable data for conservation biologists and fisheries management, ensuring fish remains a staple food for Australians for generations to come. These data critically extend the baseline from which we have to manage modern fish populations from only 50+ years into the past (~1970s onwards), a mere snapshot of people's uses of these habitats, to many thousands of years before the present-day. Archaeological and historical fisheries data is uniquely placed to inform a range of conservation issues through an examination of the factors (e.g. people, climate, etc.) that have influenced fish dynamics over thousands of years and may indeed continue to do so into the future (Alleway et al. 2016; Disspain et al. 2018; Klaer 2001).

References

Alleway, H.K., B.M. Gillanders and S.D. Connell (2016). "Neo Europe" and its ecological consequences: the example of systematic degradation in Australia's inland fisheries. *Biology Letters* 12(1).

Anderson, A. (2013a). Inshore or offshore? Boating and fishing in the Pleistocene. *Antiquity* 87(337): 879.

Anderson, A. (2013b). Response to O'Connor and Ono, Bailey and Erlandson. *Antiquity* 87(337): 892–5.

Angas, G.F. (1847). *Savage life and scenes in Australia and New Zealand: being an artist's impressions of countries and people at the antipodes. With numerous illustrations. Vol 1*, 2nd edn. London: Smith, Elder and Company.

Attenbrow, V. (2002). *Sydney's Aboriginal past: investigating the archaeological and historical records.* Sydney: UNSW Press.

Bailey, G.N. (2013). Dynamic shorelines and submerged topography: the neglected variables. *Antiquity* 87(337): 889–90.

Balme, J. (1995). 30,000 years of fishery in western New South Wales. *Archaeology in Oceania* 30(1): 1–21.

Barber, M. and S. Jackson (2015). "Knowledge Making": Issues in modelling local and Indigenous ecological knowledge. *Human Ecology* 43: 119–30.

Barber, M. and S. Jackson (2011). Aboriginal water values and resource development pressures in the Pilbara, northwestern Australia. *Australian Aboriginal Studies* 2011: 32–50.

Barker, B. (2004). *The Sea People: late Holocene maritime specialisation in the Whitsunday Islands, Central Queensland.* Canberra: Pandanus Press.

Benjamin, J., O'Leary, M., McDonald, J., Wiseman, C., McCarthy, J., Beckett, E. et al. (2020). Aboriginal artefacts on the continental shelf reveal ancient drowned cultural landscapes in northwest Australia. *PLOS ONE* 15(7): e0233912.

Bennett, M. (2007). The economics of fishing: sustainable living in colonial New South Wales. *Aboriginal History* 31: 85–102.

Berndt, R.M., C.H. Berndt and J.E. Stanton (1993). *The world that was: The Yaraldi of the Murray River and the Lakes, South Australia.* Vancouver: UBC Press.

Black, L. (1947). Aboriginal fisheries of Brewarrina. *The South African Archaeological Bulletin* 2(5): 15–16.

Bowler, J. M., Jones, R., Allen, H. and Thorne, A.G. (1970). Pleistocene human remains from Australia: a living site and human cremation from Lake Mungo, western New South Wales. *World Archaeology* 2(1): 39–60.

Butler, V.L. (1994). Fish feeding behaviour and fish capture: the case for variation in Lapita fishing strategies. *Archaeology in Oceania* 29: 81–90.

Campbell, A.H. (1965). Elementary food production by the Australian Aborigines. *Mankind* 6(5): 206–11.

Casteel, R.W. (1976). *Fish remains in archaeology and Palaeo-environmental studies.* London: Academic Press Ltd.

Chapman, M.D. (1987). Women's fishing in Oceania. *Human Ecology* 15(3): 267–88.

Clarke, P.A. (1994). Contact, conflict and regeneration: Aboriginal cultural geography of the Lower Murray, South Australia. Doctoral thesis, Geography and Anthropology, University of Adelaide, SA.

Clarkson, C., Jacobs, Z., Marwick, B., Fullagar, R., Wallis, L., Smith, M. et al. (2017). Human occupation of northern Australia by 65,000 years ago. *Nature* 547(7663): 306–10.

Clements, J. (1988). *Salmon at the Antipodes: a history and review of trout, salmon and char and introduced coarse fish in Australasia.* Ballarat: J. Clements.

Colley, S.M. (2013). Fish and fishing in colonial New South Wales: new evidence from the Quadrant Site in Sydney. *Post-Medieval Archaeology* 47: 119–35.

Colley, S.M. (1990). The analysis and interpretation of archaeological fish remains. *Archaeological Method and Theory* 2: 207–53.

Colley, S.M. (1987). Fishing for facts. Can we reconstruct fishing methods from archaeological evidence? *Australian Archaeology* 24: 16–26.

Colley, S.M. and V. Attenbrow (2012). Does technology make a difference? Aboriginal and colonial fishing in Port Jackson, New South Wales. *Archaeology in Oceania* 47: 69–77.

Colley, S.M. and R. Jones (1987). New fish bone data from Rocky Cape, North West Tasmania. *Archaeology in Oceania* 22(2): 67–71.

Disspain, M.C.F., Wallis, L.A., Fallon, S.A., Sumner, M., St Georger, C., Wilson, C. et al. (2017). Direct radiocarbon dating of fish otoliths from mulloway

(*Argyrosomus japonicus*) and black bream (*Acanthopagrus butcheri*) from Long Point, Coorong, South Australia. *Journal of the Anthropological Society of South Australia* 41, 3–17.

Disspain, M.C.F., S. Ulm, N. Draper, J. Newchurch, S. Fallon and B.M. Gillanders (2018). Long-term archaeological and historical archives for mulloway, *Argyrosomus japonicus*, populations in eastern South Australia. *Fisheries Research* 205: 1–10.

Disspain, M.C.F., S. Ulm and B.M. Gillanders (2016). Otoliths in archaeology: methods, applications and future prospects. *Journal of Archaeological Science: Reports* 6: 623–32.

Disspain, M.C.F., L.A. Wallis and B.M. Gillanders (2011). Developing baseline data to understand environmental change: a geochemical study of archaeological otoliths from the Coorong, South Australia. *Journal of Archaeological Science* 38(8): 1842–57.

Ditchfield, K., S. Ulm, T. Manne, H. Farr, D. O'Grady and P. Veth (2022). Framing Australian Pleistocene coastal occupation and archaeology. *Quaternary Science Reviews* 293: 107706.

Dufour, E., C. Holmden, W. Van Neer, A. Zazzo, W. P. Patterson, P. Degryse and E. Keppens. (2007). Oxygen and strontium isotopes as provenance indicators of fish at archaeological sites: the case study of Sagalassos, SW Turkey. *Journal of Archaeological Science* 34(8): 1226–39.

Duncan-Kemp, A.M. (1968). *Where strange gods call.* Brisbane: W.R. Smith and Paterson.

Erlandson, J.M. (2013) . Interpreting archaeological fish remains. *Antiquity* 87(337): 890–2.

Faulkner, P. (2013). *Life on the margins: an archaeological investigation of Late Holocene economic variability, Blue Mud Bay, northern Australia.* Canberra: ANU Press.

Ferguson, G., J. Earl and Q. Ye (2018). The history of fisheries in the Lower Lakes and Coorong. *Natural History of the Coorong, Lower Lakes, and Murray Mouth region (Yarluwar-Ruwe).* Royal Society of South Australia.

Fowler, A. and J. Ling (2010). Ageing studies done 50 years apart for an inshore fish species from southern Australia – contribution towards determining current stock status. *Environmental Biology of Fishes* 89(3): 253–65.

Galik, A., G. Haidvogl, L. Bartosiewicz, G. Guti and M. Jungwirth (2015). Fish remains as a source to reconstruct long-term changes of fish communities in the Austrian and Hungarian Danub. *Aquatic Science* 77: 337–54.

Gilmore, M.D. (1934). *Old days, old ways: a book of recollections.* Sydney: Angus & Robertson.

Guillaud, E., R. Elleboode, K. Mahé and P. Béarez (2017). Estimation of age, growth and fishing season of a Palaeolithic population of grayling (*Thymallus thymallus*) using scale analysis. *International Journal of Osteoarchaeology* 27(4): 683–92.

Gunn, J. (1908). *We of the Never-Never.* New York: Macmillan.

Haidvogl, G,. R. Hoffmann, D. Pont, M. Jungwirth and V. Winiwarter (2015). Historical ecology of riverine fish in Europe. *Aquatic Sciences* 77(3): 315–42.

Hale, H.M. and N.B. Tindale (1930). Notes on some human remains in the lower Murray Valley, South Australia. *Records of the South Australian Museum* 4: 145–218.

Hawdon, J. (1952). *The journal of a journey from New South Wales to Adelaide (the capital of South Australia) performed in 1838.* Melbourne: Georgian House.

Hawkins, Stuart, S. O'Connor, T.R. Maloney, M. Litster, S. Kealy, J.N. Fenner et al. (2017). Oldest human occupation of Wallacea at Laili Cave, Timor-Leste, shows broad-spectrum foraging responses to late Pleistocene environments. *Quaternary Science Reviews* 171: 58–72.

Heider, K.G. (1988). The Rashomon Effect: when ethnographers disagree. *American Anthropologist* 90(1): 73–81.

Hobday, A.J. (2011). Sliding baselines and shuffling species: implications of climate change for marine conservation. *Marine Ecology* 32(3): 392–403.

Hope, J. and G. Vines (1994). *Brewarrina Aboriginal Fisheries Conservation Plan.* Report to the Brewarrina Aboriginal Cultural Museum.

Humphries, P. (2007). Historical Indigenous use of aquatic resources in Australia's Murray-Darling Basin, and its implications for river management. *Ecological Management and Restoration* 8(2): 106–13.

Izzo, C., Z.A. Doubleday, G.L. Grammer, K.L. Gilmore, H.K. Alleway, T.C. Barnes et al. (2016). Fish as proxies of ecological and environmental change. *Reviews in Fish Biology and Fisheries* 26(3): 265–86.

Jackson, S. and M. Barber (2016). Historical and contemporary waterscapes of North Australia: Indigenous attitudes to dams and water diversions. *Water History* 8(4): 385–404.

Jones, T.L., K.W. Gobalet and B.F. Codding (2016). The archaeology of fish and fishing on the central coast of California: The case for an under-exploited resource. *Journal of Anthropological Archaeology* 41: 88–108.

Kealy, S., S. O'Connor, G. Mahirta, D.M. Sari, C. Shipton, M.C. Langley et al. (2020). Forty-thousand years of maritime subsistence near a changing shoreline on Alor Island (Indonesia). *Quaternary Science Reviews* 249: 106599.

Klaer, N.L. (2001). Steam trawl catches from south-eastern Australia from 1918 to 1957: trends in catch rates and species composition. *Marine and Freshwater Research* 52(4): 399–410.

Krefft, G. (1865). On the manners and customs of the Aborigines of the Lower Murray and Darling. In *Transactions of the Philosophical Society of New South Wales,* 357–74. Sydney: Royal Society of New South Wales.

Lahn, J. (2006). Women's gift-fish and sociality in the Torres Strait, Australia. *Oceania* 76(3): 297–309.

Lambrides, A.B.J., I.J. McNiven, S.J. Aird, K.M. Lowe, P.T. Moss, C. Rowe et al. (2020). Changing use of Lizard Island over the past 4000 years and implications for understanding Indigenous offshore island use on the Great Barrier Reef. *Queensland Archaeological Research* 23: 43–109.

Lambrides, A.B.J., I.J. McNiven and S. Ulm (2019). Meta-analysis of Queensland's coastal Indigenous fisheries: examining the archaeological evidence for geographic and temporal patterning. *Journal of Archaeological Science: Reports* 28: 102057.

Lambrides, A.B.J. and M.I. Weisler (2016). Pacific Islands ichthyoarchaeology: implications for the development of prehistoric fishing studies and global sustainability. *Journal of Archaeological Research* 24(3): 275–324.

Langley, M.C., S. O'Connor and E. Piotto (2016). 42,000-year-old worked and pigment-stained Nautilus shell from Jerimalai (Timor-Leste): evidence for an early coastal adaptation in ISEA. *Journal of Human Evolution* 97: 1–16.

Langley, M.C. and S. O'Connor (2018). Exploring red ochre use in Timor-Leste and surrounds: headhunting, burials, and beads. *The Archaeology of Portable Art: Southeast Asian, Pacific and Australian Perspectives.* Routledge: 25–36.

Leavesley, M.G. and J. Allen (1998). Dates, disturbance and artefact distributions: another analysis of Buang Meraban, a Pleistocene site on New Ireland, Papua New Guinea. *Archaeology in Oceania* 33: 63–82.

Longhurst, A. (1998). Cod: perhaps if we all stood back a bit? *Fisheries research* 38: 101–8.

Lourandos, H. (1997). *Continent of hunter-gatherers: new perspectives in Australian prehistory.* Cambridge: Cambridge University Press.

Maclean, J.L. (1978). The clam gardens of Manus. *Harvest* 4(3): 160–3.

Manne, T. and P.M. Veth (2015). Late Pleistocene and early Holocene exploitation of estuarine communities in northwestern Australia. *Quaternary International* 385: 112–23.

McNiven, I. (2006). Late moves on *Donax*: Aboriginal marine specialisation in southeast Queensland over the last 6000 years. In S. Ulm and I. Lilley, eds. *An archaeological life: Papers in honour of Jay Hall,* 109–124. Brisbane: Aboriginal and Torres Strait Islander Studies Unit, The University of Queensland.

McNiven, I. (2004). Saltwater People: spiritscapes, maritime rituals and the archaeology of Australian indigenous seascapes. *World Archaeology* 35(3): 329–349.

McNiven, I. and D. Bell (2010). Fishers and farmers: historicising the Gunditjmara freshwater fishery, western Victoria. *The La Trobe Journal* 85: 83–105.

McNiven, I.J., J. Crouch, T. Richards, N. Dolby, G. Jacobsen, Gunditj Mirring Traditional Owners Aboriginal Corporation (2012). Dating Aboriginal stone-walled fishtraps at Lake Condah, southeast Australia. *Journal of Archaeological Science* 39(2): 268–86.

McNiven, I.J. and A.B.J. Lambrides (2023). Stone-walled fish traps of Australia and New Guinea as expressions of enhanced sociality. In I.J. McNiven and B. David, eds. *The Oxford Handbook of the Archaeology of Indigenous Australia and New Guinea,* 413–48: Oxford: Oxford University Press.

McNiven, I.J., T. Manne and A. Ross (2021). Enhanced ecologies and ecosystem engineering: strategies developed by Aboriginal Australians to increase the abundance of animal resources. In I.J. McNiven and B. David, eds. *The Oxford Handbook of the Archaeology of Indigenous Australia and New Guinea,* 329–60. Oxford: Oxford University Press.

Monks, C. (2021). The role of terrestrial, estuarine, and marine foods in dynamic Holocene environments and adaptive coastal economies in Southwestern Australia. *Quaternary International* 597: 5–23.

Nicholson, R.A. (1996). Fish bone diagenesis in different soils. *Archaeofauna* 5: 79–91.

O'Connor, S. and P. Veth (2000). The world's first mariners: savannah dwellers in an island continent. In O'Connor and P. Veth, eds. *East of Wallace's Line: Studies of Past and Present Maritime Cultures of the Indo-Pacific Region,* modern qaternary research in Southeast Asia, 99–137. Rotterdam: A.A. Balkema.

O'Connor, S. and J. Chappell (2003). Colonisation and coastal subsistence in Australia and Papua New Guinea: different timing, different modes. *Pacific Archaeology: Assessments and Prospects (Cahiers de l'Archeólogie en Nouvelle-Calédonie)* 15: 17–32.

O'Connor, S., R. Ono and C. Clarkson (2011). Pelagic fishing at 42,000 years before the present and the maritime skills of modern humans. *Science* 334(6059): 1117–21.

O'Connor, T. (2000). *The archaeology of animal bones.* Gloucestershire: Sutton Publishing.

O'Connell, J.F., J. Allen and K. Hawkes (2010). Pleistocene Sahul and the origins of seafaring. In A. Anderson, J. Barrett and K. Boyle, eds. *The Global Origins and Development of Seafaring*, 57–68. Cambridge: McDonald Institute for Archaeological Research.

O'Connor, S., J. Louys, S. Kealy and S.C. Samper Carro (2017). Hominin dispersal and settlement east of Huxley's Line: the role of sea level changes, island size, and subsistence behavior. *Current Anthropology* 58(S17): S567–82.

Olsen, A.M. and D. Evans (1991). *The Coorong, a multi-species*. Adelaide: Department of Fisheries.

Pauly, D. (1995). Anecdotes and the shifting baseline syndrome of fisheries. *Trends in Ecology and Evolution* 10(10): 430.

People, Gunditjmara and G. Wettenhall (2010). *The People of Budj Bim: engineers of aquaculture, builders of stone house settlements and warriors defending country*. Heywood, Vic: em PRESS Publishing for the Gungitj Mirring Traditional Owners Corporation.

Pepperell, J.G. (2018). *Fishing for the past: casting nets and lines into Australia's early colonial history*. Dural Delivery Centre, NSW: Rosenberg.

Richards, T.H. (2012). An early-Holocene Aboriginal coastal landscape at Cape Duquesne, southwest Victoria, Australia, 2012. *Peopled Landscapes: Archaeological and Biogeographic Approaches to Landscapes*. Terra Australis 34: 121–56.

Richter, K.K., J. Wilson, A.K.G. Jones, M. Buckley, N. van Doorn and M.J. Collins (2011). Fish 'n chips: ZooMS peptide mass fingerprinting in a 96 well plate format to identify fish bone fragments. *Journal of Archaeological Science* 38(7): 1502–10.

Roberts, A. (2010). *Aboriginal women's fishing in New South Wales: a thematic history*. Sydney: Department of Environment, Climate Change and Water NSW.

Robson, H.K., A.P. Little, K.G. Jones, S. Blockley, I. Candy, I. Matthews et al. (2018). Scales of analysis: evidence of fish and fish processing at Star Carr. *Journal of Archaeological Science: Reports* 17: 895–903.

Rowell, K., K.W. Flessa, D.L. Dettman, M.J. Román, L.R. Gerber and L.T. Findley (2008). Diverting the Colorado River leads to a dramatic life history shift in an endangered marine fish. *Biological Conservation* 141: 1138–48.

Rowland, M.J. and S. Ulm (2011). Indigenous fish traps and weirs of Queensland. *Queensland Archaeological Research Queensland Archaeological Research* 14: 1–58.

Schaerlaekens, D.G., W. Dekker, H. Wickström, F. A.M. Volckaert and G.E. Maes (2011). Extracting a century of preserved molecular and population demographic data from archived otoliths in the endangered European eel (*Anguilla anguilla* L.). *Journal of Experimental Marine Biology and Ecology* 398(1–2): 56–62.

Selleslagh, J., A. Echard, C. Pécheyran, M. Baudrimont, J. Lobry, F. Daveratet (2016). Can analysis of *Platichthys flesus* otoliths provide relevant data on historical metal pollution in estuaries? Experimental and in situ approaches. *Science of The Total Environment* 557–8: 20–30.

Szpak, P. (2011). Fish bone chemistry and ultrastructure: implications for taphonomy and stable isotope analysis. *Journal of Archaeological Science* 38(12): 3358–72.

Taplin, G. (1879). The Narrinyeri. In J.D. Woods, ed. *The native tribes of South Australia*. Adelaide: E.S. Wigg and Son.

Tench, W. (1789). *Sydney's first four years: being a reprint of "A narrative of the expedition to Botany Bay" and "A complete account of the Settlement at Port Jackson"*. Sydney: Royal Australian Historical Society, Library of Australian History.

Tendi, Ngarrindjeri, Ngarrindjeri Heritage Committee and Ngarrindjeri Native Title Committee (2007). *Ngarrindjeri Nation Sea Country Plan: Caring for Ngarrindjeri Country and Culture*. Meningie: Ngarrindjeri Land Progress Association.

Thurstan, R.H., A.B. Campbell and J.M. Pandolfi (2016). Nineteenth century narratives reveal historic catch rates for Australian snapper (*Pagrus auratus*). *Fish and Fisheries* 17(1): 210–25.

Thurstan, R.H., L. Mcclenachan, L.B Crowder, J. Drew, J.N. Kittinger, P. Levin et al. (2015). Filling historical data gaps to foster solutions in marine conservation. *Ocean and Coastal Management* 115: 31–40.

Tregenza, J.M. (1980). *George French Angas, artist, traveller and naturalist 1822–1886*. Adelaide: Art Gallery Board of South Australia.

Ulm, S. (2006). *Coastal themes: an archaeology of the southern Curtis Coast, Queensland*. Canberra: Pandanus Press.

Ulm, S. (2011). Coastal foragers on southern shores: marine resource use in northeast Australia since the Late Pleistocene. In N.F. Bicho, J.A. Haws and L.G. Davis, eds. *Trekking the shore: changing coastlines and the antiquity of coastal settlement*, 441–61. New York: Springer New York.

Veth, P., K. Aplin, L. Wallis, T. Manne, T. Pulsford, E. White and A. Chappell (2007). *The archaeology of the Montebello Islands: late quaternary foragers on an arid coastline*. Volume 1668. Oxford: Archaeopress.

Veth, Peter, I. Ward, T. Manne, S. Ulm, K. Ditchfield, J. Dortch et al. (2017). Early human occupation of a maritime desert, Barrow Island, North-West Australia. *Quaternary Science Reviews* 168: 19–29.

Wallace-Carter, E. (1987). *For they were fishers*. Adelaide: Gillingham Printers Pty Ltd.

Weisler, M.I. and I.J. McNiven (2016). Four thousand years of western Torres Strait fishing in the Pacific-wide context. *Journal of Archaeological Science: Reports* 7: 764–74.

West, C.F., S. Wischniowski and C. Johnston (2012). Pacific cod (*Gadus macrocephalus*) as a paleothermometer: otolith oxygen isotope reconstruction. *Journal of Archaeological Science* 39(10): 3277–83.

Westell, C., A. Roberts, M. Morrison,G. Jacobsen and the River Murray and Mallee Aboriginal Corporation (2020). Initial results and observations on a radiocarbon dating program in the Riverland region of South Australia. *Australian Archaeology* 86(2): 160–75.

Wickler, S.K. (2001). *The prehistory of Buka: a stepping stone island in the northern Solomons.* Canberra: Department of Archaeology and Natural History, and Centre for Archaeological Research, Australian National University.

Williams, E. (1998). The archaeology of the lake systems in the middle Cooper basin, north-eastern South Australia. *Records of the South Australian Museum* 30(2): 69–91.

4

Tell me what you eat and I will tell you who you are
The socio-environmental impacts of European animal domesticates in colonial Australia

Tanja Nussbaumer and Melanie Fillios

Introduction

As Brillat-Savarin wrote, "The destiny of nations depends on the manner in which they are fed" (Brillat-Savarin 1854, 25). Indeed, establishing reliable sources of food was critical for the survival of colonies, as early historical records demonstrate in Australia. Animal bones recovered from historical sites have been well-studied from colonies in the Americas, but remain understudied in Australia, and should be central to understanding early colonial anxieties around food security. As animal domesticates share a unique, close relationship with humans and are intricately connected with human activities, delineating this relationship contributes to understanding past behaviours, such as the responses of early colonists to a new suite of social and environmental conditions during initial periods of colonisation.

In this chapter, we argue that food choice was pivotal in maintaining European identity during the first century post colonisation. In particular, the preference for consuming mutton over more readily available native species, such as kangaroo, was a way of maintaining ties to British heritage and social identity. Some have also argued that prohibiting the hunting of native species was also an initial mechanism to maintain control of the new colony (Newling 2016). Unfortunately, the preference for introduced European domesticates by the early colonists, and subsequent intensive sheep husbandry, resulted in significant environmental consequences and cultural changes, for both Aboriginal peoples and native species – changing an ancient landscape and ancient culture permanently. Here we explore the impacts of this human-animal-environmental nexus in colonial Australia with a focus on sheep, providing a zooarchaeological case study highlighting the detrimental environmental impacts of colonisation. In so doing, we also construct a high-level model for considering how different cultures adapted their food choices to challenging new colonial environments. We apply this model to Australia, examining the way in which this adaptation shaped and was shaped by foodways.

Social formation, colonisation and sheep

Social formation in early colonial settings is a fluid process, typically resulting in novel combinations of ethnic groups and resources (e.g. Deagan 2003; Stein 2005). Because these combinations tend to be dynamic and highly experimental, they are challenging to understand. Human-animal interactions are an intrinsic part of these dynamics and lay the groundwork for subsequent socio-cultural and economic structures. The presence of introduced species in colonies also had significant and lasting environmental impacts. Much of the available literature on the early colonisation of Sydney, Australia's first colony, has primarily focused on two landscape transformations. First, the shift "from an Aboriginal landscape to an organic, preindustrial town" and second, change involving "a remodelling and growth tied to farming, grazing, timbergetting and town building …" (Karskens 2010, 3).

While relatively abundant zooarchaeological remains have been recovered from well-contextualised deposits derived from development-led consulting projects, they have yet to be used as a source of socio-ecological evidence for these early stages of colonisation. This chapter uses evidence from the analysis of sheep bones to question assumptions surrounding early colonial social dynamics and foodways. In doing so, it challenges foundational stories to create new narratives and develop a more robust understanding of these early colonial social dynamics and their resulting ecological impact.

The colonisation of Australia has been studied from many angles (e.g. Flexner 2014), but surprisingly limited attention has been directed toward the species brought out on ships in the early phases, and approaches to farming them once here. Sheep have largely been examined through the lens of history, with a focus on key pastoral figures such as John Macarthur and the role they played in fuelling the colonial economy (e.g. Murray and Chesters 2012), but limited focus has been given to them from a zooarchaeological and ecological perspective. There has also been only limited historical and archaeological study devoted to the ways in which these new species (and resulting agricultural practices) impacted the environment. As an introduced species, sheep have had a critical impact on Australia's physical landscape. We know that this is true from an ecological perspective (e.g. Melville 1994), and so it is important that this species, which was simultaneously economically significant while also being fundamentally environmentally destructive, features more prominently in archaeological understandings of the colonial past.

The introduction and spread of non-native species into novel ecosystems has been a focus of anthropological research for decades (Fillios et al. 2012; Fillios and Taçon 2016; Letnic et al. 2012; Sykes 2012; Sykes et al. 2006), and while understanding how species generally impact regional environments and integrate with and/or interrupt local ecosystems has been a driving force to this type of research, sheep have received only limited attention as a non-native species. Limited scholarship has addressed how European colonisers adapted their agricultural practices to their new environment, what factors governed the choice of domesticates and whether new husbandry/agricultural techniques were adopted as a result. Even less is known of the role played by behavioural ecology and those biological variables intrinsic to sheep. Once introduced, sheep become the dominant animals in most places, but the driving force(s) behind their popularity are rarely addressed.

The examination of this more recent human-sheep relationship, specifically in the delineation of the ecological, socio-cultural and economic impacts of this relationship in colonial Australia from a zooarchaeological perspective, provides an opportunity to apply an Australian case study to pressing global questions of environmental change and resource security in the face of growing climatic instability. The continual interplay between humans and the unique suite of environmental conditions encountered in each new place (e.g. topography, geologies, soils, climates, ecologies) is not simply backdrop to social transformation in early colonial contexts but is also a series of conditions vital to understanding the experience and sort of settlement that emerged in Sydney (Karskens 2010).

The story of human history is the story of migration, and colonialism is one of its more recent chapters. Diachronically, colonialism shares several features, most commonly the "importation" of the coloniser's cultural package. These shared features mean that short, early phases of experimentation accompanying these periods can help decipher human dynamics. Faunal evidence plays a key role in understanding colonial adaptations to new environments (e.g. Landon 1996; Zierden and Reitz 2016), and the social importance of the human-animal relationship, particularly with respect to foodways, is well-recognised. Shifts in land use strategies by European colonists have been examined in North America (Arbuckle and Bowen 2002), but the pivotal role that the grazing of European stock played in altering the landscape of the Sydney basin by grazing over woodlands and pastures created by Aboriginal burning, has not received the attention it merits. The earliest colonial animal economies in Australia can be explained by the nexus between animal management and ecology. "By the 1820's, the pattern of farming and grazing lands echoed the funnel shape of the plain's arable soils precisely" (Karskens 2010, 20). For example, European modification of the landscape in the Sydney basin led to the destruction of the resources on which the Dharug people had relied for thousands of years.

The zooarchaeology of colonisation in Australia is shaped by the interplay between culture and the environment, in particular the impact of hard-hoofed European domesticates, predominantly sheep and cattle, on an environment that drastically differed from the homelands of the British colonisers. To contextualise this interplay, we briefly contrast Australian zooarchaeology against the zooarchaeology of domesticates in another area of British colonisation, the Americas.

Animals, colonisation and cultural cores: the Americas

Delineating the human-animal relationship in colonial settings offers an unrivalled view of the impacts of introduced species on novel environments the world over. Indeed, the colonial period was an important phase in history, where the tyranny of ever-increasing distances coupled with drastically different climates compared to countries of origin necessitated degrees of change, innovation and cultural adaptations to survive in new and challenging environments. Few scholars have focused on understanding reactions to new environments by looking at the role of culture as a uniquely human way of adapting to environmental constraints and opportunities (Steward 2006). External drivers are well-discussed as agents of cultural change in human history, and so too is acceptance that similar adjustments could occur within similar environments (Gunn 1980). The driver behind this premise is that people carry a "culture core" with them (particularly regarding subsistence strategies and economic arrangements) that would likely reoccur in any place with the same environmental conditions (Hardesty 2009). Bökönyi (1975) suggested that when settlers immigrate to new regions where animal husbandry is unknown, they will maintain their original animal husbandry traditions. This theory of international immigrants to new environments, and the idea of culture change versus cultural persistence and continuity (e.g. Voss 2018, 2015, 2012, 2008, 2005), is relevant to many studies of settler colonies in North, Central and South America, where the British, French and Spanish had varying degrees of success incorporating their own culture cores.

Colonial American foodways offer a wealth of extensively analysed faunal material. Drawn primarily from collections of seventeenth to nineteenth century material, the broad similarities to Australia in the historical setting provides a useful comparison, including well-documented insights into this period of adaptation and change, such as diet and subsistence practices, animal husbandry strategies, food production/distribution systems, social and cultural variation and specifically, degrees of transplantation of cultural traditions (Landon 2009, 2005). The colonial period in the Americas was characterised by the settlement and subsequent continuity/ change of several European cultures (i.e. Dutch, British, French and Spanish), and so offers the opportunity to contrast systems derived from different peoples.

Diet and subsistence

The concept of continuity and/or change is a prominent area of research into subsistence, particularly in the degree to which colonists tried to retain traditional dietary preferences or a "library of foodways" (Cheek 1998) in new environments. Many have used this concept to examine British, French, Spanish and even Dutch settlements, with specific focus on the British colonists' responses to the new environments (Bowen 1975; Fischer et al. 1997; Hodgetts 2006; Landon 1996, 1997; Lightfoot 2018; Miller 1984, 1988; Reitz 1986; Reitz and Honerkamp 1983; Reitz and Waselkov 2015; Reitz and Zierden 2014; Smith 2014; Tourigny 2020; Welker et al. 2018; Zierden and Reitz 2009). In stark contrast to Australia, Miller (1984, 1988) detailed British adaptations in subsistence strategies to the new environment of the south-eastern coast of the United States, finding the overall subsistence patterns of the colonists shifted significantly from their English antecedent by the 1700s. In this case, the environment drove change such that, despite the traditional importance of sheep in the British diet, there was a switch to cattle, which were better suited to the hot and humid Chesapeake climate (Miller 1988). Reitz and Honerkamp (1983) reached the same conclusions regarding the seminal role of the environment when explaining a dearth of sheep at Fort Frederica, Georgia.

Fischer and colleagues (1997) and Hodgetts (2006) both compared the traditional English diets with those of the colonists (Plymouth, Massachusetts Bay and Newfoundland, Canada), suggesting a desire (and ability) on the part of the colonists to retain certain domestic "English" meats – primarily beef and pork. In these colder contexts, sheep became universally redundant, as cattle and pig were better suited to the sandy and forested environment.

Differences between rural and urban diets have also been widely recognised in colonial areas – but the role of environmental factors as drivers in these contexts has been less well-addressed. In general, similar patterns appear across time and space, with urban contexts including more domestic animals and rural diets being more diverse with the inclusion of wild species. This pattern has been identified among British colonists in Massachusetts, South Carolina and Georgia (Landon 1996, 1997; Reitz 1986).

Military contexts also conform to the rural/urban colonial pattern. Welker and colleagues (2018) examined the diet of the British colonial militia at Fort Shirley, Pennsylvania, which indicated a distinctive dietary patterning whereby consumption of domesticates lessened over time. The inaccessible nature of the fort's location was heavily influenced by road infrastructure, fostering a reliance on wild game within colonial military provisioning (Welker et al. 2018). Similarly, in a study of British and American settlers in Upper Canada, Tourigny (2020) suggested initial foodways were heavily influenced by traditional diets, with beef and pork important food staples at the beginning of settlement. Over time, however, a cuisine characteristic of the region developed (Tourigny 2020).

The influence of Indigenous peoples also shaped dietary practice in the Americas, especially in rural contexts. Data on French subsistence practices in the mid-western United States (Fort Michilimackinac, Fort Ouiatenon, Cahokia wedge) suggest that compared to their English counterparts, French traders had far greater interaction and trade with Native Americans, significantly altering their diets to incorporate higher rates of wild mammals – with an almost complete dearth of sheep (Cleland 1970; Martin 1986, 1988, 1991; Scott 1991, 1996). Additional research finds variability. Greenfield (1989) examined faunal remains to differentiate Dutch and British households, suggesting that as the Dutch New Amsterdam became the English New York, pig became less desirable as the popularity of sheep and cattle increased. Janowitz (1993) examined seventeenth century New Amsterdam foodways, finding faunal assemblages dominated by the three main domestic taxa, and that, despite adding native species to the diets, the Dutch retained their European food preparation methods.

Notably, traditional Spanish subsistence practices appear to have changed in colonial North America, with major dietary changes driven by an unsuitable environment for sheep which meant Spanish livestock failed to thrive. Beef began to supplant traditional Spanish species and was accompanied by a marked increase in wild species consumption (Opishinski 2019; Reitz 1979, 1991, 1992a, 1992b, 1993, 1994; Reitz and Cumbaa 1983; Reitz and Scarry 1985; Reitz and Waselkov 2015; Sunseri 2017). In a comparison between Spanish, French and British diets, colonists appear to have transplanted subsistence practices from their homelands in varying degrees, but adapted to their new environment by altering their reliance on certain domesticates, thereby reflecting local social, economic and especially environmental factors (Reitz and Waselkov 2015).

In Central and South America, the degree to which the Spanish colonists adapted their foodways to new environments, and the degree to which local Indigenous communities assimilated the imposed diets has been well-studied (deFrance

1996, 2003; deFrance and Hanson 2008; deFrance et al. 2016; De Nigris et al. 2010; Freiwald and Pugh 2018; Jamieson 2008; Kennedy and VanValkenburg 2016; Kennedy et al. 2019; Newman 2010). Here, Spanish colonisation generally meant a fusion of traditional Andean culture and European customs – whereby the majority of Indigenous settlements rapidly accepted and integrated Eurasian domesticates (particularly sheep, goat and pig) into their diets, with a continued, though diminished, reliance on local resources. Again, here too there is variability. DeFrance (2003) suggested that wealthy Spanish inhabitants of Potosi (Bolivia) were more likely to maintain their Iberian cultural traditions rather than adapt Andean cuisine. Data from parts of Argentina and Peru suggests that there was no indication of the introduction of Eurasian animals but rather a persistence of Indigenous dietary practices. This may have resulted from brief colonial occupations and failed settlements due to the maladaptation of domesticates in high elevation environments (deFrance et al. 2016; De Nigris et al. 2010).

The confluence of European colonists, new environments and local Indigenous peoples also came together to produce changes in husbandry, and thereby diet. Sarah Boston's Farmstead in Massachusetts established that the New England Native American households incorporated and adapted European animal husbandry strategies into their Native Nipmuc practices (Allard 2015). Morphometric data from cattle have been used to explain how husbandry strategies were a contributor to changes in cattle size (e.g. Arbuckle and Bowen 2004; Reitz and Ruff 1994). Changes in land use strategies including access to less forage, coupled with static husbandry strategies, resulted in less nutrition and thus decreased cattle size (Arbuckle and Bowen 2004). Additional research examined how husbandry strategies affected the environment, with the rapid rate of settlement and cotton growing in Ozan Township, Arkansas, resulting in drought and soil erosion (Proebsting 2016).

In other areas of the Americas, particularly Spanish missions in southern Arizona and northern Mexico, extensive cattle ranching was introduced by Spanish colonists who exploited Indigenous communities as a labour force (e.g. Pavão-Zuckerman 2011, 2017; Pavão-Zuckerman and LaMotta 2007; Pavão-Zuckerman and Martinez-Ramirez 2020). Cattle were also used for secondary products, particularly hides and tallow, which were vital for Spanish mining activities in the regions (Pavão-Zuckerman 2011; Pavão-Zuckerman and LaMotta 2007). Elsewhere, Wallman (2018) focused on the ecological consequences of colonialism and the sugar monoculture plantation era in the Caribbean (Martinique, Barbados and Dominica), highlighting that the subsistence practices and small-scale animal husbandry that began during slavery are still evident today.

This survey illustrates that despite variability, there are several consistent patterns in colonial contexts whereby early colonists initially tried to adhere to the foodways of their native land. Subsequently, however, diets evolved, ultimately adapting in response to a suite of environmentally determined factors, including climate, topography and availability of wild species. These adaptations to new environments, coupled with influences from Indigenous communities and new sources of labour, resulted in the distinctive foodways which now characterise different geographical regions. These patterns form a significant base for comparison with early colonial contexts in Australia.

Australia – a colonial anomaly?

Colonial Australian diets initially follow patterns evident in other areas of British colonisation – but instead of evolving to incorporate Indigenous resources and novel foodways, they generally remained stubbornly static (but see Allen 2008 for Port Essington as a notable exception). The choice to maintain British foodways could be argued to be wrapped in a firmly British identity for at least the first century of Australia's colonial history.

From an archaeological perspective, historical zooarchaeology is a young discipline in Australia in which discussions over the human-animal-environmental nexus have largely centred around megafaunal extinctions (e.g. Brook and Johnson 2006; Cosgrove et al. 2010; David et al. 2021; DeSantis et al. 2017; Dortch et al. 2016; Field 2006; Field and Dodson 1999; Field et al. 2008; Field et al. 2013; Fillios et al. 2009; Gillespie et al. 2006; Grellet-Tinner et al. 2016; Hocknull et al. 2020; Langley 2020; Price et al. 2011; Trueman et al. 2005; Turney et al. 2008; Wroe et al. 2013) and Australian pre-European history (primarily the Pleistocene and the early Holocene) (e.g. Cosgrove and Allen 2001; Garvey 2006, 2007, 2011; Garvey and Sandy 2009; Garvey et al. 2011, 2016; Fillios et al. 2012; Fillios and Taçon 2016; Langley et al. 2016). Faunal analyses from colonial contexts often fall under the larger umbrella of historical archaeology and so are often buried within broader research – such as overviews of Oceania (Flexner 2014), Australia and New Zealand (Harvey 2013; Lawrence and Davies 2009; Winter 2013) and thematically convict archaeology in New South Wales (Gojak 2001). The small number of extant overviews focused specifically on Australian foodways, and none focused on the environmental effects of introduced animal domesticates, demonstrating the limited research in colonial contexts (e.g. Cosgrove 2002; Crabtree 2016; Manne et al. 2016; Garvey and Field 2011).

Of the published analyses, those with a colonial focus (c. 1780s–1860s) have a strong emphasis on diet. The concept of continuity and change in foodways (so prevalent in the Americas) is still an emerging theme in colonial Australian zooarchaeology, as is a socio-economic perspective examining the rural/urban and convict/free settler dichotomies. Research on early colonial Sydney by historian Grace Karskens leads the discussion (e.g. 1997, 1999, 2003 and 2010), with detailed findings on the interplay between subsistence, diet and the environment drawn from excavations at the Cumberland/Gloucester site in The Rocks. Karskens (2003) suggested that convicts and ex-convict families in The Rocks were in fact eating well, and that the foodways of early colonial Sydney reflected the traditional and well-known habits of England. In this case, the consumption of heads and feet (less desirable parts of an animal) was not a sign of poverty and oppression, but rather an indication of the transplantation of native customs and preferences.

Some suggest that diets of the wealthy show similar dietary patterns to those of freed convicts in early colonial Sydney (e.g. Karskens 2003), with deposits from the oldest "wealthy" colonial site in Australia – the first Government House – yielding evidence for cattle hocks and suckling pig (Crook et al. 2006; Lawrence and Davies 2009), species also found in common contexts. Sarah Colley (2006, 2013) proposed a preference for European domesticates as a way that free settlers could distinguish themselves from convicts, thereby providing a useful comparison against which to contextualise further analyses of the interplay between cultural preferences and diet. More research is needed on convict settlements to test this theory.

Status and identity markers in rural areas are comparable to patterns noticed in North America. Blake's (2010) comparative analysis of urban and rural diets from Sydney (Cumberland Street) and surrounds (Parramatta and Old Marulan) suggested a consistency of dietary preference across colonial Sydney (i.e. primacy of mutton) in line with Karskens (1999; 2010), but also variability due to geographical differences, such as the consumption of Australian native species away from urban centres. Documentary evidence further indicates that British cultural traditions were desirable and were retained in the early post-convict period (Blake 2010). Native species were also consumed in early Hobart, with kangaroo eaten during a time in which no European domesticates were imported from the mainland (Fillios 2016). In this case, rural diets were blind to class – with evidence the wealthy ate as the poor – suggesting that access also played a key role in one's ability to maintain cultural food preferences.

In Tasmania, D'Gluyas and colleagues (2015) contrasted subsistence patterns and quality of life of civilians, the military and incarcerated occupants of Port Arthur prisoner barracks. The faunal assemblages suggested diets included traditional European domesticates, as well as wild native taxa, suggesting a reasonably varied diet in contrast to the urban mainland. Sheep and pig remains were the most prevalent, with on-site processing suggested, as one would expect in this remote location. D'Gluyas and colleagues (2015) noted ration size changed across classes (i.e. from prisoners to privileged convicts, military or civilian overseers), suggesting standardised rations for higher status people. Whether meat quality also changed is not known.

In colonial Melbourne, Howell-Meurs (2000) and Simons and Maitri (2006) both utilised species abundance, skeletal part representation, butchery marks and age determinations to establish diet. Howell-Meurs (2000) discussed socio-economic patterns in light of high-quality cuts of cattle and sheep consumed at the Viewbank homestead site in Heidelberg. Howell-Meurs (2000) also advocated further intra-assemblage studies using the Viewbank assemblage for socio-economic insights (rural representations) and the environmental impact of colonisation on flora and fauna. Guiry and colleagues (2014) introduced the first stable isotope study of domesticates in Australia from the Commonwealth Block site. Isotopic analyses established the species consumed, finding domestic species were raised locally, with a few imported/non-local animals (Guiry et al. 2014).

Isotopic analyses have been applied to the analysis of faunal remains infrequently. In addition to Guiry, Pate focused primarily on human remains (e.g. 1995, 1997, 2012, 2017) and native Australian species (e.g. 1998, 2008) to examine Aboriginal diets, mobility and provenance. Lastly, whilst Owen and colleagues (2017) examined the isotopic signatures of human rather than domestic animal remains, the study provided valuable insight into early Sydney colonial diet. Owen and colleagues (2017) suggested the main meats consumed were pork and mutton with the occasional beef, facilitating comparisons with the diets of other colonial Australian settlements, as well as the documented diets from nineteenth-century England and Ireland.

Dietary remains recovered from shipwrecks provides strong insight into foodways and trade networks. English (1990) focused on the salted meats from the *William Salthouse* wreck (on the Pope's Eye Shoal). Analysing mainly a beef and pork cargo, he suggested that butchery mark location and morphology may facilitate the identification of salted meats at terrestrial sites. In a similar vein, Guiry and colleagues (2015) used stable isotopes from cattle and pig remains to establish the origin and dietary life histories of the animals on board the *William Salthouse*, concluding that a single ship could have contained animals with a relatively wide range of origins. Lastly, Nash's (2002) analysis of animal remains from the *Sydney Cove* shipwreck (at Preservation Island) suggested that necessary provisions for the early colonies, such as salted meat (including sheep) were being imported from India. Nash's (2002) study has important implications for understanding the adaptation process of the colonisers and the importation of certain meats (i.e. that they were not solely imported from Britain).

Finally, dietary insight from analysis of faunal remains at whaling stations provides additional support for the seminal role of the transplantation/adaptation process of the British cultural core. Meat diets from nineteenth-century Tasmanian whaling stations (Adventure Bay, Bruny Island and Lagoon Bay, Forestier Peninsula) suggest that men in whaling parties had access to a varied and nutritious diet, with mutton always preferred, especially when fresh, and thus was most likely to be locally raised and butchered on-site (Lawrence 2001; Lawrence and Tucker 2002). Meanwhile beef was commonly brought in as barrelled beef, a diet heavily influenced by Britain (Lawrence 2010).

Gibbs (2005) likewise established the same in his study of a Western Australian whaling station (Cheyne Beach), where he noted a high frequency of sheep (fresh mutton) in the assemblage, alongside an absence of cattle and pigs. James-Lee (2014) examined both Australian (Lagoon Bay, Adventure Bay and Cheyne Beach) and New Zealand (Te Hoe and Oashore) nineteenth-century whaling stations to better understand the interactions between the immigrants and the Aboriginal peoples and Māori peoples. James-Lee (2014) established that all the communities studied mostly maintained their traditional whaling station rations but also supplemented with local and exotic species in varying degrees, as dependent on land access and interactions with local peoples. For example, in New Zealand, intermarriage with Māori women provided supplementations of seafood into diets, but colonisation also introduced pork (from Polynesia) and new varieties of pig and chicken (from Europe), followed by mutton becoming the most dominant meat (James-Lee 2014). In Australia, less trade with Aboriginal communities, larger areas of land to farm and access to native land mammals meant that there was an increased frequency of local animal husbandry predicated on imported European domesticates as well as ration supplementation with opportunistic hunting.

In an interesting contrast to whaling stations, Dooley and colleagues (2020) examined the subsistence practices of nineteenth-century enslaved Aboriginal pearl divers at Bandicoot Bay in Western Australia and suggested that the provisioning arrangements were very different to those in whaling stations, with no domestic animals recovered. Explanations for this dissimilarity include the suggestion that whaling stations were occupied for larger portions of the year than Bandicoot Bay, which represented only brief occupations, and that the complete absence of imported domesticate meats could be explained by the depletion of provisioned meats on ships, whereby wild meats were then used to substitute.

This brief review highlights what appears to be lack of interest in foodways beyond species lists in Australia. However, there is a vast body of data from historical sites in the grey literature, either as subsections within larger archaeological consultancy reports, or as unpublished academic theses. For example, English's (1991) paper on *William Salthouse* stemmed from a much larger, unpublished research project on mutton. Similarly, Piper's (1991) thesis remains unpublished. Others include Torres (1997), who focused on the meat diet of the working class in Sydney, Baylem (2009) who examined socio-economic status in colonial Adelaide and Hart (2018) who examined wild versus domestic faunal remains from Cottage Green, Hobart. Many more faunal assemblages remain unpublished and unanalysed – representing a rich but untapped source of data on early colonial Australian lifeways. Encouragingly, Connor's research delineating the meat diet of women at the Hyde Park Barracks in Sydney has recently been published (2016; 2021).

Foodways and the human-animal-environmental nexus

Foodways offer a nuanced understanding of the past interplay between humans, animals and the environment. Domesticated species in particular function as proxies for social, cultural, economic, technological and environmental change (Thomas and Fothergill 2014). Delineating past diets of a particular cultural group, town or region addresses the specific choices people made, and importantly for this discussion, the drivers for those decisions. Here, we argue that the single largest factor in Australian colonial food choice was cultural connection with Britain. Not only do the historical sources, including cookery books, evidence the dedication to British cuisine, but the faunal record clearly and strongly supports this preference.

In colonial Australia, most historical sources suggest that mutton, preferably locally raised, was the overall preferred meat. Beef and pork were also prevalent, although, being more expensive, were consumed less by the working class and more so by the elite. The archaeological record supports this picture, with "English" food seen as desirable and thus retained. Mutton was comfort food from home, while native fauna, like kangaroo, were not widely consumed – especially in comparison with other areas of British colonisation. The question that has still to be adequately addressed is why English colonists in Australia remained steadfast in their adherence to traditional foods, whereas in the Americas, local foods were more readily incorporated into the diet. Perhaps some of this difference can be attributed to the unfamiliarity of Australian native animals (e.g. marsupials) as opposed to the relative familiarity of animals such as deer in the Americas, as well as to the different socio-economic backgrounds of many of Australia's first European inhabitants, which were initially drawn from the lower classes. Certainly, in rural areas and in periods of scarcity, native fauna were consumed. In the early nineteenth century, New South Wales experienced a period of scarcity and so sheep were not exported to the colonists in Hobart who quickly turned to kangaroo to fill the gap (Fillios 2016; Hart 2018). Similar patterns are apparent at Port Arthur (D'Gluyas et al. 2015) and rural areas near Sydney (Blake 2010).

Australia's British colonists likely did not consider the impact that their food choices would have on this new and very different place – and, in particular, the way in which the choice to manage one species over another would shape and alter the environment with which colonists came into contact. Environmental change driven by cultural food preference was an unintentional process, but one that has had dire consequences for almost every environment into which both plant and animal domesticates were introduced.

Husbandry strategies altered animals, humans and the environment. Not only have the drivers behind Australia's cultural adherence to British foods not been adequately addressed, but neither have the resultant impacts on the environment. In Australia, the environment was the limiting factor in sheep husbandry, most notably water and feed. Karskens (2010) notes that European grazing species were initially introduced to fertile landscapes around the Sydney Basin, which were the product of Aboriginal firing. These areas were ideally suited to cattle and sheep, who quickly altered the landscape for good through overgrazing. As sheep moved westward, the climate was drastically different - hotter, more arid, with less water and food. This different climate necessitated changing the genetic composition of the flock – the first steps toward creating the Australian Merino.

In other areas of European colonisation, a similar mix of environmental and socio-cultural factors governed the extent to which, and whether, sheep became part of a national industry. Sheep could be a proxy indicator for former areas of British rule, as today, most former British colonies contain sheep: South Africa, South America, North America, New Zealand and Australia. In the New World, during the fifteenth century, the Spanish transported sheep from Spain on Columbus' second voyage (likely Churra breed). In the sixteenth century, Cortés brought sheep to Mexico, and the flocks spread into what is now the south-western United States via Spanish colonists. Churras were eventually introduced to the Navajos and became a key part of their livelihood and culture, with the modern Navajo-Churra breed a result of this heritage (Melville 1994).

In North America, the sheep industry was already beginning in the early seventeenth century. By the 1640s, there were 100,000 sheep across the 13 colonies, with a dedicated wool mill in Watertown, Massachusetts, 20 years later (Melville 1994). The relative ease with which sheep took hold in North America is likely in part thanks to similar environmental conditions to England, coupled with the transplantation of an already established medieval wool industry from home. In the late seventeenth century, the *Wool Act* of 1698 banned the export of wool from the American colonists. This continued into the eighteenth century, with the British government banning further export of sheep to the Americas, or wool from it, in an attempt to stifle any threat to the wool trade in Britain and Ireland – one of many restrictive trade measures that precipitated the American Revolution. The sheep industry in the north-east grew despite the bans. In the nineteenth century, sheep production moved west and this migration culminated in range wars over grazing and water rights for sheep and cattle (Gulliford 2021). It seems that economic factors have always driven production – and in Australia the story is no different.

The importance of learning from the past

In addition to the novel understandings of socio-economic and cultural adaptations arising from colonial encounters, foodways provide a way of looking at adaptations to a new suite of environmental conditions. The historic period, in particular, was one of rapid environmental change, whereby European colonisation spread plants, animals and diseases around the world (Landon 2009, 2005). Research on colonial Australian foodways holds great potential to understand not only how the climate influenced past peoples, but also how colonists influenced new environments by responding to, adapting to and changing them (Steele 2015). Indeed, in recent decades there has been a growing number of archaeological studies with multidisciplinary approaches acting as proxies for information on past climate and environment, and changes in both (Emery 2004, 2007, 2010; Emery and Thornton 2008a, 2008b, 2012a, 2012b; Sandweiss and Kelley 2012). Faunal remains can be used as proxies for climate conditions and therefore aid in understanding local human interactions and responses to environmental changes, such as the economic strategies used to cope with them (Jones and Britton 2019).

Combining traditional approaches with advanced methodologies has therefore become increasingly useful in exploring these human-environmental interactions, not only on local and regional, but also on global scales (Jones and Britton 2019). Domesticates in particular can "reveal anthropogenic modifications to their environments, diets, physiologies and life histories", as direct results of human activity (Birch 2013; Jones and Britton 2019; Makarewicz 2016; Pilaar Birch et al. 2019a; Zangrando et al. 2014; Zavodny et al. 2019). Part of the domesticate life histories include their management by past human societies, and because animal husbandry strategies were influenced by particular environments, this can reveal tailored management strategies to suit the specific conditions encountered (Jones and Britton 2019). This adjustment of the animal management strategies of past humans to suit certain conditions can be seen in studies by Balasse and colleagues (2006) and Britton and colleagues (2008) who examined sheep in areas of prehistoric Britain to reveal they were eating seaweed and grazing in salt marshes. Additionally, Gron and colleagues (2016) revealed that certain cattle in Neolithic Scandinavia were being manipulated to have multiple birth seasons, while Balasse and colleagues (2021) examined the environmental constraints within Neolithic European cattle seasonal calving, and the resulting impacts on milk availability and cheese making.

Colonial foodways provide a better understanding of the past impacts of human decisions, and this understanding should be used to inform present and future food choices. Understanding "the nature and extent of environmental and climatic changes in the past, and how societies responded to such changes, may be crucial to being able to predict and adapt to the contemporary climatic challenges" (Jones and Britton 2019, 969). Australia has a vastly different climate to Britain and understanding the environmental and social impacts that European animal husbandry had can provide didactic insights into the very real challenge we currently face to create a stable food supply with a future of rising global temperatures and climatic extremes.

The future of food (and the environment) from the past

The real value of understanding the interplay between human food choice and the environment may lie in learning to change our cultural preferences in deference to local environmental conditions – especially in the face of a future with an increasingly variable climate. This may mean turning away from lamb, beef and pork – animals with high water requirements, and some with narrower food preferences – toward more sustainable choices, such as kangaroo and even goat, as understood by Aboriginal peoples and underscored by Pascoe (2014) and many others.

It is commonly held that colonial Australia was built on the back of sheep. Sheep have shaped the culture and industry, creating what would eventually become one of the most the iconic images of Australia. Sheep, and other hard-hoofed animals like cattle, have also caused widespread environmental degradation of their grazing environments, and with their high-water requirements, were, and still are, difficult to manage sustainably in a country of climactic extremes.

Animal remains offer a different type of evidence again – and therefore, a potentially different story. For example, applying a molecular toolkit consisting of radiometric dating, isotopic and genetic analyses to more "standard" morphological and metrical faunal analyses, offers a variety of unique insights into the early dynamics of animal management in new areas – from cultural choices surrounding diet and foodways, to pasturing, husbandry practices and the environmental impacts of introduced species.

Most areas of European colonisation reflect the same general zooarchaeological trends, suggesting that colonisation spatio-temporally progresses on a similar trajectory. For example, most colonial periods can be roughly divided into an initial phase, in which faunal diversity is high, consisting of a variety of wild and introduced domesticates. These patterns make sense, as when faced with a new environment, food security and population health are both unstable as the colonisers attempt to adapt to a new suite of environmental and social conditions. This initial phase is also characterised by social, economic and nutritional instability, and often results in the depletion of native species, as exemplified by the crash in kangaroo numbers in the Sydney Basin shortly following European colonisation. Subsequent periods show a marked decline in species diversity, with an especially large decrease in the use of native species. Reliance on a handful of introduced, European domesticates follows, with an associated growth in population and specialised economic structures built off the back of these animals, including textile and meat industries. The general trend is then one of decreased species richness and increased intensification of specialised or species-targeted animal husbandry – as aptly exemplified by the growth of the Australian sheep industry.

Sheep provide an excellent insight into the development of Australia, specifically Sydney, and an exploration of the origins of colonial Australian rural life and culture. As Karskens (2010) adeptly illustrates, cities emerge from "kaleidoscopic complexity". Sydney was a different place to different people, with "different groups vying for control of urban culture, spaces and places, and for economic and social dominance, all within overarching environmental imperatives..." (Karskens 2010, 3). The early livestock industry was tied to the same geographical constraints and opportunities as the Aboriginal peoples whose Country the colonial settlers claimed – and understanding the way in which water and grazing land shaped the growth of Sydney and the hinterland is reflected in this early grazing economy.

Historical zooarchaeology in Australia remains underdeveloped, with volumes of data derived from commercial consulting projects not available through peer-reviewed publication, and so the European, colonial cultural drivers of the Australian diet have received little attention. The influence of these domesticates on the environment and Australian native species has received even less attention – perhaps because to address this places Australia in a social predicament. That is, it would mean a move away from British foods and toward native species such as kangaroo, emu and bush foods. Interestingly, however, some alternative foods have gained prominence in recent years – and much of this might be attributed to a new wave of cultural groups from South-East Asia, coupled with a growing focus on the environmental requirements of the traditional European trio (i.e. sheep, cattle and pigs).

Understanding historical foodways offers a way forward. Discussing the drivers behind food choice, coupled with a clear understanding of the environmental impacts of this choice, facilitates an open and robust conversation about future foodways. This makes possible previously unattainable avenues of research, allowing for a much broader understanding of the complex interplay between culture, environment and a burgeoning new economic system. In turn, this provides a promising way forward for the future of food – one that is sustainable and suited to an ever more fragile world. Learning from the past enables us to contextualise present day situations, increasing our ability to inform current mitigation strategies in response to changing global pressures on the environment – both natural and human induced.

References

Allard, A. (2015). Foodways, animal husbandry and Nipmuc Identity: faunal analysis from Sarah Boston's farmstead, Grafton, MA, 1790–1840. *International Journal of Historical Archaeology* 19: 208–31.

Allen, J. (2008). *Port Essington. The historical archaeology of a north Australian ninteenth century miliary outpost.* Sydney: Sydney University Press.

Arbuckle, B.S. and J. Bowen (2002). Zooarchaeology and agricultural colonization: an example from the colonial Chesapeake. In M. Mondini, S. Muñoz and S. Wickler eds. *Colonisation, migration, and marginal areas*, 20–7. Oxford: Oxbow Books.

Arnold, E.R., H.J. Greenfield and R.A. Creaser (2013). Domestic cattle mobility in early farming villages in southern Africa: harvest profiles and strontium (87Sr/86Sr) isotope analyses from Early Iron Age sites in the lower Thukela River Valley of South Africa. *Archaeological and Anthropological Sciences* 5: 129–44.

Balasse, M., R.E. Gillis, I. Živaljević et al. (2021). Seasonal calving in European prehistoric cattle and its impacts on milk availability and cheese-making. *Scientific Reports* 11: 8185.

Balasse, M., A.B. Smith, S.H. Ambrose and S.R. Leigh (2003). Determining sheep birth seasonality by analysis of tooth enamel oxygen isotope ratios: the late Stone Age site of Kasteelberg (South Africa), *Journal of Archaeological Science* 30: 205–15.

Balasse, M., A. Tresset and S.H. Ambrose (2006). Stable Isotope evidence (δ13C, δ18O) for winter feeding on seaweed by Neolithic sheep of Scotland. *Journal of Zoology* 270: 170–6.

Balasse, M., A. Tresset, G. Obein, D. Fiorillo and H. Gandois (2019). Seaweed-eating sheep and the adaptation of husbandry in Neolithic Orkney: new insights from Skara Brae. *Antiquity* 93(370): 919–32.

Baylem, V. (2009). Faunal remains and issues of socioeconomic status in nineteenth century. Master's thesis, Flinders University, Adelaide, SA.

Beinart, W. and L. Hughes (2007). *Environment and empire.* Oxford: Oxford University Press.

Blake, N. (2010). Diet in urban and rural nineteenth-century New South Wales: the evidence from the faunal remains. *Australasian Historical Archaeology* 24: 25–34.

Bocherens, H., E. Hofman-Kamińska, D.G. Drucker, U. Schmölcke and R. Kowalczyk (2015). European bison as a refugee species? Evidence from isotopic data on early Holocene bison and other large herbivores in northern Europe. *PLOS ONE*: 1–19.

Bökönyi, S. (1975). Effects of environmental and cultural changes on prehistoric fauna assemblages. In M.C. Arnott, ed. *Gastronomy. The anthropology of food and food habits,* 3–12. The Hague: Mouton.

Bowen, J. (1998). To market, to market: animal husbandry in New England. *Historical Archaeology* 32(3): 137–52.

Bowen, J. (1975). Probate inventories: an evaluation from the perspective of zooarchaeology and agricultural history at Mott Farm. *Historical Archaeology* 9: 11–25.

Brillat-Savarin, J.A. (1854). *The physiology of taste: or transcendental gastronomy.* Translated by F. Robinson. Philadelphia: Lindsay and Blakistan.

Britton, K., G. Müldner and B. Martin (2008). Stable isotope evidence for salt-marsh grazing in the Bronze Age Severn Estuary, UK: implications for palaeodietary analysis at coastal sites. *Journal of Archaeological Science* 35: 2111–8.

Brook, B.W. and C.N. Johnson (2006). Selective hunting of juveniles as a cause of the imperceptible overkill of the Australian Pleistocene megafauna. *Alcheringa: An Australasian Journal of Palaeontology* 30(S1): 39–48.

Brunache, P.L. (2011). Enslaved women, foodways, and identity formation: the archaeology of Habitation La Mahaudière, Guadeloupe, circa late-18th century to mid-19th century. Doctoral thesis, The University of Texas, Austin.

Brunson, K., R. Lele, Z. Xin, D. Xiaoling, W. Hui, Z. Jing and R. Flad (2020). Zooarchaeology, ancient mtDNA, and radiocarbon dating provide new evidence for the emergence of domestic cattle and caprines in the Tao River Valley of Gansu Province, northwest China. *Journal of Archaeological Science: Reports* 31: 102262.

Buckley, M., S.W. Kansa, S. Howard, S. Campbell, J. Thomas-Oates and M. Collins (2010). Distinguishing between archaeological sheep and goat bones using a single collagen peptide. *Journal of Archaeological Science* 37: 13–20.

Cai, D.W., L. Han, X.L. Zhang, H. Zhou and H. Zhu (2007). DNA analysis of archaeological sheep remains from China. *Journal of Archaeological Science* 34: 1347–55.

Cai, D.W., N. Zhang, X. Shao, W. Sun, S. Zhu and D.Y. Yang (2018). New ancient DNA data on the origins and spread of sheep and cattle in northern China around 4000BP. *Asian Archaeology* 2: 51–57.

Campana, M.G., T. Robinson, P.F. Campos and N. Tuross (2013). Independent confirmation of a diagnostic sheep/goat peptide sequence through DNA analysis and further exploration of its taxonomic utility within the Bovidae. *Journal of Archaeological Science* 40: 1421–24.

Cheek, C.D. (1998). Massachusetts Bay foodways: regional and class influences. *Historical Archaeology* 32 (3): 153–172.

Cleland, C. (1970). Comparison of the faunal remains from French and British Refuse Pits at Fort Michilimackinac: A study in changing subsistence practices. *Canadian Historic Sites Occasional Papers in Archaeology and History* 3: 8–23.

Cobden, R., C. Clarkson, G.J. Price, B. David, J-M. Geneste, J-J. Delannoy et al. (2017). The identification of extinct megafauna in rock art using geometric morphometrics: A *Genyornis newtoni* painting in Arnhem Land, northern Australia? *Journal of Archaeological Science* 87: 95–107.

Colley, S. (2013). Fish and fishing in colonial New South Wales: new evidence from the Quadrant site in Sydney. *Post-Medieval Archaeology* 47: 119–35.

Colley, S. (2006). A preliminary beef meat cuts typology for nineteenth-century Sydney and some methodological issues. *Australasian Historical Archaeology* 24: 47–54.

Connor, K. (2021). To make the emigrant a better colonist: transforming women in the Female Immigration Depot, Hyde Park Barracks. *World Archaeology* 52(3): 451–68.

Connor, K. (2016). Feeding the confined: a faunal analysis of Hyde Park Barracks. Honours thesis, the University of Sydney, Sydney, NSW.

Cosgrove, R. (2002). The role of zooarchaeology in archaeological interpretation: a view from Australia. *Archaeofauna* 11: 173–204.

Cosgrove, R. and J. Allen (2001). Prey choice and hunting strategies in the late Pleistocene: evidence from Southwest Tasmania. In A. Anderson, S. O'Connor and I. Lilley, eds. *Histories of old ages: essays in honour of Rhys Jones,* 397–430. Canberra: Australian National University, Coombs Academic Publishing.

Cosgrove, R., J. Field, J. Garvey, J. Brenner-Coltrain, A. Goede, B. Charles et al. (2010). Overdone overkill – the archaeological perspective on Tasmanian megafaunal extinctions. *Journal of Archaeological Science* 37: 2486–503.

Cossette, É. and M.P. Horard-Herbin (2003). A contribution to the morphometrical study of cattle in colonial North America. *Journal of Archaeological Science* 30: 263–74.

Crabtree, P.J. (2016). Zooarchaeology in Oceania: an overview. *Archaeology in Oceania* 51: 1–6.

Crass, D.C. and D.L. Wallsmith (1992). Where's the beef? Food supply at an antebellum frontier post. *Historical Archaeology* 26(2): 3–23.

Crook, P., L. Ellmoos and T. Murray (2005). *Keeping up with the McNamaras: a historical archaeological Study of the Cumberland and Gloucester Streets site, The Rocks, Sydney.* The Mint, Sydney: Historic Houses Trust of NSW.

D'GLuyas, C., M. Gibbs, C. Hamilton and D. Roe (2015). Everyday artefacts: subsistence and quality of life at the Prisoner Barracks, Port Arthur, Tasmania. *Archaeology in Oceania* 50(3): 130–37.

Daly, K.G., P.M. Delser, V.E. Mullin, A. Scheu, V. Mattiangeli and M.D. Teasdale et al. (2018). Ancient goat genomes reveal mosaic domestication in the Fertile Crescent. *Science* 361: 85–8.

Dappert-Coonrod, C.P. and S.R. Kuehn (2017). A boarder, a widow, and a tenant sit down for dinner: foodway comparisons in the Goose Hill Neighborhood, East St. Louis, Illinois. *Midcontinental Journal of Archaeology* 42(1): 4–36.

David, B., L.J. Arnold, J.J. Delannoy, J. Freslov, C. Urwin, F. Petchey et al. (2021). Late survival of megafauna refuted for Cloggs Cave, SE Australia: implications for the Australian late Pleistocene megafauna extinction debate. *Quaternary Science Reviews* 253(106781):1–15.

De Nigris, M.E., P.S. Palombo and M.X. Senatore (2010). Craving for hunger: a zooarchaeological study at the edge of the Spanish Empire. In D. Campana, P. Crabtree, S.D. deFrance, J. Lev-Tov and A. Choyke, eds. *Anthropological approaches to zooarchaeology,* 131–8. Oxford: Oxbow Books.

deFrance, S.D. (1996). Iberian foodways in the Moquegua and Torata Valleys of southern Peru. *Historical Archaeology* 30(3): 20–48.

deFrance, S.D. (2003). Diet and provisioning in the High Andes: a Spanish colonial settlement on the outskirts of Potosi, Bolivia. *International Journal of Historical Archaeology* 7(2): 99–125.

deFrance, S.D. and C.A. Hanson (2008). Labor, population movement, and food in sixteenth-century Ek Balam, Yucatán. *Latin American Antiquity* 19(3): 299–316.

deFrance, S.D., S.A. Wernke and A.E. Sharpe (2016). Conversion and persistence: analysis of faunal remains from an early Spanish colonial doctrinal settlement in Highland Peru. *Latin American Antiquity* 27(3): 300–17.

Delsol, N. (2020). Disassembling cattle and enskilling subjectivities: butchering techniques and the emergence of new colonial subjects in Santiago de Guatemala. *Journal of Social Archaeology* 20(2): 189–213.

Desantis, L.R.G., J.H. Field, S. Wroe and J.R. Dodson (2017). Dietary responses of Sahul (Pleistocene Australia–New Guinea) megafauna to climate and environmental change. *Paleobiology* 43(2): 181–95.

Dooley, T., T. Manne and A. Paterson (2020). Power in food on the maritime frontier: a zooarchaeology of enslaved pearl divers on Barrow Island, Western Australia. *International Journal of Historical Archaeology* 25(2): 544–76.

Doppler, T., C. Gerling, V. Heyd, C. Knipper, T. Kuhn, M. Lehmann, A. Pike and J. Schibler (2017). Landscape opening and herding strategies: carbon isotope analyses of herbivore bone collagen from the Neolithic and Bronze Age lakeshore site of Zurich-Mozartstrasse, Switzerland. *Quaternary International* 436: 18–28.

Dortch, J., M. Cupper, R. Grün, B. Harpley, K. Lee and J. Field (2016). The timing and cause of megafauna mass deaths at Lancefield Swamp, south-eastern Australia. *Quaternary Science Reviews* 145: 161–82.

Emery, K.F. (2010). *Dietary, environmental, and societal implications of ancient Maya animal use in the Petexbatún: a zooarchaeological perspective on the collapse.* Nashville, TN: Vanderbilt University Press.

Emery, K.F. (2007). Assessing the impact of ancient Maya animal use. *Journal of Nature Conservation* 15: 184–95.

Emery, K.F. (2004). Environments of the Maya collapse: zooarchaeological perspective from the Petexbatún, Guatemala. In K.F. Emery, ed. *Maya zooarchaeology: new directions in method and theory*, 81–96. Los Angeles, CA: UCLA Press.

Emery, K.F. and E.K. Thornton (2012a). Tracking climate change in the ancient Maya world through zooarchaeological habitat analysis. In G. Iannone, ed. *The Great Maya Droughts in Cultural Context*, 301–25. Boulder: University Press of Colorado.

Emery, K.F. and E.K. Thornton (2012b). Using animal remains to reconstruct landscapes and climate of the ancient Maya world. In C. Lefèvre, ed. *Proceedings of the General Session of the 11th ICAZ Conference*. Paris, France: Archaeopress, Oxford England.

Emery, K.F. and E.K. Thornton (2008a). A regional perspective on biotic change during the Classic Maya occupation using zooarchaeological isotopic chemistry. *Quaternary International* 191: 131–43.

Emery, K.F. and E.K. Thornton (2008b). Zooarchaeological habitat analysis of Ancient Maya landscape changes. *Journal of Ethnobiology* 28(2): 154–79.

English, A.J. (1990). Salted meats from the wreck of the "William Salthouse": archaeological analysis of nineteenth century butchering patterns. *Australasian Society for Historical Archaeology* 8: 63–9.

English, A.J. (1991). This muttonous diet. Aspects of faunal analysis and site comparison in Australian historical archaeology. Honours thesis, the University of Sydney, Sydney, NSW.

Fenner, J.N., R.K. Jones, P.J. Piper, M. Llewellin, M. Gagan, B. Prasetyo and A. Calo (2018). Early goats in Bali, Indonesia: stable isotope analyses of diet and movement. *The Journal of Island and Coastal Archaeology* 13(4): 563–81.

Field, J. and J. Dodson (1999). Late Pleistocene megafauna and archaeology from Cuddie Springs, southeastern Australia. *Proceedings of the Prehistoric Society* 65: 275–301.

Field, J., M. Fillios and S. Wroe (2008). Chronological overlap between humans and megafauna in Sahul (Pleistocene Australia–New Guinea): a review of the evidence. *Earth-Science Reviews* 89: 97–115.

Field, J., S. Wroe, C.N. Trueman, J. Garvey and S. Wyatt-Spratt (2013). Looking for the archaeological signature in Australian megafaunal extinctions. *Quaternary International* 285: 76–88.

Field, J.H. (2006). Trampling through the Pleistocene: does taphonomy matter at Cuddie Springs? *Australian Archaeology* 63: 9–20.

Fillios, M., M.S. Crowther and M. Letnic (2012). The impact of the dingo on the thylacine in Holocene Australia. *World Archaeology* 44(1): 118–34.

Fillios, M., J. Field and B. Charles (2009). Investigating human and megafauna co-occurrence in Australian prehistory: mode and causality in fossil accumulations at Cuddie Springs. *Quaternary International*: 1–21.

Fillios, M.A. and P.S.C. Taçon (2016). Who let the dogs in? A review of the recent genetic evidence for the introduction of the dingo to Australia and implications for the movement of people. *Journal of Archaeological Science: Reports*: 7: 782–92.

Fillios, M.A. (2016). *The faunal remains from Cottage Green (Monteplier Estate), Hobart.* Report to Austral Archaeology Pty Ltd.

Fischer, J.B., L.H. Mcarthur and J.B. Petersen (1997). Continuity and change in the food habits of the seventeenth-century English colonists in Plymouth and Massachusetts Bay. *Ecology of Food and Nutrition* 36: 65–93.

Fisher, A. and R. Thomas (2012). Isotopic and zooarchaeological investigation of later medieval and post-medieval cattle husbandry at Dudley Castle, West Midlands. *The Journal of Human Palaeoecology* 17(2): 151–67.

Flexner, J.L. (2014). Historical archaeology, contact and colonialism in Oceania. *Journal of Archaeological Research* 22: 43–87.

Flexner, J.L. (2011). Foreign animals, Hawaiian practices: zooarchaeology in the leprosarium at Kalawao, Moloka'i Hawaii'. *Journal of Pacific Archaeology* 2: 82–92.

Fradkin, A. and T.L. Walter (2018). Foodways at a colonial military frontier outpost in northern New Spain: the faunal assemblage from Presidio San Sabá, 1757–1772. *Historical Archaeology* 52: 397–419.

Frantz, L.A.F., J. Haile, A.T. Lin and G. Larson (2020). Ancient pigs reveal a near-complete genomic turnover following their introduction to Europe. *Proceedings of the National Academy of Sciences of the U.S.A. (PNAS)* 116(35): 17231–8.

Freiwald, C. and T. Pugh (2018). The origins of early colonial cows at San Bernabé, Guatemala: strontium isotope values at an early Spanish Mission in the Petén Lakes Region of northern Guatemala. *Environmental Archaeology* 23: 80–96.

Frémondeau, D., T. Cucchi, F. Casabianca, J. Ughetto-Monfrin, M.P. Horard-Herbin and M. Balasse (2012). Seasonality of birth and diet of pigs from stable isotope analyses of tooth enamel (d18O, d13C): a modern reference data set from Corsica, France. *Journal of Archaeological Science* 39: 2023–35.

Garvey, J. (2011). Bennett's wallaby (*Macropus rufogriseus*) marrow quality vs quantity: evaluating human decision-making and seasonal occupation in late Pleistocene Tasmania. *Journal of Archaeological Science* 38: 763–83.

Garvey, J. (2007). Surviving an ice age: the zooarchaeological record from southwestern Tasmania. *PALAIOS* 22(6): 583–5.

Garvey, J.M. (2006). Preliminary zooarchaeological interpretations from Kutikina Cave, south-west Tasmania. *Australian Aboriginal Studies* 2006(1): 57–62.

Garvey, J., B. Cochrane, J. Field and C. Boney (2011). Modern emu (*Dromaius novaehollandiae*) butchery, economic utility and analogues for the Australian archaeological record. *Environmental Archaeology* 16(2): 97–112.

Garvey, J. and J. Field (2011). Recent studies in Australian palaeoecology and zooarchaeology: a volume in honour of the late Su Solomon. *Environmental Archaeology* 16(2): 79–81.

Garvey, J., G. Roberts and R. Cosgrove (2016). Economic utility and nutritional value of the Common wombat (*Vombatus ursinus*): evaluating Australian Aboriginal hunting and butchery patterns. *Journal of Archaeological Science: Reports* 7: 751–63.

Garvey, J. and J.R. Sandy (2009). The first record of palaeopathology from the zooarchaeological record of late Pleistocene, southwest Tasmania. *International Journal of Osteoarchaeology* 19: 742–48.

Gibbs, M. (2005). The archaeology of subsistence on the maritime frontier: faunal analysis of the Cheyne Beach whaling station 1845–1877. *Australasian Historical Archaeology* 23: 115–22.

Gillespie, R., B.W. Brook and A. Baynes (2006). Short overlap of humans and megafauna in Pleistocene Australia. *Alcheringa: An Australasian Journal of Palaeontology* (S1): 163–86.

Gojak, D. (2001). Convict archaeology in New South Wales: an overview of the investigation, analysis and conservation of convict heritage sites. *Australasian Historical Archaeology* 19: 73–83.

Greenfield, H.J. (1989). From pork to mutton: a zooarchaeological perspective on colonial New Amsterdam and early New York City. *Northeast Historical Archaeology* 18: 85–110.

Grellet-tinner, G., N.A. Spooner and T.H. Worthy (2016). Is the "Genyornis" egg of a mihirung or another extinct bird from the Australian dreamtime? *Quaternary Science Reviews* 133: 147–64.

Gron, K.J., J. Montgomery, P.O. Nielsen, G. Nowell, J. Peterkin, L. Sorensen and P. Rowely-Conwy (2016). Strontium isotope evidence of early Funnel Beaker Culture movement of cattle. *Journal of Archaeological Science: Reports* 6: 248–51.

Guiry, E. (2016). Tracing colonial animal trade and husbandry using stable isotope analyses. Doctoral thesis, University of British Colombia, Canada.

Guiry, E., P. Szpak and M.P. Richards (2017). Isotopic analyses reveal geographical and socioeconomic patterns in historical domestic animal trade between predominantly wheat-and maize-growing agricultural regions in eastern North America. *American Antiquity* 82(2): 341–52.

Guiry, E.J., B. Harpley, Z. Jones and C. Smith (2014). Integrating stable isotope and zooarchaeological analyses in historical archaeology: a case study from the urban nineteenth-century Commonwealth Block site, Melbourne, Australia. *International Journal of Historical Archaeology* 18: 415–40.

Guiry, E.J., B.M. Jones, S. deFrance, J.E. Bruseth, J. Durst and M.P. Richards (2018). Animal husbandry and colonial adaptive behaviour: isotopic insights from the La Belle Shipwreck fauna. *Historical Archaeology* 52(4): 684–99.

Guiry, E. J., S. Noël and E. Tourigny (2012a). Stable-isotope bone chemistry and human animal interactions in historical archaeology. *Northeast Historical Archaeology* 41(7): 126–43.

Guiry, E.J., S. Noël, E. Tourigny and V. Grimes (2012b). A stable isotope method for identifying transatlantic origin of pig (*Sus scrofa*) remains at French and English fishing stations in Newfoundland. *Journal of Archaeological Science* 39: 2012–22.

Guiry, E.J., M. Staniforth, O. Nehlich, V. Grimes, C. Smith, B. Harpley, S. Noel and M. Richards (2015). Tracing historical animal husbandry, meat trade, and food provisioning: a multi-isotopic approach to the analysis of shipwreck faunal remains from the *William Salthouse*, Port Phillip, Australia. *Journal of Archaeological Science: Reports* 1: 21–8.

Gulliford, A. (2021). *The woolly west: Colorado's hidden history of sheepscapes*. Texas: A&M University Press.

Gunn, M.C. (1980). Cultural Ecology: A brief overview. *Nebraska Anthropologist* 5: 19–27.

Hamilton, J. and R. Thomas (2012). Pannage, pulses and pigs: isotopic and zooarchaeological evidence for changing pig management practices in Later Medieval England. *Medieval Archaeology* 56: 234–59.

Hammond, C. and T. O'Connor (2013). Pig diet in medieval York: carbon and nitrogen stable isotopes. *Archaeological and Anthropological Sciences* 5: 123–7.

Hardesty, D.L. (2009). Historical archaeology and the environment: a North American perspective. In T. Majewski and D. Gaimster, eds. *International Handbook of Historical Archaeology*, 67–75. New York: Springer-Verlag.

Hart, N. (2018). Reverand Knopwood's Kangaroos. Unpublished Honours Thesis, University of New England, Armidale.

Hartman, G., G. Bar-Oz, R. Bouchnick and R. Reich (2013). The pilgrimage economy of Early Roman Jerusalem (1st century BCE–70 CE) reconstructed from the d15N and d13C values of goat and sheep remains. *Journal of Archaeological Science* 40: 4369–76.

Haruda, A.F. (2017). Separating sheep (*Ovis aries* L.) and goats (*Capra hircus* L.) using geometric morphometric methods: an investigation of Astragalus morphology from late and final Bronze Age Central Asian contexts. *International Journal of Osteoarchaeology* 27(4): 551–62.

Haruda, A.F., V. Varfolomeev, A. Goriachev, A. Yermolayeva and A.K. Outram (2019). A new zooarchaeological application for geometric morphometric methods: distinguishing *Ovis aries* morphotypes to address connectivity and mobility of prehistoric Central Asian pastoralists. *Journal of Archaeological Science* 107: 50–7.

Harvey, C.S. (2013). An overview of historical archaeology in Queensland, Australia. *International Journal of Historical Archaeology* 17(3): 428–44.

Hattori, E.M. and J.L. Kosta (1990). Packed pork and other foodstuffs from the California Gold Rush. In A.G. Pastronand E.M. Hatton, eds. *The Hoff Store site and Gold Rush merchandise from San Francisco, California*, 82–93. Pennsylvania: Society for Historical Archaeology, California.

Hocknull, S.A., R. Lewis, L.J. Arnold, T. Pietsch, R. Joannes-Boyau, G. Price et al. (2020). Extinction of eastern Sahul megafauna coincides with sustained environmental deterioration. *Nature Communications* 11: 1–14.

Hodgetts, L.M. (2006). Feast or famine? Seventeenth-century English colonial diet at Ferryland, Newfoundland. *Historical Archaeology* 40(4): 125–38.

Howell-Meurs, S. (2000). Nineteenth-century diet in Victoria: the faunal remains from Viewbank. *Australasian Historical Archaeology* 18: 39–46.

James-Lee, T. (2014). Subsistence activities at 19th-century shore whaling station sites in New Zealand and Australia: a zooarchaeological perspective. *Anthropozoologica* 49(1): 79–98.

Jamieson, R.W. (2008). The market for meat in colonial Cuenca: a seventeenth-century urban faunal assemblage from the southern highlands of Ecuador. *Historical Archaeology* 42(4): 21–37.

Janowitz, M.F. (1993). Indian corn and Dutch pots: seventeenth-century foodways in New Amsterdam/New York. *Historical Archaeology* 27(2): 6–24.

Jones, E.L., J. Dombrosky and C.S. Ainsworth (2018). New directions in southwestern zooarchaeology. *Journal of Southwestern Anthropology and History* 84: 46–50.

Jones, J. and K. Britton (2019). Multi-scale, integrated approaches to understanding the nature and impact of past environmental and climatic change in the archaeological record, and the role of isotope zooarchaeology. *Journal of Archaeological Science: Reports* 23: 968–72.

Kamjan, S., R.E. Gillis, C. Çakırlar and D.C.M. Raemaekers (2020). Specialized cattle farming in the Neolithic Rhine-Meuse Delta: results from zooarchaeological and stable isotope (δ18O, δ13C, δ15N) analyses. *PLOS ONE* 15 (10): e0240464.

Karskens, G. (2010). *The colony: a history of early Sydney.* Sydney: Allen & Unwin.

Karskens, G. (2003). Revisiting the worldview: the archaeology of convict households in Sydney's Rocks neighborhood. *Historical Archaeology* 37(1): 34–55.

Karskens, G. (1999). *Inside the Rocks: the archaeology of a neighbourhood.* Alexandria: Hale & Iremonger Pty Ltd.

Karskens, G. (1997). The dialogue of townscape: the Rocks and Sydney, 1788–1820. *Australian Historical Studies* 27: 88–112.

Kennedy, S.A., K.L. Chiou and P. VanValkenburgh (2019). Inside the Reducción: crafting colonial foodways at Carrizales and Mocupe Viejo, Zaña Valley, Peru (1570–1700). *International Journal of Historical Archaeology* 23: 980–1010.

Kennedy, S.A. and P. VanValkenburgh (2016). Zooarchaeology and changing food practices at Carrizales, Peru following the Spanish Invasion. *International Journal of Historical Archaeology* 20(1): 73–104.

Klippel, W. E. (2001). Sugar monoculture, bovid skeletal part frequencies, and stable carbon isotopes: interpreting enslaved African diet at Brimstone Hill, St Kitts, West Indies. *Journal of Archaeological Science* 28: 1191–8.

Kornmayer, R.I. (2018). Investigating socioeconomic status in historic Charleston through dietary analysis of *Sus scrofa*. Master of Arts thesis, North Carolina State University.

Koungoulos, L. (2020). Old dogs, new tricks: 3D geometric analysis of cranial morphology supports ancient population substructure in the Australian dingo. *Zoomorphology* 139: 263–75.

Lampard, S. (2006). Approaches to faunal analysis: a Port Adelaide comparative case study. *The Artefact 2006* 29: 22–33.

Landon, D.B. (2009). An update on zooarchaeology and historical archaeology: progress and prospects. In T. Majewski and D. Gaimster, eds. *International Handbook of Historical Archaeology*, 77–104. New York: Springer.

Landon, D.B. (2005). Zooarchaeology and historical archaeology: progress and prospects. *Journal of Archaeological Method and Theory* 12: 1–35.

Landon, D.B. (1997). Interpreting urban food supply and distribution systems from faunal assemblages: an example from colonial Massachusetts. *International Journal of Osteoarchaeology* 7: 51–64.

Landon, D.B. (1996). Feeding colonial Boston: a zooarchaeological study. *Historical Archaeology* 30: 1–153.

Langley, M.C. (2020). Re-analysis of the "engraved" Diprotodon tooth from Spring Creek, Victoria, Australia. *Archaeology in Oceania* 55: 33–41.

Langley, M.C., S. O'Connor and K. Aplin (2016). A >46,000-year-old kangaroo bone implement from Carpenter's Gap 1 (Kimberley, northwest Australia). *Quaternary Science Reviews* 154: 199–213.

Larson, G., U. Albarella, K. Dobney, P. Rowely-Conwy, J. Schibler, A. Tresset et al. (2007a). Ancient DNA, pig domestication, and the spread of the Neolithic into Europe. *Proceedings of the National Academy of Sciences of the U.S.A. (PNAS)* 104(39): 15276–15281.

Larson, G., T. Cucchi, M. Fujita, E. Matisoo-Smith, J. Robins, A. Anderson et al. (2007b). Phylogeny and ancient DNA of Sus provides insights into neolithic expansion in Island Southeast Asia and Oceania. *Proceedings of the National Academy of Sciences of the U.S.A. (PNAS)* 104(12): 4834–4839.

Larson, G., K. Dobney, U. Albarella, M. Fang, E. Matisoo-Smith, J. Robins et al. (2005). Worldwide phylogeography of wild boar reveals multiple centers of pig domestication. *Science* 307: 1618–1621.

Larson, G., R. Liu, X. Zhao, J. Yuan, D. Fuller, L. Barton et al. (2010). Patterns of East Asian pig domestication, migration, and turnover revealed by modern and ancient DNA. *Proceedings of the National Academy of Sciences of the U.S.A. (PNAS)* 107(17): 7686–7691.

Lawrence, S. (2010). Feeding workers: food and drink in early colonial Australia. In J. Symonds, ed. *Table Settings: the material culture and social context of dining, AD 1700–1900,* 144–53. Oxford: Oxbow Books.

Lawrence, S. (2001). Foodways on two colonial whaling stations: archaeological and historical evidence for diet in nineteenth-century Tasmania. *Journal of the Royal Australian Historical Society* 87: 209–28.

Lawrence, S. and D. Peter (2009). Natives and newcomers in the Antipodes: historical archaeology in Australia and New Zealand. In T. Majewski and D. Gaimster, eds. *International handbook of historical archaeology,* 629–46. New York: Springer.

Lawrence, S. and C. Tucker (2002). Sources of meat in colonial diets: faunal evidence from two nineteenth century Tasmanian whaling stations. *Environmental Archaeology* 7: 23–34.

Letnic, M., Fillios, M., Crowther, M.S. (2012). Could the direct killing by larger dingoes have caused the extinction of the thylacine from mainland Australia? *PLOS ONE.* 7(5): e34877.

Lightfoot, D.E. (2018). "God sends meat and the Devil sends cooks": meat usage and cuisine in eighteenth-century English colonial America. Doctoral thesis, College of William & Mary, Williamsburg, Virginia.

Lyman, R.L. (1994). *Vertebrate taphonomy.* Cambridge Manuals in Archaeology. Cambridge: Cambridge University Press.

Machugh, D.E., G. Larson and L. Orlando (2017). Taming the past: ancient DNA and the study of animal domestication. *Annual Review of Animal Bioscience* 5: 329–51.

Mackinnon, M. (2018). Zooarchaeology: reconstructing the natural and cultural worlds from archaeological faunal remains. In W. Scheidel, ed. *The science of Roman history,* 95–122. New Jersey: Princeton University Press.

Makarewicz, C.A. (2016). Toward an integrated isotope zooarchaeology. In G.M. Grupe and G.C. McGlynn, eds. *Isotopic landscapes in bioarchaeology,* 189–209. Berlin, Heidelberg: Springer.

Makarewicz, C.A. (2014). Winter pasturing practices and variable fodder provisioning detected in nitrogen (δ15N) and carbon (δ13C) isotopes in sheep dentinal collagen. *Journal of Archaeological Science* 41: 502–10.

Makarewicz, C. and N. Tuross (2012). Finding fodder and tracking transhumance: isotopic detection of goat domestication processes in the Near East. *Current Anthropology* 53(4): 495–505.

Martin, T.J. (1991). Modified animal remains, subsistence, and cultural interaction at French colonial sites in the Midwestern United States. In J.R. Purdue, W.E. Klippel and B.W. Styles, eds. *Beamers, Bob Whites, and blue points: tributes to the career of Paul W. Parmalee,* 409–19. Springfield: Illinois State Museum.

Martin, T.J. (1988). Animal remains from the Cahokia Wedge Site. In B.L. Gums, ed. *Archaeology at French Colonial Cahokia,* 221–34. Springfield: Illinois Historic Preservation Agency.

Martin, T.J. (1986). A faunal analysis of Fort Ouiatenon, an eighteenth-century trading post in the Wabash Valley of Indiana. Doctoral thesis, Michigan State University, MI.

Manne, T., J. Balme and M. Weisler (2016). News from the south: current perspectives in Australian zooarchaeology. *Journal of Archaeological Science: Reports* 7: 687–8.

Mate, G. and S. Ulm (2016). Another snapshot for the album: a decade of Australian Archaeology in Profile survey data. *Australian Archaeology* 82(2): 168–83.

Melville, E.G.K. (1994). *A plague of sheep: environmental consequences of the conquest of Mexico.* Cambridge: Cambridge University Press.

Michalk, D.L. (1980a). Sheep production in Australia. *Rangelands* 2(5): 189–91.

Michalk, D.L. (1980b). Production systems on Australian sheep ranches. *Rangelands* 2(1): 11–14.

Millard, A.R., N.G. Jimenez-Cano, O. Lebrasseur and Y. Sakai (2013). Isotopic investigation of animal husbandry in the Welsh and English periods at Dryslwyn Castle, Carmarthenshire, Wales. *International Journal of Osteoarchaeology* 23: 640–50.

Miller, H.M. (1988). An archaeological perspective on the evolution of diet in the colonial Chesapeake, 1620–1745. In L.G. Carr, P.D. Morgan and J.B. Russo, eds. *Colonial Chesapeake Society,* 176–99. Chapel Hill, NC: University of North Carolina Press.

Miller, H.M. (1984). Colonization and subsistence change on the 17th century Chesapeake Frontier. Doctoral thesis, Michigan State University, MI.

Milne, C. and P.J. Crabtree (2001). Prostitutes, a rabbi, and a carpenter – dinner at the Five Points in the 1830s. *Historical Archaeology* 35(3): 31–48.

Morgan, P.D. (1995). Slaves and livestock in eighteenth-century Jamaica: Vineyard Pen, 1750–1751. *The William and Mary Quarterly* 52(1): 47–76.

Mudar, K. (1978). The effects of socio-cultural variables on food preferences in early 19th century Detroit. *Conference on Historic Sites Archaeology Papers 1977* 12: 322–91.

Müldner, G., K. Britton and A. Ervynck (2014). Inferring animal husbandry strategies in coastal zones through stable isotope analysis: new evidence from the Flemish coastal plain (Belgium, 1st–15th century AD). *Journal of Archaeological Science* 41: 322–32.

Müldner, G. and M.P. Richards (2005). Fast or feast: reconstructing diet in later medieval England by stable isotope analysis. *Journal of Archaeological Science* 32: 39–48.

Murray, G. and J. Chesters (2012). Economic Wealth and Political Power in Australia, 1788–2010. *Labour History* 103: 1–16.

Nash, M. (2002). The *Sydney Cove* shipwreck project. *The International Journal of Nautical Archaeology* 31: 39–59.

Nelson, D.E., J. Heinemeier, J. Møhl and J. Arneborg (2012). Isotopic analyses of the domestic animals of Norse Greenland. *Journal of the North Atlantic* Special Volume 3: 77–92.

Newling, J. (2016). Phillips' table: food in the early Sydney settlement. *Sydney Journal* 5(1): 68–82.

Newman, E.T. (2010). Butchers and shamans: zooarchaeology at a central Mexican hacienda. *Historical Archaeology* 44(2): 35–50.

Okumura, M. and A.G.M. Araujo (2019). Archaeology, biology and burrowing: a critical examination of geometric morphometrics in archaeology. *Journal of Archaeological Science* 101: 149–58.

Opishinski, A.C. (2019). Eat this in remembrance: the zooarchaeology of secular and religious sites in 17th-century New Mexico. Master of Arts, University of Massachusetts, Boston.

Otto, J.S. (1984). *Cannon's Point Plantation, 1794–1860: living conditions and status patterns in the Old South.* Orlando, FL: Academic Press.

Ottoni, C., L. G. Fink, A. Evin, C. Geörg, B. De Cupere, W. Van Neer et al. (2012). Pig domestication and human-mediated dispersal in western Eurasia revealed through ancient DNA and geometric morphometrics. *Molecular Biology and Evolution* 30(4): 824–32.

Owen, J., K. Dobney, A. Evin, T. Cucchi, G. Larson and U.S. Vidarsdottir (2014). The zooarchaeological application of quantifying cranial shape differences in wild boar and domestic pigs (*Sus scrofa*) using 3D geometric morphometrics. *Journal of Archaeological Science* 43: 159–67.

Owen, T., M. Casey and N. Pitt (2017). The Old Sydney Burial Ground: an inference of early colonial diet in Sydney and Britain. *Australasian Historical Archaeology* 35: 34–42.

Pálsdóttir, A.H., A. Bläuer, E. Rannamäe, S. Boessenkool and J.H. Hallsson (2019). Not a limitless resource: ethics and guidelines for destructive sampling of archaeofaunal remains. *Royal Society Open Science* 6: 1–11.

Parés-Casanova, P.M. (2015). Geometric morphometrics to the study of skull sexual dimorphism in a local domestic goat breed. *Journal of Fisheries and Livestock Production* 3(3): 1–4.

Parés-Casanova, P.M. (2014). Does the application of geometric morphometric methods on skull allow a differentiation of domestic sheep breeds? *Journal of Zoological and Bioscience* 4: 27–31.

Parés-Casanova, P.M. (2013). Allometric shape variation in *Ovis aries* mandibles: a digital morphometric analysis. *Journal of Morphological Science* 30(4): 1–3.

Parés-Casanova, P.M. and J. Sabaté (2013). Shape, not only size, differentiate wild and domestic Ovis. *Indian Journal of Applied Research* 3(7): 633–6.

Pascoe, B. (2014). *Dark emu: black seeds: agriculture or accident?* Broome: Magabala Books.

Pate, F.D. (2017). Diet, mobility and subsistence-settlement systems in the late Holocene Lower Murray River Basin of South Australia: testing models of Aboriginal seasonal mobility and sedentism with isotopic and archaeological data. *Journal of the Anthropological Society of South Australia* 41: 123–71.

Pate, F.D. (1997). Bone chemistry and paleodiet: reconstructing prehistoric subsistence-settlement systems in Australia. *Journal of Anthropological Archaeology* 16(2): 103–20.

Pate, F.D. (1995). Palaeodietary inferences from bone collagen stable carbon isotopes at Roonka Flat, South Australia. *Australian Archaeology* 40: 57.

Pate, F.D. and T.J. Anson (2008). Stable nitrogen isotope values in arid-land kangaroos correlated with mean annual rainfall: potential as a palaeoclimatic indicator. *International Journal of Osteoarchaeology* 18: 317–26.

Pate, F.D. and T.J. Anson (2012). Stable isotopes and dietary composition in the mid-late 19th century anglican population, Adelaide, South Australia. *Journal of the Anthropological Society of South Australia* 35: 1–16.

Pate, F.D., T.J. Anson, A.H. Noble and M.J. Schoeninger (1998). Bone collagen stable carbon and nitrogen isotope variability in modern South Australian mammals: a baseline for palaeoecological inferences. *Quaternary Australasia* 16(1): 43–51.

Paterson, A. (2011). Considering colonialism and capitalism in Australian historical archaeology: two cases of culture contact from the pastoral domain. In S.K.W. Croucher and L. Weiss, eds. *The Archaeology of Capitalism in Colonial Contexts: Postcolonial Historical Archaeologies*, 243–67. London: Springer.

Pavão-Zuckerman, B. (2017). Missions, livestock, and economic transformations in the Pimería Alta. In J.G. Douglass and W.M. Graves, eds. *New Mexico and the Pimería Alta,* 289–309. Colorado: University Press of Colorado.

Pavão-Zuckerman, B. (2011). Rendering economics: Native American labor and secondary animal products in the eighteenth-century Pimería Alta. *American Antiquity* 76(1): 3–23.

Pavão-Zuckerman, B., D.T. Anderson and M. Reeves (2018). Dining with the Madisons: elite consumption at Montpelier. *Historical Archaeology* 52: 372–96.

Pavão-Zuckerman, B. and V.M. Lamotta (2007). Missionization and economic change in the Pimería Alta: the zooarchaeology of San Agustín de Tucson. *International Journal of Historical Archaeology* 11(3): 241–68.

Pavão-Zuckerman, B. and J. Martínez-Ramírez (2020). Zooarchaeology of Mission Nuestra Señora del Pilar y Santiago de Cocóspera. *International Journal of Historical Archaeology* 24: 456–82.

Peng, L., K. Brunson, Y. Jing and L. Zhipeng (2017). Zooarchaeological and genetic evidence for the origins of domestic cattle in ancient China. *Asian Perspectives* 56(1): 92–120.

Peres, T.M. (2017). Foodways Archaeology: a decade of research from the southeastern United States. *Journal of Archaeological Research* 25: 421–60.

Peres, T.M. (2008). Foodways, economic status, and the antebellum upland south in central Kentucky. *Historical Archaeology* 42(4): 88–104.

Pilaar Birch, S.E. (2013). Stable Isotopes in zooarchaeology: an introduction. *Archaeological and Anthropological Sciences* 5: 81–3.

Pilaar Birch, S.E., L. Atici and B.I. Erdoğu (2019a). Spread of domestic animals across Neolithic western Anatolia: new stable isotope evidence from Uğurlu Höyük, the island of Gökçeada, Turkey. *PLOS ONE*: 1–18.

Pilaar Birch, S.E., A. Scheu, M. Buckley and C. Çakirlar (2019b). Combined osteomorphological, isotopic, aDNA and ZooMS analyses of sheep and goat remains from Neolithic Ulucak, Turkey. *Archaeological and Anthropological Sciences* 11: 1669–81.

Piper, A. (1991). Butchery analysis in Australian historical archaeology. Master of Arts (Honours), University of New England, Armidale.

Pitt, J., P.K. Gillingham, M. Maltby, R. Stafford and J.R. Stewart (2019). Changing cultures, changing environments: a novel means of investigating the effects of introducing non-native species into past ecosystems. *Journal of Archaeological Science: Reports* 23: 1066–75.

Pölläth, N., R. Shafberg and J. Peters (2019). Astragular morphology: approaching the cultural trajectories of wild and domestic sheep applying geometric morphometrics. *Journal of Archaeological Science: Reports* 23: 810–21.

Price, G.J., G.E. Webb, J.-X. Zhao, Y-x Feng, A. Murray, B. Cooke, S. Hocknull and I. Sobbe (2011). Dating megafaunal extinction on the Pleistocene Darling Downs, eastern Australia: the promise and pitfalls of dating as a test of extinction hypotheses. *Quaternary Science Reviews* 30: 899–914.

Proebsting, E. (2016). Plowing prairies and raising stock: historical ecology and community life on the cotton frontier of southwest Arkansas. *Historical Archaeology* 50(1): 114–34.

Reitsema, L.J., T.E. Brown, C.S. Hadden, R.B. Cutts, M.E. Little and B.T. Ritchison (2015). Provisioning and urban economy: Isotopic perspectives on landscape use and animal sourcing on the Atlantic Coastal plain. *Southeastern Archaeology* 34(3): 237–54.

Reitsema, L.J., T. Kozłowski and D. Makowiecki (2013). Human-environment interactions in medieval Poland: a perspective from the analysis of faunal stable isotope ratios. *Journal of Archaeological Science* 40: 3636–46.

Reitz, E.J. (1994). The wells of Spanish Florida: using taphonomy to identify site history. *Journal of Ethnobiology* 14: 141–60.

Reitz, E.J. (1993). Evidence for animal use at the missions of Spanish Florida. In B.G. Mcewan, ed. *The Spanish Missions of La Florida,* 376–98. Gainesville, FL: University Press of Florida.

Reitz, E.J. (1992a). The Spanish colonial experience and domestic animals. *Historical Archaeology* 26(4): 84–91.

Reitz, E.J. (1992b). Vertebrate fauna from seventeenth-century St. Augustine. *Southeastern Archaeology* 11(2): 79–94.

Reitz, E.J. (1991). Animal use and culture change in Spanish Florida. In P. Crabtree and K. Ryan, eds. *Animal use and culture change,* 62–78. Philadelphia: University of Pennsylvania Museum.

Reitz, E.J. (1986). Urban/rural contrasts in vertebrate fauna from the southern Atlantic coast. *Historical Archaeology* 20(2): 47–58.

Reitz, E.J. (1979). Spanish and British subsistence strategies at St. Augustine, Florida, and Frederica, Georgia, between 1565 and 1733. Doctoral thesis, University of Florida, Gainesville, FL.

Reitz, E.J. and B.G. Mcewan (1995). Animals, environment, and the Spanish diet at Puerto Real. In K.A. Deagan, ed. *Puerto Real: the archaeology of a sixteenth-century Spanish town in Hispaniola,* 287–334. Gainesville, FL: University Press of Florida.

Reitz, E.J. and B. Ruff (1994). Morphometric data for cattle from North America and the Caribbean prior to the 1850s. *Journal of Archaeological Science* 21: 699–713.

Reitz, E.J. and C.M. Scarry (1985). *Reconstructing historic subsistence with an example from sixteenth century Spanish Florida.* New Jersey: Glassboro.

Reitz, E.J. and G.A. Waselkov (2015). Vertebrate use at early colonies on the southeastern coasts of eastern North America. *International Journal of Historical Archaeology* 19: 21–45.

Reitz, E.J. and M.A. Zierden (2014). Wildlife in urban Charleston, South Carolina, USA. *Anthropozoologica* 49(1): 33–46.

Reitz, E. and N. Honerkamp (1983). British colonial subsistence strategy on the southeastern coastal plain. *Historical Archaeology* 17: 4–26.

Reitz, E.J. and S.L. Cumbaa (1983). Diet and foodways of eighteenth century Spanish St. Augustine. In K.A. Deagan, ed. *Spanish St. Augustine: the archaeology of a colonial Creole community,* 147–81. New York: Academic.

Reynolds, C.R., B. Kendall, W.E. Whittaker and T.H. Charlton (2014). Nineteenth-century butchery and transport for a market economy: Plum Grove as a case study for commercial transactions in the Midwestern USA. *Anthropozoologica* 49(1): 47–61.

Roberts, G.L., J. Towers, M.K. Gagan, R. Cosgrove and C. Smith (2019). Isotopic variation within Tasmanian bare-nosed wombat tooth enamel: implications for archaeological and palaeocological research. *Palaeogeography, Palaeoclimatology, Palaeoecology* 523: 97–115.

Salvagno, L. and U. Albarella (2017). A morphometric system to distinguish sheep and goat postcranial bones. *PLOS ONE* 12: 1–37.

Sandweiss, D.H. and A.R. Kelley (2012). Archaeological contributions to climate change research: the archaeological record as a paleoclimatic and paleoenvironmental archive. *Annual Review of Anthropology* 41: 371–91.

Schmitt, D.N. and C.D. Zeier (1993). Not by bones alone: exploring household consumption and socioeconomic status in an isolated historic mining community. *Historical Archaeology* 27(4): 20–38.

Schulz, P.D. and S.M. Gust (1983). Faunal remains and social status in 19th century Sacramento. *Historical Archaeology* 17: 44–53.

Scott, E.M. (1996). Who ate what? Archaeological food remains and cultural diversity. In E. Reitz, L. Newsom and S. Scudder, eds. *Case studies in environmental archaeology,* 339–56. New York: Plenum Press.

Scott, E.M. (1991). "Such diet as befitted his station as clerk": the archaeology of subsistence and cultural diversity at Fort Michilimackinac, 1761–1781. Doctoral thesis, University of Minnesota, Minneapolis.

Scott, K.P., Plug, I. (2016). Osteomorphology and osteometry versus aDNA in taxonomic identification of fragmentary sheep and sheep/goat bones from archaeological deposits: Blydefontein Shelter, Karoo, South Africa. *Southern African Humanities* 28: 61–79.

Simons, A. and M. Maitri (2006). The food remains from Casselden Place, Melbourne, Australia. *International Journal of Historical Archaeology* 10(4): 357–73.

Skippington, J., T. Manne and P. Veth (2018). Macropods and measurables: a critical review of contemporary isotopic approaches to palaeo-environmental reconstructions in Australian zooarchaeology. *Journal of Archaeological Science: Reports* 17: 144–54.

Slim, F.G., C. Çakırlar and C.H. Roosevelt (2020). Pigs in sight: Late Bronze Age pig husbandries in the Aegean and Anatolia. *Journal of Field Archaeology* 45(5): 315–33.

Smith, S.M. (2014). Foodways in colonial western Pennsylvania: an analysis of faunal remains from Hanna's Town (36WM203). Master of Arts, Indiana University of Pennsylvania.

Sportman, S., C. Cipolla and D. Landon (2007). Zooarchaeological evidence for animal husbandry and foodways at Sylvester Manor. *Northeast Historical Archaeology* 36: 127–42.

Sportman, S.P. (2014). Beyond beef: dietary variability and foodways in the late 19th-century mining town of Hammondville, New York, USA. *Anthropozoologica* 49(1): 63–78.

Steele, T.E. (2015). The contributions of animal bones from archaeological sites: the past and future of zooarchaeology. *Journal of Archaeological Science* 56: 168–76.

Stein, G. 2005. *The archaeology of colonial encounters: comparative perspectives.* Albuquerque, NM: SAR Press.

Steward, J. (2006). The concept and method of cultural ecology. In N. Haenn and R. Wilk, eds. *The environment in anthropology: a reader in ecology, culture and sustainable living,* 5–9. New York and London: New York University Press.

Stewart-Abernathy, L.C. and B.L. Ruff (1989). A good man in Israel: zooarchaeology and assimilation in antebellum Washington, Arkansas. *Historical Archaeology* 23: 96–112.

Sugiyama, N., A.D. Somerville and M.J. Schoeninger (2015). Stable isotopes and zooarchaeology at Teotihuacan, Mexico reveal earliest evidence of wild carnivore management in Mesoamerica. *PLOS ONE* 10: 1–14.

Sunseri, J.U. (2017). Grazing to gravy: faunal remains and indications of Genízaro foodways on the Spanish colonial frontier of New Mexico. *International Journal of Historical Archaeology* 21(3): 577–97.

Sykes, N. (2012). A social perspective on the introduction of exotic animals: the case of the chicken. *World Archaeology* 44(1): 158–69.

Sykes, N., White, J., Hayes, T.E., Palmer, M. (2006). Tracking animals using strontium isotopes in teeth: the role of fallow deer (*Dama dama*) in Roman Britain. *Antiquity* 80: 948–59.

Tarcan, C. and J. Driver (2010). The adoption and use of domestic animals at Zuni. In D.C. Campana, P. Crabtree, S.D. DeFrance, J. Lev-Tov and A. Choyke, eds. *Anthropological Approaches to Zooarchaeology,* 159–67. Oxford: Oxbow Books.

Thomas, R. and B.T. Fothergill (2014). Foreword animals, and their bones, in the "modern" world: a multiscalar zooarchaeology. *Anthropozoologica* 49: 11–18.

Torres, C.F. (1997). Behind every bone, there is a great animal: analysis of faunal remains from the CSR site at Pyrmont. Honours thesis, the University of Sydney, Sydney, NSW.

Tourigny, E. (2009). What Ladies and Gentlemen ate for dinner: the analysis of faunal materials recovered from a seventeenth-century high-statue English household, Ferryland, Newfoundland. Masters thesis, Memorial University of Newfoundland, St. John's.

Tourigny, E.D. (2020). Maintaining traditions: food and identity among early immigrants to upper Canada. *Historical Archaeology* 54: 354–74.

Tourigny, E.D. (2017). Eating barrelled meat in upper Canada: cultural and archaeological implications. *International Journal of Historical Archaeology* 22: 843–64.

Tourigny, E.D. (2016). Upper Canada foodways: an analysis of faunal remains recovered from urban and rural domestic sites in Toronto (York), AD 1794–1900. Doctoral thesis, University of Leicester, Leicester.

Towers, J., A. Gledhill, J. Bond and J. Montgomery (2014). An investigation of cattle birth seasonality using δ13 C and δ18 O profiles within first molar enamel. *Archaeometry* 56: 208–36.

Towers, J., M. Jay, I. Mainland, O. Nehlich and J. Montgomery (2011). A calf for all seasons? The potential of stable isotope analysis to investigate prehistoric husbandry practices. *Journal of Archaeological Science* 38: 1858–68.

Trueman, C.N.G., J.H. Field, J. Dortch, B. Charles and S. Wroe (2005). Prolonged coexistence of humans and megafauna in Pleistocene Australia. *Proceedings of the National Academy of Sciences of the U.S.A. (PNAS)* 102(23): 8381–5.

Turney, C.S.M., T.F. Flannery, R.G. Roberts, C.S.M. Turney, T.F. Flannery, R.G. Roberts et al. (2008). Late-surviving megafauna in Tasmania, Australia, implicate human involvement in their extinction. *Proceedings of the National Academy of Sciences of the U.S.A. (PNAS)* 105(34): 12150–12153.

Ulm, S., G. Mate, C. Dalley and S. Nichols (2013). A working profile: the changing face of professional archaeology in Australia. *Australian Archaeology* 76: 34–43.

Van de Noort, R. (2011). Conceptualising climate change archaeology, *Antiquity* 85: 1039–48.

van Wijngaarden-Bakker, L.H. (1984). Faunal analysis and the historical record. In C. Grigson and J. Clutton-Brock, eds. *Animals and archaeology: husbandry in Europe.* Oxford: BAR International Series.

Voss, B.L. (2015). What's new? Rethinking ethnogenesis in the archaeology of colonialism. *American Antiquity* 80(4): 655–70.

Voss, B.L. (2012). Status and ceramics in Spanish colonial Archaeology. *Historical Archaeology* 46(2): 39–54.

Voss, B.L. (2008). Gender, race, and labor in the archaeology of the Spanish colonial Americas. *Current Anthropology* 49(5): 861–93.

Voss, B.L. (2005). From *Casta* to *Californio*: social identity and the archaeology of culture contact. *American Anthropologist* 107(3): 461–74.

Voss, B.L., J.R. Kennedy, J.S. Tan and L.W. Ng (2018). The archaeology of home: *Qiaoxiang* and nonstate actors in the archaeology of the Chinese diaspora. *American Antiquity* 83(3): 407–26.

Walczesky, K.A. (2013). An examination of dietary differences between French and British households of post-conquest Canada. Masters thesis, Illinois State University, Normal.

Wallman, D. (2018). Histories and trajectories of socio-ecological landscapes in the lesser Antilles: implications of colonial period zooarchaeological research. *Environmental Archaeology* 23: 13–22.

Welker, M., S. Billings, J. Burns and S. Mcclure (2018). Roads and military provisioning during the French and Indian War (1754–1763): the faunal remains of Fort Shirley, PA in Context. *Open Quaternary* 4: 1–15.

Winter, S. (2013). Historical archaeological research in Western Australia: a critical review and suggestions for future research. *Australasian Society for Historical Archaeology* 31: 49–59.

Wroe, S., J.H. Field, M. Archer, D. Grayson, G. Price, J. Louys et al. (2013). Climate change frames debate over the extinction of megafauna in Sahul (Pleistocene Australia-New Guinea). *Proceedings of the National Academy of Sciences of the U.S.A. (PNAS)* 110(22): 8777–81.

Yalcin, H., M.A. Kaya and A. Arslan (2010). Comparative geometrical morphometrics on the mandibles of Anatolian wild sheep (*Ovis gmelini anatolica*) and Akkaraman sheep (*Ovis aries*). *Kafkas Universitesi Veterinarer Fakultesi Dergisi* 16(1): 55–61.

Zangrando, A.F., A. Tessone, A. Ugan and M.A. Gutierrez (2014). Applications of stable isotope analysis in zooarchaeology: an introduction. *International Journal of Osteoarchaeology* 24: 127–33.

Zavodny, E., S.B. Mcclure, B.J. Culleton, E. Podrug and D.J. Kennett (2015). Identifying Neolithic animal management practices in the Adriatic using stable isotopes. *Documenta Praehistorica*: 261–74.

Zavodny, E., S.B. Mcclure, B.J. Culleton, E. Podrug and D.J. Kennett (2014). Neolithic animal management practices and stable isotope studies in the Adriatic. *Environmental Archaeology* 19(3): 184–95.

Zavodny, E., S.B. Mcclure, M.H. Welker, B.J. Culleton, J. Balen and D.J. Kennett (2019). Scaling up: stable isotope evidence for the intensification of animal husbandry in Bronze-Iron Age Lika, Croatia. *Journal of Archaeological Science: Reports* 23: 1055–65.

Zeder, M.A. (2012). The domestication of animals. *Journal of Anthropological Research* 68(2): 161–90.

Zeder, M.A. (2008). Domestication and early agriculture in the Mediterranean Basin: origins, diffusion, and impact. *Proceedings of the National Academy of Sciences of the U.S.A. (PNAS)* 105(33): 11597–604.

Zeder, M.A. (2006). A critical assessment of markers of initial domestication in goats (*Capra hircus*). In M.A. Zeder, D.G. Bradley, E. Emshwiller and B.D. Smith, eds. *Documenting Domestication: New Genetic and Archaeological Paradigms*, 181–208. Berkeley: University of California Press.

Zhang, H., J. L.A. Paijmans, F. Chang, X. Wu, G. Chen, C. Lei et al (2013). Morphological and genetic evidence for early Holocene cattle management in northeastern China. *Nature Communications* 4: 1–7.

Zhang, K., J.A. Lenstra, S. Zhang, W. Liu and J. Liu (2020). Evolution and domestication of the Bovini species. *International Foundation for Animal Genetics* 51: 637–57.

Zierden, M.A. and E.J. Reitz (2009). Animal use and the urban landscape in colonial Charleston, South Carolina, USA. *International Journal of Historical Archaeology* 13: 327–65.

"Suitable food for old and worn out persons …"[4]
Archaeological evidence of institutional foodways in Australia

Kimberley G. Connor

Introduction

The archaeology of institutions holds an outsized place in Australian historical archaeology. This is in part due to their continued physical presence in the cultural landscape, but also stems from a popular narrative which cites the origins of the Australian identity in convictism, in particular, and institutionalisation, more broadly (Casella and Fredericksen 2004). While only a small proportion of Australian migrants in the early colonial period experienced confinement in institutions, focusing on food highlights the impact that these places had on culture beyond their walls. For example, we see how forms of institutionalisation spread beyond the confines of prisons and barracks into whaling camps, ration depots and the domestic sphere. Surprisingly limited attention has been given to the specific roles of food both within Australian residential institutions and in Australian society more broadly by archaeologists to date. This is a significant oversight given the ways in which food has been used to control and manage populations historically, but also how significant it has been in the formation of identities and as a means of resistance. This chapter provides an overview of the emergent archaeology of institutional food in Australia, showing how institutional forms of consumption have shaped Australian foodways and colonial identities more widely. At the same

---

4 Frederic King quoted in Hughes 2004, 89.

time, this survey points to the need for improved methodologies and increasingly sophisticated analytical frameworks that are specifically adapted for historical archaeology in Australia.

What is institutional food?

Institutions are organisations dedicated to the care, confinement or mobilisation of a particular population, encompassing not just the physical facilities, but also the people and organisational structures that make up the institution. Importantly, they are characterised by the presence of two distinct non-familial groups between which there is an inherent power imbalance, with one supervising the other, for example teachers and schoolchildren, or staff and patients (Goffman 1961). Institutions also mark inhabitants spatially and temporally by association with a set location and time period. Since institutions occupy a spectrum from the totally voluntary (such as community associations) to fully coercive (such as prisons), the extent of this marking varies greatly (Winter 2015). In voluntary institutions, such as many religious institutions or community groups, the members are marked only briefly during the time they come together as a group. At the other end of the spectrum, Erving Goffman (1961) calls the most coercive institutions "total institutions" because of their all-encompassing nature. They are characterised by a lack of separation between places of sleep, play, and work. In institutions like prisons, inmates are marked by separation from the community for the length of their sentence.

Institutional food, then, is the food that is prepared and consumed within the context of an institution. By food I mean substances (including beverages) taken into the body orally to nourish the body, including those consumed for recreational purposes and sociability, such as alcohol and tobacco. Medicine is not examined in detail here, but it is acknowledged that some substances once considered medicinal would now be categorised as foods, and that nutrition continues to be an integral part of disease prevention and health care.

Food in disciplinary institutions serves a variety of functions, including fuelling labour and creating a social hierarchy, but it is used most broadly as a form of coercive control for punishment and/or reform (Brisman 2008; Farrish 2015; Godderis 2006; Johnston 1985). At the same time, institutional residents can use food and its associated material culture to subvert the rules, create and maintain identities, and exercise power over others (Dusselier 2002; Earle and Phillips 2012; Godderis 2006; Ugelvik 2011). Finally, the unofficial trading and selling of food can be used to solidify relationships between inmates and to create social obligations (Casella 2007, 80; Cate 2008). Archaeology adds to discussions about these functions because of its ability to see illicit and hidden behaviours that are rarely recorded in official records and which inhabitants may be unwilling to discuss with ethnographers (Casella 2009).

In this chapter I categorise institutional food in two ways: 1) rationing, which is the provision of fixed quantities of ingredients or the components of a meal, and 2) institutional dining, where prepared meals are served inside institutions like prisons, schools and hospitals. The details of these two types are explored below, but the distinction is important because it teases apart the logistical and affective differences between these modes of institutional provisioning, which are generally collapsed. Archaeologically, these two forms of institutional food leave different material traces and the type of institutional food system in use at a site should inform both method and interpretation.

Rationing refers here to the organised distribution of ingredients (or, occasionally, meal components such as bread) in set quantities to individuals or groups at given intervals of time. Rationing as a technique for managing populations is highly transferable, meaning that it can be applied to different groups. In the Australian colonial context, for example, rationing was used for sailors and the military, for convicts, First Nations communities and free settlers. The exact contents of the rations varied depending on age, gender, occupation and function (e.g. to reward or punish certain behaviours). For those doing the rationing, whether individuals, philanthropic groups or government entities, it provides a measure of surveillance and control over the diet of the population. Anthropologist Tim Rowse (1998) has shown, for example, how rationing systems used on Aboriginal families in central Australia served a variety of purposes including producing flexible labour forces, establishing European norms around food and enforcing the transition to waged labour.

Notwithstanding the fact that ration systems are highly coercive and associated with limited quantities of poor-quality food, counterintuitively, they also provide a certain measure of agency. Since uncooked ingredients are the foundation of rationing systems, ration users can choose how to prepare their meals, when they want to eat, who they want to eat with, how to spread the food over the time before the next distribution, whether to barter some of their supplies and how to supplement their rations.

By contrast, institutional dining is characterised by the provision of cooked meals and by a lack of choice about what, when and where to eat. In institutions like prisons and workhouses, food is produced on a large scale for the whole institution at once and meals occur on a strict schedule with everyone eating together, or in shifts. This is true even in more open institutions such as homeless shelters or school dining halls where the choice to attend requires acceptance of the given hours and menu. Other options to acquire food are typically limited, leading to illicit acquisition of food through trade, smuggling, theft and unsanctioned food production, although it is also common for food to be available to purchase (as in a commissary) to encourage participation in work or in return for good behaviour.

In practice, rationing and institutional food provisioning are two sides of the same coin, and institutions may alternate between the two systems or apply them to different groups. Prior to the New Poor Law in Britain, for example, workhouses often provided both indoor and outdoor relief simultaneously. Indoor relief, where individuals entered the workhouse for accommodation and meals, constituted a form of institutional dining, while outdoor relief included a rationing system with money and food distributed to people living in the community. While these two types of institutional food have notable differences, they are both ways of managing populations through regulation of individual bodies or what Michel Foucault (2003) calls "biopower" or power focused on human life at two levels – the individual body and the population as a whole. Food served in institutions functions to normalise certain behaviours through regulation, producing subjugated citizens who are more efficient and more obedient (Foucault 1995 [1975], 128–9, 138). In institutional settings, the emphasis on repetition and uniformity leads to standardisation of consumption patterns and individuals learn self-regulation, which encourages adherence to norms even after leaving the institution. Tim Rowse's (1998) analysis of rationing in Aboriginal communities in central Australia illustrates this duality (see also Farry 2021; Nettelbeck and Foster 2012). By bringing groups of First Nations peoples together at the mission or the ration depot, rationing facilitated surveillance and the construction of a body of administrative knowledge about the population as a whole, while simultaneously making available a flexible pool of labour (Rowse 1998, 5–8, 17, 86–8). At the level of the individual, rationing normalised consumption of European foodstuffs, their material corollaries (indoor dining, cutlery and crockery) and associated norms (of the nuclear family, for example) (Rowse 1998, 5–8).

Institutional food in Australia

Earliest rations

The first dietary scale (the written daily or weekly food allowance) in the Australian colonies was produced for the convicts on board the 11 ships of the First Fleet in 1788 and was developed from the British navy dietary. By the end of the eighteenth century, the British navy was responsible for keeping hundreds of ships provisioned. It used a dietary laid down in the late-seventeenth century which remained remarkably stable until the introduction of canned meat in 1847 (Macdonald 2014). Governor Philip, who led the British colonisation of New South Wales, was fully aware of the health consequences of long voyages on naval rations due to his experience as a naval captain and he made careful preparations for provisioning the fleet and insisted on sourcing fresh food in intermediate ports.

Upon their arrival, marines and convicts alike moved to a weekly shore ration of 7 lb bread or flour; 7 lb salt beef or 4 lb salt pork; 3 pt pease (dried peas, split peas or lentils); 6 oz butter, and 1 lb flour or 1/2 lb rice. Marines and male convicts received the full ration, while women received two-thirds of the male ration and children between one- and two-thirds (Government Printing Office 1892, 143, 184). The rations were supplemented with fresh fruit and vegetables, soft bread (instead of hard tack), and fresh meat when possible. The only official distinction in diet between the marines and the convicts was the addition of 1/2 pt spirits per day for the marines, which was not enough to avoid resentment since the marines expected to have better rations than the convicts (Gilling 2016; Newling 2021, 38–9).

Convict rations varied over time as food supplies were more or less abundant and as the convict system developed between 1788 and the 1860s (Steele 1997). Maize was substituted for wheat in the early years, while tea and sugar were added over time, especially for women (Cushing 2007; Steele 1997). Some of the items introduced in the early convict rations period, such as pumpkin, would become signatures of the Australian diet, while others like maize, tainted by the association with the convict rations, would almost completely disappear for the remainder of the nineteenth century (Cushing 2007; Santich 2012, 5–12).

In spite of these variations, the basic convict rationing system laid out the essential ingredients of the Australian institutional and indeed the wider diet for most of the nineteenth century: meat (salted beef or pork at first, later fresh mutton or beef), bread or flour, tea and sugar. Different versions of this system would be used on board ships for assisted immigrants, in post-convict institutional settings and in partial payment of wages by employers (Byrne 1848, 99; Haines 1997, 49; Malone 1854, 258).

Convicts

While convict life is marked by incarceration in the popular imagination, the lives of convicts varied depending on their legal status, assignment, location and the timing of their transportation. Many convicts lived freely in the community where they had substantial control over their lives and consumption practices, whereas those living on their employers' properties or in institutional settings had much less choice in what and how they ate.

Excavations in The Rocks neighbourhood on the western side of Sydney Cove, an area strongly associated with the convict and emancipist (ex-convict) community, gives us a fascinating insight into their food and foodways. A large excavation of parts of two city blocks – called the Cumberland/Gloucester Streets site – in 1994 provided insight into the lives and diets of early residents and, particularly, convict butcher George Cribb. Transported in 1808, Cribb was able to take advantage of opportunities for skilled convicts by working as a butcher almost as soon as he arrived. He received a conditional pardon in 1813 and amassed substantial property in The Rocks until the failure of his businesses around 1824 (Karskens 1994, 23–27, 2009). Cribb's business served a community which reflected his own household where convicts, probationers, ex-convicts, those born in the colony and free settlers lived side by side. Since the population of The Rocks was mobile and residents moved fluidly between legal statuses, it is generally not possible to assign the archaeological material to particular households, but it is possible to associate the material with the convict and ex-convict community more broadly. Looking at these assemblages gives us a broad understanding of the food and foodways of this community as a whole (e.g. Voss 2008).

Faunal assemblages at both convict institutions and convict homes are dominated by four species not native to Australia: sheep, goat, cow and pig.[5] During the earliest period of convict occupation of the Cumberland/Gloucester Streets site (1788 to c. 1810) most of the bones came from cows (55 per cent) and sheep (40 per cent), but by the end of the second phase when Cribb was active (c. 1810 to c. 1833), the proportion of beef and mutton decreased to 51 per cent and 35 per cent respectively as the total number of species represented increased (Table 5.1) (Godden Mackay, Steele and Johnson 1996). The predominance of beef and mutton is consistent with documentary evidence of the early Australian economy, but the proportions of different animals and changes in consumption over time remain poorly understood. Pig bones are particularly underrepresented compared to the historical documentation of convict rations. This could be the result of the provision of imported salt pork or the use of boneless products like bacon, which would explain the limited recovery of pig bones at sites like Cribb's butchery (on salt pork in archaeology see Simmons 2011).

The extent to which colonists consumed native Australian foods has been hotly debated by historians. Settlers starving in a land of plenty because they refused to eat local foods has become a trope, but more recent scholarship suggests that colonists consumed a variety of indigenous plants, seafood, shellfish, birds and mammals

---

5   Goat and sheep bones are difficult to differentiate so are often grouped together although sheep probably predominate.

(for rejection of ignorance of native foods see Beckett 1984; Davey, Macpherson and Clements 1945, 193; Jupp 2004, 176; McIntyre and Wisbey 2009; Newton 2014, 243–4; for use of native foods see Bannerman 2006, 2019; Newling 2021; O'Brien 2016; Santich 2011, 2012, 28–75). The archaeology at the Gloucester/ Cumberland Streets site provides interesting insight into this debate because it provides evidence for the collection of shellfish and fish, but not of birds and mammals. The almost complete absence of native mammals has been interpreted as evidence of cultural conservatism on the part of European settlers: "The lower orders were conservative in their taste, sticking rigidly to mutton and beef and a little pork. They seem to have had a deep distaste, even horror, of eating strange meats from other animals..." (Karskens 2003, 46). This raises the question of how much class played into the adoption or rejection of different native foods and whether, for example, convicts were particularly conservative in their tastes because of their social precarity or if this resulted from differential access to particular species and equipment for acquiring them.

Interesting evidence comes from one of the few faunal collections reported from a convict institution, the Port Arthur Prisoner Barracks in Tasmania (c. 1835 to 1877). Bones from medium-sized mammals including sheep (NISP = 166)[6] and pigs (NISP = 161) were most frequent, while cow bones were less abundant (NISP = 38). However, wallaby (NISP = 38), unidentified macropod (NISP = 26), wombat (NISP =1), leopard seal (NISP = 1), rabbit (NISP = 2), chicken (NISP = 7), duck (NISP = 2) and pheasant (NISP = 1) as well as more than 1,400 fish bones and nearly 1,000 shells including oysters, periwinkles, abalone, mussels, clams and sea-snails were found (D'Gluyas et al. 2015, Supplementary Table 1; Hamilton 2013, 41–2). D'Gluyas and colleagues (2015) point to the complexity of interpreting these remains where the presence of native species could be the result of illicit hunting by convicts, officially sanctioned supplementation of the diet when food supplies were unstable, or of recreational hunting by civilians and officers within the institution.

Plant remains provide another potential source of information for convict diets. At the Cumberland/Gloucester Streets site, identified species included apricot, cherry, coconut, fig, grape, hazelnut, lemon, melon, passionfruit, peach, pea, plum, pumpkin, raspberry/blackberry and perhaps apple, brassicas, mustard and prickly pear (Godden Mackay, Lawrie, et al. 1996; Godden Mackay, Steele, et al. 1996, 14). However, the lack of a formal botanical report or clear provenance of the plant remains complicates their interpretation. Pollen from imported fruit and nut trees as well as vegetables, cereals and herbs is found in samples from nearby Parramatta,

---

6   number of identified specimens (NISP).

Table 5.1 Species present in Phase 1 (1788–1810) and Phase 2 (1810–1833) of convict occupation of the Cumberland/Gloucester Streets site. Data from Godden Mackay, Steele and Johnson 1996.

	1788–1810	1810–1833
Mammals	cow	cow
	sheep	sheep
	pig	pig
	goat	goat
	cat	cat
	dog	dog
		horse
		rabbit
		rodent
Bird	chicken	chicken
		turkey
		unidentified (at least 2 types)
Fish	non-diagnostic	unidentified (at least 3 types)
		snapper (*Pagrus auratus*)
		bream (*Acanthopagrus australis*)
		flathead (*Platycephalidae*)
		shark (*Elasmobranch*)
Shellfish	rock oyster (*Saccostrea cuccullata*)	rock oyster (*Saccostrea cuccullata*)
	mud oyster (*Ostrea angasi*)	mud oyster (*Ostrea angasi*)
	hairy mussel (*Trichomya hirsuta*)	hairy mussel (*Trichomya hirsuta*)
	Hercules club whelk (*Pyrazus ebeninus*)	Hercules club whelk (*Pyrazus ebeninus*)
	sea snail (*Cacozeliana granarium*)	sea snail (*Cacozeliana granarium*)
	auger shell (*Terebridae*)	ribbed periwinkle (*Austrocochlea constricta*)
	cowry shell (*Cypraeidae*)	black nerite (*Nerita atramentosa*)
	sand plough (*Conuber conicum*)	striped-mouth conniwink (*Bembicium nanum*)

	1788–1810	1810–1833
Shellfish	abalone (*Haliotidae*)	gold-mouthed conniwink (*Bembicium auratum*)
		limpet (*Scutellastra peronii*)
		Comtesse's top shell (*Calthalotia fragum*)
		fig cone (*Conus figulinus*)
		snakehead cowry (*Monetaria caputserpentis*)
		friend's cowry (*Zoila friendii*)
		thick-edged cowry (*Erronea caurica*)
		Spengler's trumpet (*Cabestana spengleri*)
		dog cockle (*Glycymeris striatularis*)
		pearly nautilus (*Nautilus pompilius*)
		marlinspike auger (*Oxymeris maculata*)
		mud creeper (*Batillaria australis*)
		helmet snails (*Cassidae*)
		cone shells (*Conidae*)
		cowry shell (*Cypraeidae*)
		olive shell (*Olividae*)
		limpet (*Patellidae*)
		scallop (*Pectinidae*)
		auger shell (*Terebridae*)
		turban snail (*Turbinidae*)
		conch (*Strombidae*)

painting a picture of the remarkably varied range of foods available in early Sydney (Macphail 2004; Macphail and Casey 2008).

Analysis of ceramics, glass and metal also provides insights into food production and dining practices. In penal institutions like Hyde Park Barracks (Sydney, NSW) and the Ross Female Factory (Tasmania), ceramic pipes and alcohol bottles found in underfloor occupation deposits speak to illicit consumption by convicts and to a trade in prohibited goods, while the discovery of an illegal still stashed in George Cribb's well shows that such behaviours were also present among convicts living in the community (Casella 2010; Karskens 2003, 44; Starr 2015). The use of drug foods and intoxicants to alleviate the challenges of convict life are not a surprise, but the presence of decorative, high-quality imported ceramics, Chinese porcelain and glassware may be. Evidence from The Rocks and other residential sites suggests that the convicts and emancipists who had the choice were enmeshed in global consumer markets and chose increasingly ornate tableware (Karskens 2003; see also Brooks and Connah 2007).

Work camps

From the earliest period of colonisation, the organisation of labour gangs in a remote and frequently harsh environment was critical, initially for convicts and later for free migrants working in agriculture, infrastructure and resource extraction. Sustaining these remote workers was not without its challenges. Anthropologist Richard Wilk (2004) argues that labour gangs were provisioned by an early globalised food system adapted from semi-industrial rationing systems previously used to feed European navies and militaries. The components of these diets will be familiar from the convict system described above: bread or hard tack, salted meat or fish, and stimulants including alcohol, coffee, tobacco and sugar. Demand for these products not only reshaped environments globally and facilitated technological developments in food preservation (such as canning and refrigerated shipping) but also produced new food cultures.

Archaeology provides evidence of the experiences of those labouring in work camps, which are often poorly recorded historically. In Australia, there has been extensive survey and excavation of camps for a variety of industries including sealing, whaling, fish-curing, pearling, agriculture, logging, mining and manufacturing (Lawrence and Davies 2011). The evidence suggests that the diet at these sites was dominated by bread or flour, meat from domesticated animals, sugar and tea. This was supplemented with purchased condiments, alcohol and tobacco, as well as opportunistic hunting and gathering of native resources such as fish, shellfish, birds and mammals as diverse as emus and quokkas (Davies 2002; Gibbs 2005; Lawrence and Tucker 2002).

As with many of the other forms of institutional food discussed in this chapter, scholars understand the broad components of diets at these sites but have paid less attention to how food in these institutions shaped people's identities and relationships. On the one hand, the historical tendency to focus on rural, masculine sites of pastoralism, mineral extraction and industry has excluded both women and Aboriginal and Torres Strait Islander peoples from histories of colonial Australia

(Ireland 2003, 62). Even within the stereotypically male work camp, women were often present. Focusing on women's food-related work presents the opportunity to recognise their contribution more fully. This challenges the central place of masculine mateship in the Australian story, enhancing the visibility of women and their contribution to these industries and the economy (Lawrence 2010).

On the other hand, to what extent did male-only work camps produce new food cultures? Frontier communities were based on homosocial bonding promoted by men working, drinking and gambling together in an environment often marked by deprivation and violence (Perry 2001, 21; on masculine food cultures see Conlin 1979; Earle and Phillips 2012; Vester 2015; Wilk and Hintlian 2005). In a North American context, Wilk and Hintlian (2005) have conjectured that this environment produced a pattern in which quantity was more important than quality, with a staple diet of plainly cooked preserved foods punctuated by occasional bingeing. It is interesting to consider what specifically Australian forms of bush masculinity can be inferred from the presence of delicate teawares, fashionable transfer-printed ceramics or the stem of a glass cake plate in a miner's tent (Cheney 1992, 40; Lawrence 2010).

The construction, maintenance and negotiation of ethnic and racial identities through food is another potentially significant theme for the study of institutional food in ethnically segregated camps and settlements. Archaeologically, sites associated with Chinese labour have attracted the most attention (see Chapter 6), but studies of foodways relating to Afghan cameleers, South Sea Islander sugarcane workers, Cornish miners, Indian hawkers, and Italian, Polish, German and Irish settlers may be equally fruitful.

Chinese migrants to the Australian colonies played a large role in the development of the mining, fishing and agricultural sectors, and a number of camps are specifically associated with Chinese labourers (Bowen 2008; Mitchell 1999; Rains 2003; Smith 2003). Interpretations of Chinese foodways have moved away from cultural conservatism to emphasise cultural fluidity and individual agency, with sites showing both efforts to import traditional Chinese ingredients, utensils and tablewares, and simultaneous integration of European products (Lawrence and Davies 2011, 234–6; Rains 2003). The benefits of such analysis are borne out in studies of worksites overseas which demonstrate the complexity of assigning artefacts to a single ethnic origin (Ross 2012; for an Australian example see Harrison 2002). Attending to the complicated meanings of such "transnational artifacts" (items with fluid identities and global origins) also raises the question of how artefacts can link different types of institutional sites and forms of institutional food provisioning. How, for example, did the structures set up to provision Chinese labourers affect Australian cuisine more broadly? The presence of longan, loquat and lychee fruits at sites in Sydney, including within the institutions of Hyde Park Barracks, points to the importation of fruit trees and/or fruit for the Chinese market spreading to consumers who were probably not of Chinese heritage (Connor 2023; Fairbairn 2007; Lydon 1993; Porter 2019). Gordon Grimwade's chapter in this volume (Chapter 6) highlights the role that roast pork played in mining communities throughout Australasia.

Institutions of First Nations incarceration

As a part of the colonial process, First Nations peoples in Australia were incarcerated and institutionalised from the early nineteenth century. Places such as missions and "Native Institutes" focused on control of the population, as well as racial and cultural assimilation. While much has been written of missions and institutionalisation of First Nations peoples, little attention has been played to the role of food in these places (for an exception see Morrison et al. 2010; for missions and institutionalisation see Andrew and Hibberd 2022; Burke et al. 2023; Casella and Fredericksen 2004; Dewar and Fredericksen 2003; Paterson 2006, 2011, 2017; Paterson and Veth 2020; Roberts et al. 2021; Winter et al. 2020; for food beyond those discussed below, see Harrison 2002; Smith 2000).

The most commonly excavated sites associated with institutional food for Aboriginal communities in Australia are missions (using the expansive definition offered by Graham 1998). The nature and chronology of the Australian mission system varied from colony to colony but was inherently both racist and carceral in nature. Its ostensible goals were to convert, protect and "civilise" First Nations peoples, both through "education" and control of reproduction and family networks (Middleton 2020). The success of the missions' program of cultural assimilation was measured by the extent to which inhabitants adopted British material culture and practices, including foodways (Lydon 2015). Archaeological evidence, often in conjunction with oral histories, shows both the long-term effects that these institutions had on Aboriginal lives and cultures, and the failures of colonial authorities to fully enact their goals.

The archaeological evidence for dining and food at mission sites is locally and temporally specific, but a striking feature to emerge from studies of many missions is the combination of Aboriginal and/or Torres Strait Islander food cultures with that of European food cultures. Continued traditions of hunting, gathering and consumption of bush foods, especially game and shellfish but also plants and wild honey, is evident from the Torres Strait to the Bass Strait (Ash, Manas and Bosun 2010; Birmingham and Wilson 2010; Dalley and Memmott 2010; Morrison, McNaughton and Shiner 2010; Ebenezer Mission in Victoria is a rare exception, see Lydon 2009). These foodstuffs complemented institutional diets which could incorporate both rationing and institutional dining. At Killalpaninna Mission, for example, rations were distributed to people living at campsites around the mission while Aboriginal women on the mission produced meals for the communal mess hall (Birmingham 2000).

One of the challenges for many missions was their remoteness and, as a result, their reliance on sometimes tenuous supply routes. How much bush foods contributed to the diet and the extent to which such supplementation was officially encouraged is often unclear. At the Weipa Mission (1892–1966) in the Western Cape York Peninsula, mission residents exchanged sea turtle, dugong, wallaby, kangaroo, emu, duck, fish, crab, shellfish, wild honey (sugarbag), fruits, nuts and tubers for credit at the mission store (Morrison et al. 2010, 2015). Evidence for the scale of this practice, especially the extent of sugarbag harvesting, led the archaeologists to conclude that not only did bush food contribute substantially to the mission diet but also that "Unlike language, marriage, religious practices, or other Indigenous social institutions, knowledge around food does not seem to have been targeted by the missionaries for reform" (Morrison et al. 2010, 107).

However, given that the archaeological, anthropological and historical literatures suggest that food was routinely targeted for reform within mission, an alternate reading might be that the meaning of food was contested within the institution (Birmingham 2000; Birmingham and Wilson 2010; Foster 2000; Lydon 2009, 2015; for American examples see Lindauer 2009; Surface-Evans 2016). Rowse (1998), in particular, has argued that a key feature of rationing systems for First Nations peoples was their openness to different interpretations by the missionaries and First Nations communities. Bush foods could be both "a site of resistance to assimilation" and provided ongoing connection to Country, culture and an opportunity for inter-generational knowledge and skill transmission (Morrison et al. 2010, 107). Conversely, for missionaries, trading bush foods for European commodities was part of the strategy of "mercantile evangelism" with bartering understood as an intermediate stage on the way to participation in the wage economy (Rowse 1998, 89; see also Fowler, Roberts and Rigney 2016; Griffin 2010, 163). In particular, missionaries might support First Nations women's food production, including gathering of bush foods, because it could facilitate men's participation in waged industries such as pearling and fishing by freeing up male labour (Ash et al. 2010).

Beyond the missions, two recent studies of the animal bones and charcoal from a late nineteenth-century pearl diving site on Barrow Island in Western Australia have revealed some of the dynamics of food provisioning in an Aboriginal work camp (Byrne et al. 2020; Dooley, Manne and Paterson 2021). Intriguingly, there is no evidence for domesticated animals in the faunal record, but instead, the archaeologists recovered evidence of bandicoot, possum, wallaby, wallaroo and sea turtle as well as various fish and birds (Dooley et al. 2021, 3). The authors interpret this as demonstrating insufficient provisioning of Aboriginal divers by the colonial pearlers as well as ration supplementation by the divers in order to provide themselves with sufficient food and to perform traditional forms of masculinity (Dooley et al. 2021, 568). Yet the over-representation of the lower limbs of macropods may also demonstrate how hunting practices were affected by the institutional setting (Dooley et al. 2021, 567).

There is significant potential to understand the ways in which rations were distributed, consumed and supplemented through archaeological study of food at other institutions associated with First Nations peoples, including reserves and stations, Native Mounted Police camps, and ration depots. Archaeological studies of the different locations associated with rationing including "the pastoral lease, the mission enclave, the police station, the welfare settlement," would contribute to a burgeoning historical literature on ration systems and their effects (Rowse 1998, 5; on rationing see Brock 2008; Farry 2021; Levi 2006; Nettelbeck and Foster 2012; Smith 2000). While the rationing that developed for Aboriginal peoples in Australia was an amplification of the use of state power against a population, it was not a new invention, but an adaptation of the existing rationing system. The system which reached its apogee in the ration depots of outback Australia had already shown its value for surveilling and managing convicts, marines and settlers. More research is required to understand the relationships between the two systems, but they clearly shared a number of functions including surveillance and integration into capitalist forms of production by giving food in return for labour (Farry 2021; Newling 2021).

Confinement and care

In the post-convict era, two major types of institutions dominated the Australian landscape: institutions of confinement, like prisons and reformatories, and institutions of care like lazarets, hospitals and asylums. While the aims of these institutions may seem remarkably different, in practice many institutions like industrial schools and quarantine stations combined the functions of care and confinement, and there was often significant overlap in the ways that they were organised, particularly with regards to food.

Recent research from the St John's girls' reformatory in South Australia points to the potential of artefact studies at these types of institutions. Decorated ceramics, primarily food-service dishes and teawares, evince a domestic rather than a uniformly institutional setting and highlight the ambiguous nature of care institutions, perhaps especially those for young women (De Leiuen 2015, 149; see also Connor 2023).

These sites – which were often designed to explicitly and/or implicitly train women in gendered roles and housekeeping skills – may lack the extreme uniformity popularly associated with punitive institutions like prisons. At the same time, the mismatched ceramics suggest an ad hoc approach to sourcing, reflecting that the idealised function of institutions was constrained by the practicalities of funding and a lack of choice in the goods that were available (De Leiuen 2015, this argument mirrors what De Cunzo [1995] argued for the Magdalen Asylum in Philadelphia). While many recent studies of the physical infrastructure of lunatic asylums, destitute asylums and reformatories have yielded interesting results (e.g. Kay 2015; Longhurst 2017; Piddock 2007), artefact-focused studies have not been as forthcoming, even though they are likely to be equally informative.

Institutions of immigration are another group with potentially important implications for institutional food, because they were liminal spaces where immigrants were introduced to the norms of Australian food cultures (Connor 2021, 2023). Several Australian states had networks of immigration depots in the nineteenth century to facilitate the movement of newly arrived immigrants into regional areas, to find them employment and to protect vulnerable populations on arrival. My research at the Female Immigration Depot (1848–1887) in Sydney demonstrates how a British style of cooking, eating and dining was normalised for working-class women arriving on subsidised passages. Analysis of food remains from other Australian depots, and of British emigration depots at the other end of the journey, would permit comparison of different immigration policies across Australia.

These sites also highlight how grey the line between food and medicine was in the period under review. At the North Head Quarantine Station (1832–1984), where immigrants could be quarantined on arrival in accommodation segregated by ticket class, a small collection of twentieth-century items reveals the multiple uses of alcohol in institutions: to produce a compliant population and staff, as a reward, but also to fight disease (Longhurst 2018). Tablewares from the same institution tell a similarly complex story. Longhurst argues that Wedgewood ceramics at the quarantine station have survived in part because they were understood as less likely to transmit disease, partly because of their material qualities and partly because they were associated with first- and second-class passengers arriving in the station (Longhurst 2018, 523–4). From the moment that they arrived in Australia, the food and dining arrangements for immigrants reflected and created distinctions based on class, race and health status.

Future directions

This chapter has covered the major forms of institutional food currently being studied by archaeologists in Australia, though they are rarely thought of as a single, cohesive whole. From the examples outlined here, it is clear that defining institutional food as a distinct field facilitates different types of questions and a distinctive approach to the themes that mobilise Australian historical archaeology. It pushes us to consider the relationship between institutional regimes aimed at different groups, for example, how rationing as a technology was transferred from the navy and military to convicts, settlers and First Nations peoples. Thinking about the spread of institutional technologies in this way provides an avenue for understanding the conundrum that Casella and Fredericksen (2004) pose: why is there such a strong belief in a history of shared confinement when a relatively small proportion of colonial Australians spent time in penal institutions? By focusing on food, we can see that elements of institutionalisation spread beyond the walls of individual sites. Developing a cohesive sub-field, however, requires archaeologists to apply methods from archaeological science more systematically, expand to new types of sites, and, most importantly, to develop comparative multi-material analyses. Doing so will not only allow us to better understand the functions and material correlates of institutional food historically and in the present, but it will enable us to explain how modern Australia came into being. In a nation defined by its institutional history, it is not enough to study just the impressive standing buildings, but it is essential to understand the lived experience of institutionalisation through the remains of daily life.

References

Andrew, B. and L. Hibberd (2022). The Blacktown Native Institution as a living, embodied being: decolonizing Australian First Nations zones of trauma through creativity. *Space and Culture* 25(2): 168–83. DOI: 10.1177/12063312211073048.

Ash, J., L. Manas and D. Bosun (2010). Lining the path: a seascape perspective of two Torres Strait missions, northeast Australia. *International Journal of Historical Archaeology* 14(1): 56–85. DOI: 10.1007/s10761-009-0095-9.

Bannerman, C. (2019). *The people's cuisine: origins of Australia's cookery*. Fremantle, WA: Vivid Publishing.

Bannerman, C. (2006). Indigenous food and cookery books: redefining Aboriginal cuisine. *Journal of Australian Studies* 30(87): 19–36. DOI: 10.1080/14443050609388048.

Beckett, R. (1984). *Convicted tastes: food in Australia.* Sydney: George Allen & Unwin.

Birmingham, J. (2000). Resistance, creolization or optimal foraging at Killalpaninna Mission, South Australia. In A. Clarke and R. Torrence, eds. *The archaeology of difference: negotiating cross-cultural engagements in Oceania*, 368–414. London: Routledge.

Birmingham, J. and A. Wilson (2010). Archaeologies of cultural interaction: Wybalenna Settlement and Killalpaninna Mission. *International Journal of Historical Archaeology* 14(1): 15–38. DOI: 10.1007/s10761-009-0092-z.

Bowen, A.M. (2008). *Archaeology of the Chinese fishing industry in colonial Victoria.* Sydney: Sydney University Press: Australasian Society for Historical Archaeology.

Brisman, A. (2008). Fair fare?: Food as contested terrain in U.S. prisons and jails. *Georgetown Journal on Poverty Law and Policy* XV(1): 49–93.

Brock, P. (2008). Two-way food: bush tucker and Whitefella's food. *Journal of Australian Studies* 32(1): 19–32. DOI: 10.1080/14443050801993792.

Brooks, A. and G. Connah (2007). A hierarchy of servitude: ceramics at Lake Innes Estate, New South Wales. *Antiquity* 81(311): 133–47. DOI: 10.1017/S0003598X00094898.

Burke, H., L.A. Wallis, N. Hadnutt, I. Davidson, G. Ellwood and L. Sullivan (2023). The difficult, divisive and disruptive heritage of the Queensland Native Mounted Police. *Memory Studies* 17(4): 904–22. DOI: 10.1177/17506980231170353.

Byrne, C., T. Dooley, T. Manne, A. Paterson and E. Dotte-Sarout (2020). Island survival: the anthracological and archaeofaunal evidence for colonial-era events on Barrow Island, north-west Australia. *Archaeology in Oceania* 55(1):15–32. DOI: 10.1002/arco.5202.

Byrne, J.C. (1848). *Emigrant's guide to New South Wales proper, Australia Felix, and South Australia [with a map.]* 8th edn. London: Effingham Wilson.

Casella, E.C. (2010). Landscapes of punishment and resistance: a female convict settlement in Tasmania, Australia. In R.W. Preucel and S.A. Mrozowski, eds. *Contemporary archaeology in theory: the new pragmatism*, 92–128. Chichester, UK: Wiley-Blackwell.

Casella, E.C. (2009). On the enigma of incarceration: philosophical approaches to confinement in the modern era. In A.M. Beisaw and J.G. Gibb, eds. *The archaeology of institutional life*, 17–32. Tuscaloosa, AL: The University of Alabama Press.

Casella, E.C. (2007). *The archaeology of institutional confinement.* Gainesville, FL: University Press of Florida.

Casella, E.C. and C. Fredericksen (2004). Legacy of the "fatal shore": the heritage and archaeology of confinement in post-colonial Australia. *Journal of Social Archaeology* 4(1): 99–125. DOI: 10.1177/1469605304039852.

Cate, S. (2008). "Breaking bread with a spread" in a San Francisco county jail. *Gastronomica: The Journal of Critical Food Studies* 8(3): 17–24. DOI: 10.1525/gfc.2008.8.3.17.

Cheney, S.L. (1992). Uncertain migrants: the history and archaeology of a Victorian goldfield community. *Australasian Historical Archaeology* 10: 36–42.

Conlin, J.R. (1979). Old boy, did you get enough of pie? A social history of food in logging camps. *Journal of Forest History* 23(4): 164–85.

Connor, K.G. (2023). From immigrant to settler: food and dining in a nineteenth-century institution of immigration. Doctoral thesis, Stanford University, Stanford, CA.

Connor, K.G. (2021). "To make the emigrant a better colonist": transforming women in the Female Immigration Depot, Hyde Park Barracks. *World Archaeology* 53(3): 451–68. DOI: 10.1080/00438243.2022.2037454.

Cushing, N. (2007). The mysterious disappearance of maize: food compulsion and food choice in colonial New South Wales. *Food, Culture and Society* 10(1): 109–31.

Dalley, C. and P. Memmott (2010). Domains and the intercultural: understanding Aboriginal and missionary engagement at the Mornington Island Mission, Gulf of Carpentaria, Australia from 1914 to 1942. *International Journal of Historical Archaeology* 14(1): 112–35. DOI: 10.1007/s10761-009-0097-7.

Davey, L., M. Macpherson and F.W. Clements (1945). The hungry years: 1788–1792: a chapter in the history of the Australian and his diet. *Historical Studies: Australia and New Zealand* 3(11): 187–208. DOI: 10.1080/10314614508594858.

Davies, P. (2002). "A little world apart ...": domestic consumption at a Victorian forest sawmill." *Australasian Historical Archaeology* 20: 58.

De Cunzo, L.A. (1995). Reform, respite, ritual: an archaeology of institutions; the Magdalen society of Philadelphia, 1800–1850. *Historical Archaeology* 20(3): i–168.

De Leiuen, C. (2015) "Corporal punishment and the grace of God": the archaeology of a nineteenth century girls' reformatory in South Australia." *Archaeology in Oceania* 50(3): 145–52. DOI: 10.1002/arco.5071.

Dewar, M. and C. Fredericksen (2003). Prison heritage, public history and archaeology at Fannie Bay Gaol, northern Australia. *International Journal of Heritage Studies* 9(1): 45–63. DOI: 10.1080/1352725022000056622.

D'Gluyas, C., M. Gibbs, C. Hamilton and D. Roe (2015). Everyday artefacts: subsistence and quality of life at the prisoner barracks, Port Arthur, Tasmania. *Archaeology in Oceania* 50(3): 130–37. DOI: 10.1002/arco.5072.

Dooley, T., T. Manne and A. Paterson (2021). Power in food on the maritime frontier: a zooarchaeology of enslaved pearl divers on Barrow Island, Western Australia. *International Journal of Historical Archaeology* 25(2): 544–76. DOI: 10.1007/s10761-020-00575-3.

Dusselier, J. (2002). Does food make place? Food protests in Japanese American concentration camps. *Food and Foodways* 10(3): 137–65. DOI: 10.1080/07409710213923.

Earle, R. and C. Phillips (2012). Digesting men? Ethnicity, gender and food: perspectives from a "prison ethnography". *Theoretical Criminology* 16(2): 141–56. DOI: 10.1177/1362480612441121.

Fairbairn, A. (2007). Seeds from the slums: archaeobotanical investigations at Mountain Street, Ultimo, Sydney, New South Wales. *Australian Archaeology* 64: 1–8.

Farrish, C. (2015). Theft, food labour, and culinary insurrection. In J.J. Wallach, ed. *Dethroning the deceitful pork chop: rethinking African American foodways from slavery to Obama*, 151–63. Fayetteville, AR: University of Arkansas Press.

Farry, S. (2021). Living (and dying) on dry bread: rationing and biopower in Jack Davis's *Kullark* and *No Sugar*. *Food, Culture and Society* 24(4): 579–99. DOI: 10.1080/15528014.2021.1884437.

Foster, R. (2000). Rations, co-existence, and the colonisation of Aboriginal labour in the South Australian pastoral industry, 1860–1911. *Aboriginal History Journal* 24: 1–27. DOI: 10.22459/AH.24.2011.01.

Foucault, M. (1995 [1975]). *Discipline and punish: the birth of the prison*. New York: Vintage Books.

Foucault, M. (2003). *Society must be defended: lectures at the Collège de France, 1975–76*. 1st ed. M. Bertani, A. Fontana and F. Ewald, eds. New York: Picador.

Fowler, M., A. Roberts and L.-I. Rigney (2016). The "very stillness of *things*": object biographies of sailcloth and fishing net from the Point Pearce Aboriginal Mission (Burgiyana) Colonial Archive, South Australia. *World Archaeology* 48(2): 210–25. DOI: 10.1080/00438243.2016.1195770.

Gibbs, M. (2005). The archaeology of subsistence on the maritime frontier: faunal analysis of the Cheyne Beach Whaling Station 1845–1877. *Australasian Historical Archaeology* 23: 115–22.

Gilling, T. (2016). *Grog: a bottled history of Australia's first 30 years*. Sydney: Hachette Australia.

Godden Mackay, R. Lawrie, C. Everett and M. MacPhail (1996). *Cumberland/ Gloucester Streets Site. Archaeological investigation 1994. Volume 4 Part 6. Specialist Reports. [Soil Analysis, Parasites and Plant Remains, Pollen Analysis]*. Report to the Sydney Cove Authority, New South Wales.

Godden Mackay, D. Steele and W. Johnson (1996). *Cumberland/Gloucester Streets Site. Archaeological investigation 1994. Volume 4 Part 5. Specialist Reports. [Bone and Shell, Coins, Tokens and Medals]*. Report to the Sydney Cove Authority, New South Wales.

Godderis, R. (2006). Dining in: the symbolic power of food in prison." *The Howard Journal of Criminal Justice* 45(3): 255–67. DOI: 10.1111/ j.1468-2311.2006.00420.x.

Goffman, E. (1961). *Asylums: essays on the social situation of mental patients and other inmates*. Garden City, NY: Anchor Books.

Government Printing Office (1892). *Historical Records of New South Wales*. Vol. 1. Pt. 2–Phillip. Sydney, NSW: Charles Potter, Government Printer.

Graham, E. (1998). Mission Archaeology. *Annual Review of Anthropology* 27: 25–62.

Griffin, D. (2010). Identifying domination and resistance through the spatial organization of Poonindie Mission, South Australia. *International Journal of Historical Archaeology* 14(1): 156–69. DOI: 10.1007/s10761-009-0099-5.

Haines, R. (1997). *Emigration and the Labouring Poor*. London: Palgrave Macmillan UK.

Hamilton, C. (2013). Consumption and convicts: faunal analysis from the Port Arthur Prisoner Barracks. Honours thesis, the University of Sydney, Sydney, NSW.

Harrison, R. (2002). Australia's Iron Age: Aboriginal post-contact metal artefacts from Old Lamboo Station, Southeast Kimberley, Western Australia. *Australasian Historical Archaeology* 20: 67–76.

Hughes, J.N. (2004). Hyde Park Asylum for Infirm and Destitute Women, 1862–1886: an historical study of government welfare for women in need of residential care in New South Wales. MA (Honours) thesis, University of Western Sydney, Sydney.

Ireland, T. (2003). "The absence of ghosts": landscape and identity in the archaeology of Australia's settler culture. *Historical Archaeology* 37(1): 56–72. DOI: 10.1007/ BF03376592.

Johnston, V.J. (1985). *Diet in workhouses and prisons 1835–1895*. New York: Garland Publishing.

Jupp, J. (2004). *The English in Australia*. Cambridge: Cambridge University Press.

Karskens, G. (2009). *Lifeway: George Cribb.* Sydney: The Big Dig Archaeology Education Centre.

Karskens, G. (2003). Revisiting the worldview: the archaeology of convict households in Sydney's Rocks neighborhood. *Historical Archaeology* 37(1): 34–55.

Karskens, G. (1994). *The Cumberland/Gloucester Streets Sites, The Rocks: an historical discourse.* Sydney, NSW: Prepared for Godden Mackay Logan and the Sydney Cove Authority.

Kay, E. (2015). Containment of "wayward" females: the buildings of Abbotsford Convent, Victoria. *Archaeology in Oceania* 50(3): 153–61. DOI: 10.1002/arco.5077.

Lawrence, S. (2010). At home in the bush: material culture and Australian nationalism. In S. Lawrence, ed. *Archaeologies of the British*, 211–23. London: Routledge.

Lawrence, S. and P. Davies (2011). *An archaeology of Australia since 1788.* New York: Springer-Verlag.

Lawrence, S. and C. Tucker (2002). Sources of meat in colonial diets: faunal evidence from two nineteenth century Tasmanian whaling stations. *Environmental Archaeology* 7(1): 23–34. DOI: 10.1179/env.2002.7.1.23.

Levi, T.J. (2006). Food, control, and resistance: rations and Indigenous Peoples in the American Great Plains and South Australia. Doctoral thesis, University of Nebraska, Lincoln, NE.

Lindauer, O. (2009). Individual struggles and institutional goals: small voices from the Phoenix Indian School Track Site. In A.M. Beisaw and J.G. Gibb, eds. *The archaeology of institutional life*, 86–104. Tuscaloosa, AL: The University of Alabama Press.

Longhurst, P. (2018). Contagious objects: artefacts of disease transmission and control at North Head Quarantine Station, Australia. *World Archaeology* 50(3): 512–29. DOI: 10.1080/00438243.2018.1494624.

Longhurst, P. (2017). Madness and the material environment: an archaeology of reform in and of the asylum. *International Journal of Historical Archaeology* 21(4): 848–66. DOI: 10.1007/s10761-017-0399-0.

Lydon, J. (1993). *Archaeological Investigation "Jobbins Building" 103–111 Gloucester Street, The Rocks, Sydney.* Report to the Sydney Cove Authority, New South Wales.

Lydon, J. (2015). Intimacy and distance: life on the Australian Aboriginal Mission. In N. Ferris, R. Harrison and M.V. Wilcox, eds. *Rethinking colonial pasts through archaeology*, 232–50. Oxford: Oxford University Press.

Lydon, J. (2009). Imagining the Moravian Mission: space and surveillance at the former Ebenezer Mission, Victoria, southeastern Australia. *Historical Archaeology* 43(3): 5–19. DOI: 10.1007/BF03376757.

Macdonald, J. (2014). *Feeding Nelson's navy: the true story of food at sea in the Georgian era.* London: Frontline Books.

Macphail, M. (2004). *Pollen Analysis of Soil Samples, Parramatta Children's Court Development Site, Corner of George and O'Connell Streets, Parramatta. Palynological Report prepared 17 November 2004 for Casey and Lowe Pty Ltd.* Report to NSW Department of Commerce.

Macphail, M. and M. Casey (2008). "News from the interior": what can we tell from plant microfossils preserved on historical archaeological sites in colonial Parramatta? *Australasian Historical Archaeology* 26: 45–69.

Malone, R.E. (1854). *Three years' cruise in the Australasian colonies.* London: Richard Bentley.

McIntyre, P. and C. Wisbey (2009). Sally Wise discovers colonial era food. *ABC Local*, 29 May.

Middleton, A. (2020). Missionization and mission archaeology in New Zealand and Australia. In C. Smith, ed. *Encyclopedia of global archaeology*, 7237–53. Cham, Switzerland: Springer International Publishing.

Mitchell, S. (1999). Dog's dinner? Archaeological evidence for meat consumption on Chinese historic sites in the Pine Creek Region. *Australian Archaeology* 48: 23–28.

Morrison, M., McNaughton and J. Shiner (2010). Mission-based Indigenous production at the Weipa Presbyterian Mission, Western Cape York Peninsula (1932–66). *International Journal of Historical Archaeology* 14(1): 86–111. DOI: 10.1007/s10761-009-0096-8.

Morrison, M., D. McNaughton and C. Keating (2015). "Their God is their Belly": Moravian Missionaries at the Weipa Mission (1898-1932), Cape York Peninsula." *Archaeology in Oceania* 50(2): 85–104. DOI:10.1002/arco.5061.

Nettelbeck, A. and R. Foster (2012). Food and governance on the frontiers of colonial Australia and Canada's north west territories. *Aboriginal History* 36: 21–41.

Newling, J.A. (2021). First Fleet fare: food and food security in the founding of colonial New South Wales, 1788-1790. PhD thesis, the University of Sydney, Sydney, NSW.

Newton, J. (2014). Terra Nullius, Culina Nullius: the contradictions of Australian food culture. Doctoral thesis, University of Technology, Sydney, NSW.

O'Brien, C. (2016). *The colonial kitchen: Australia 1788–1901.* Lanham, MD: Rowman & Littlefield.

Paterson, A.G. (2011). Considering colonialism and capitalism in Australian historical archaeology: two case studies of culture contact from the pastoral domain. In S.K. Croucher and L. Weiss, eds. *The archaeology of capitalism in colonial contexts: postcolonial historical archaeologies, contributions to global historical archaeology*, 243–67. New York, NY: Springer New York.

Paterson, A. (2017). Unearthing Barrow Island's past: the historical archaeology of colonial-era exploitation, northwest Australia. *International Journal of Historical Archaeology* 21(2): 346–68. DOI: 10.1007/s10761-017-0411-8.

Paterson, A. (2006). "Towards a historical archaeology of Western Australia's northwest. *Australasian Historical Archaeology* 24: 99–111.

Paterson, A. and P. Veth (2020). The point of pearling: colonial pearl fisheries and the historical translocation of Aboriginal and Asian workers in Australia's northwest. *Journal of Anthropological Archaeology* 57: 101143. DOI: 10.1016/j.jaa.2020.101143.

Perry, A. (2001). *On the edge of empire: gender, race, and the making of British Columbia, 1849–1871*. Toronto: University of Toronto Press.

Piddock, S. (2007). *A space of their own: the archaeology of nineteenth century Lunatic asylums in Britain, South Australia and Tasmania*. New York, NY: Springer New York.

Porter, J. (2019). *115b Victoria Parade, Fitzroy – H7822–2368. Volume 2: Historical Archaeological Artefact Report*. Report to Australian Catholic University, Abbotsford, Victoria.

Rains, K. (2003). Rice bowls and beer bottles: interpreting evidence of the overseas Chinese at a Cooktown dumpsite. *Australasian Historical Archaeology* 21: 30–41.

Roberts, A., H. Burke, M. Tutty, C. Westell and the River Murray and Mallee Aboriginal Corporation (RMMAC) (2021). From loop-holes to labour: Aboriginal connections to Calperum and Chowilla Pastoral Stations, South Australia. *Transactions of the Royal Society of South Australia* 145(2): 218–41. DOI: 10.1080/03721426.2021.1998298.

Ross, D.E. (2012). Transnational artifacts: grappling with fluid material origins and identities in archaeological interpretations of culture change" *Journal of Anthropological Archaeology* 31(1): 38–48. DOI: 10.1016/j.jaa.2011.10.001.

Rowse, T. (1998). *White flour, white power: from rations to citizenship in Central Australia*. Cambridge: Cambridge University Press.

Santich, B. (2012). *Bold palates: Australia's gastronomic heritage*. South Australia: Wakefield Press.

Santich, B. (2011). Nineteenth-century experimentation and the role of Indigenous foods in Australian food culture. *Australian Humanities Review* (51): 1.

Simmons, A. (2011). "Salty as sailors boots"; salt-cured meat, the blessing and bane of the soldier and the archaeologist. In H. Saberi, ed. *Cured, Smoked, and Fermented: Proceedings of the Oxford Symposium on Food and Cookery 2010*, 288–301. Totnes, UK: Prospect Books.

Smith, L. (2003). Identifying Chinese ethnicity through material culture: archaeological excavations at Kiandra, NSW. *Australasian Historical Archaeology* 21(2003): 18.

Smith, P.A. (2000). Station camps: legislation, labour relations and rations on pastoral leases in the Kimberley Region, Western Australia. *Aboriginal History* 24: 75–97.

Starr, F. (2015). An archaeology of improvisation: convict artefacts from Hyde Park Barracks, Sydney, 1819–1848. *Australasian Historical Archaeology* 33: 37–54.

Steele, D. (1997). *An Historical Assessment of Convict Diet in Sydney 1788–1840*. Report held by Hyde Park Barracks.

Surface-Evans, S.l. (2016). A landscape of assimilation and resistance: the Mount Pleasant Indian Industrial Boarding School. *International Journal of Historical Archaeology* 20(3): 574–88. DOI: 10.1007/s10761-016-0362-5.

Ugelvik, T. (2011). The hidden food mealtime resistance and identity work in a Norwegian prison." *Punishment and Society* 13(1): 47–63. DOI: 10.1177/1462474510385630.

Vester, K. (2015). *A taste of power: food and American identities*. Berkeley, CA: University of California Press.

Voss, B.L. (2008). Between the household and the world system: social collectivity and community agency in overseas Chinese archaeology. *Historical Archaeology* 42(3): 37–52. DOI: 10.1007/BF03377098.

Wilk, R. (2004). The extractive economy: an early phase of the globalization of diet. *Review (Fernand Braudel Center)* 27(4): 285–306.

Wilk, R. and P. Hintlian (2005). Cooking on their own: cuisines of manly men. *Food and Foodways* 13(1–2): 159–68. DOI: 10.1080/07409710590915418.

Winter, S. (2015). The archaeology of Australian institutions. *Archaeology in Oceania* 50(3): 121–22. DOI: 10.1002/arco.5076.

Winter, S., C. Forsey, E. Dotte-Sarout and A. Paterson (2020). The settlement at Barmup: Britain's first farm in Western Australia. *Australasian Historical Archaeology* 34: 32–43. DOI: 10.3316/informit.500740913818464.

6

Pigs, temples and feasts
Australian Chinese pig ovens

Gordon Grimwade

Introduction

In the 1970s, historical archaeologists began questioning the function of large cylindrical, stone structures on nineteenth-century Australian-Chinese mining camps. Their possible use as forges or ovens was canvassed widely. By piecing together the physical evidence, oral histories and documentary records, it gradually emerged that many were used to roast whole pigs for elaborate feasts and celebrations. Mouth-watering slices of roast pork and chunks of crispy crackling are popular among many societies and were no less so among the many Chinese who migrated to Australia in the 1800s.

In this chapter I examine the diversity of "pig ovens", a generic term that is, admittedly, challenged by the existence of some smaller structures which were more likely associated with cooking smaller joints of meat. It describes their form and distribution, considering their social importance and role in religious festivals among one of Australia's largest migrant groups and how contemporary use of similar ovens has enabled archaeologists to better understand their importance. First, however, attention focuses on the significance of the pig in Chinese history and culture.

Pigs have long played an important role in Chinese heritage not only for their nutritional values, but in relation to religious rituals, astrology and social events. The pig is considered to be a symbol of virility, is the last of the 12 Chinese zodiac signs and is included in the list of the "six domestic animals" – along with the

Figure 6.1 Wei Jin Dynasty (c. 221–317 AD) pictograph showing a pig being prepared for cooking. Photo: Gordon Grimwade 2012.

horse, ox, sheep, dog and chicken (Eberhard 1993, 236). As a further indication of the pig's importance in Chinese culture, there was a "God of the Pigsty" whose origins are lost in the mists of time, but whose role was to ensure a farmer's stock grew fat and healthy (Wang 2004,130).

As far back as the Chinese Neolithic period (10,000–2,000 BP) archaeological and historical records indicate that pigs were not only domesticated but also held important roles in the socio-cultural environment of that period. Pig skulls associated with Neolithic burials indicate a close association with this important domesticate (Seung 1994, 124). Pictographs from Wei Jin Dynasty (c. 221–317 AD) burial sites near Jiayuguan, Gansu Province, China, include one of a pig being prepared for cooking (Figure 6.1), offering archaeological evidence of the importance of pork in that period.

It is probable that the role of pigs in folk religion gradually evolved to manifest into a central role in ritual feasts. Chinese religion is a rich amalgam derived from Daoism, Buddhism and Confucian philosophy into which folk religion is inextricably interwoven (Grimwade 2024, 4). In the process, the practical attributes of pork as a nutritional source has been integrated into religious festivities.

Quite how humans discovered the delights of eating roast pork is lost to antiquity, and, although it is avoided by Muslims and Jews, no one can dispute its widespread popularity in regions as far apart as China, New Guinea and Europe. Nineteenth-century essayist Charles Lamb's fanciful *A Dissertation upon Roast Pig* jestingly suggests that accidental pyrotechnics led to the discovery of roast pork. This folkloric presentation suggests Bo-bo, a Chinese youth, burnt down the family home along with the pigsty and its occupants. Bo-bo was attracted by the aroma of roasted pork and sampled the meat, which hitherto had always been eaten raw. He was gorging himself when his irate father, Ho-ti, returned home but whose furore turned to pleasure when he too sampled the roasted flesh. Subsequent dwellings met with similar conflagrations each time the sow farrowed, resulting in father and son being brought before the court. Officials sampled the meat, agreed that "burnt meat" was indeed a new-found delicacy and discharged the duo. In time, it was decided that it was not essential to destroy the family home each time and, eventually, more acceptable cooking methods were adopted. Perhaps roasting meat was indeed an accidental discovery but there is no argument with the well validated claim that pork is one of the most popular foods in Chinese cuisine.

Chinese migrants flocked to Australia in the nineteenth century and, whilst most sought gold, others saw opportunities in commerce and horticulture. They brought many important aspects of their culture to Australia, and inevitably, this extended to their food and foodways. Rice was a staple commodity and was imported along with preserved spices, ginger, teas, soy sauce and pickled vegetables packaged in a diverse range of ceramic jars and crates, the remains of which are frequently encountered during archaeological excavations. Fresh vegetables, including spinach, cabbages, carrots and celery, were essential to maintaining good health and their production led to market gardening becoming a major source of employment. In many cases, pigs and chickens were also reared to provide both essential protein-rich food and manure for fertilising the crops.

Chinese culture and world views differed markedly from those of both Aboriginal peoples and European migrants which, inevitably, led to discrimination, vilification and the development of what we now refer to as "Chinatowns", segregated settlements in which Chinese people were the dominant occupants. English language newspapers frequently reported on Chinese festivities and celebrations in which roast pork featured. Those reports were often derogatory, but tinged with curiosity, as they highlighted events and customs that were alien to contemporaneous British Australian practices.

In parts of China, full-grown pigs were roasted in a preheated woodfired oven to produce wonderfully flavoursome meat and crunchy crackling. This was enjoyed by revellers at religious festivals and special events – highlighting the cultural significance of pork in feasting. Archaeological and historical evidence demonstrates that Chinese migrants took this technique with them when they migrated around the Pacific Rim during the nineteenth century. The ovens they built have, in some cases, remained near intact (Figure 6.2), subsequently puzzling late twentieth-century archaeologists who first contemplated their use. In order to better understand their purpose, researchers have been fortunate in being able to document and analyse contemporary cooking practices and to interview older Chinese people and their descendants who could recall how their forebears used the ovens.

Stone pig ovens once featured in the Australian landscape from north-east Tasmania, east to Perth and north to Pine Creek, Northern Territory, and across to Cape York, indicating a widespread association between pig roasting and Chinese colonial settlements. The human and physical resources needed to construct ovens capable of roasting an entire pig are as important as the knowledge of how and why they were used. In simplistic terms, stone ovens are just man-made structures, but when considered in association with their morphological diversity, tools, cooking processes and the allied rituals, they take on a much greater role within the Chinese diaspora.

Pigs in history

Charles Darwin (1868) classified pigs as either *Sus scrofa* or *Sus indicus.* More recent genetic research suggests that there are in fact upwards of sixteen subspecies (Ruvinsky and Rothschild 1998 quoted in Giuffra et al. 2000). Modern pigs are descended from the Eurasian wild boar *(Sus scrofa)* and have been domesticated for some 9,000 years; a practice that probably evolved in the Near East (Giuffra et al. 2000, 1785). The domestication process is closely related to the early evolution of humans from hunter and gatherer to horticultural and agricultural societies. While Chinese pigs developed their own characteristics, there is little evidence to suggest Chinese migrants experienced any significant challenges in adapting to locally-available domesticates when they arrived in Australia.

The crossbreeding of Asian and European pigs increased during and after the eighteenth century, no doubt associated with expanding trade and mobility. It is well established that pigs were carried on both merchant and some naval vessels, released in remote locations and allowed to colonise regions as feral animals (see, for example, Clarke and Dzieciolowski 1991). Their proliferation as breeding stock to sustain mariners has led to widespread detrimental environmental impacts (Department of Sustainability, Environment, Water, Population and Communities 2011, 1). Pigs were introduced to Australia with the arrival of the First Fleet; escapees from that and subsequent importations are blamed for their proliferation in the wild, while there are suggestions that feral pigs may have been introduced to Cape Yorke via Papua New Guinea (Baldwin 1986) and that domestic pigs were released when the Coburg Peninsula, Northern Territory settlement was abandoned in 1849 (Bengsen et al. 2017). Market gardeners often kept pigs and chickens not only for food but

Figure 6.2 The remains of a ramped oven in the Palmer Goldfield, Queensland. Photo: Gordon Grimwade 2007.

for fertilising their crops. There is no evidence to indicate the Chinese sourced feral animals for cooking given that domesticates were widely stocked.

Along with the spread of pigs, a fascinating divergence of cooking techniques has evolved among those who now regard pork as a staple food (Brown 2017). Modern Chinese pork dishes reflect diverse cooking styles. *Shih Tzu Tou* from the Shanghai region blends lean pork, water chestnuts and ginger, along with spinach. Belly pork, black beans, tomato and ginger are core ingredients for twice cooked pork, *Hui Kwo Juo,* in Szechuan, while barbecued spare ribs, *Kao P'ai Ku* with an enticing mix of sauces, is a popular Cantonese dish (Morris 1984). Ground ovens (*hangi* [Maori], *kup marri* [Torres Strait]) are common among Pacific nations. Meat, yam, sweet potato and other vegetables are wrapped in banana leaves or – nowadays – aluminium foil, placed in shallow pits lined with pre-heated rocks, covered with damp sacks and sealed with earth to retain the heat – producing a mouthwatering meal within a few hours. In western societies, the rotisserie, or spit roast, is a popular method of roasting a suckling pig while others resort to the time-honoured oven-roasted joint of pork.

Almost every part of the pig was used, highlighting its economic significance beyond just food. As Ka Bo Tsang (1996, 53) has noted, not only was pork a source of protein, but the fat could be "burned in lamps; pig bristles could be made into brushes; pig skin provided raw materials for shoes and garments and its manure could be used as fertilizer".

In colonial Australasia, pork was the most favoured protein source for Chinese communities (Ritchie 1986, 600; Adamson and Bader 2013). There are colourful accounts of Chinese feasts and religious festivals in which whole roast pigs loom large. Few, however, detail the method by which the pigs were actually cooked. Festivities at Peters, Barnard and Co, Launceston, Tasmania (importers and general storekeepers), included "a pig roasted, and placed upon the table whole in a large trough made specially for the purpose" (*Weekly Examiner* 1872, 10). A few months later, at Omeo in the Victorian highlands, a spring celebration included a banquet which was considered "*recherché* (exotic) in the extreme [where] there were pigs and fowls done to a turn, sufficient to appease the appetite of a fair score of famished bullock drivers" (*Ovens and Murray Advertiser* 1872, 1). Not to be outdone, festivities in "a building adjoining [the Ararat temple] some dozen more of pigs, several goats, and fowls by the score were undergoing the process of cooking at the hand of professed cooks, who evidently understood their business" (*Portland Guardian and Normanby General Advertiser* 1873, 4). Feasting reached the dizzy heights of gastronomic indulgence at Emmavale, NSW, in 1887 with "some twenty pigs roasted whole being placed on the floor before the god" (*Sydney Mail and New South Wales Advertiser* 1887, 959).

6 Pigs, temples and feasts

Some news reports are marginally more informative. The opening of the new temple at Breakfast Creek, Brisbane, Queensland, in January 1886 noted:

> Outside [the temple] a number of Chinese butchers were slaughtering and cooking pigs and fowls. There were about a dozen pigs slain, and the bodies were cooked in a large brick oven erected for the purpose in one corner of the ground (*Queenslander* 1886, 186).

Far to the north, in Cairns, the description of an 1896 feast at the Lit Sung Goong offers further clues about the cooking process:

> At the banquet itself fifty-six tables had been laid out, all of which were occupied by eight guests, making a total of 448. In addition to all this, some twenty Europeans, representing the leading men of Cairns, put in an appearance. In order to feed this multitude it was, of course, necessary to make great preparations, and we are informed that thirty cooks were employed in the holocaust of the young spring chicken and the succulent duck; while the great brick oven of the Joss House was laid under tribute in order to roast good sized pigs and other dainties on a wholesale scale (*Queenslander* 1896, 347).

Pig ovens were capable of processing large amounts of meat relatively quickly so were clearly associated with larger concentrations of population. Cuff (1992) reports swine weights in the United States during the nineteenth century with a 200 lb (90 kg) dressed weight pig being in the upper weight range. There is a subsequent loss of weight with further cutting resulting in a "take home" yield of around 59 kg (based on Hollis 2002). Assuming an average serve of pork per person of around 250 gm, there is thus enough for about 300 people per pig; however, average consumption figures can vary markedly, and such calculations must be considered only as broad indicators. It is interesting to note that it has been separately argued, by "Hum Lee (1960, 58), that 390 people was the critical mass for a viable Chinatown; below this, essential services, such as temples, could not be sustained" (Burke and Grimwade 2013, 124). Pig ovens are therefore likely to be associated with a population of similar size to that necessary to sustain a "Chinatown" settlement.

Feasts attracted large crowds, and it was common for several pigs to be roasted for large events. Social gatherings of this nature, particularly among migrant communities, were not only based on the desire to respect the ancestors but also to draw residents together as a unifying act. The role of the clan or extended family was important, and little expense was spared for many events. The proliferation of food was a source of pride among those who could afford it.

There is no archaeological evidence to indicate what might have happened to any uneaten pork produced for festivals and other celebrations. In the absence of refrigeration, salting or smoking offered the only realistic options for retaining leftovers. Popular modern sources certainly suggest meat preservation techniques were well established in Chinese culture:

> Pork is the most common base of preserved meat in China. The legs of the pig are reserved for the more expensive whole hams, and high-quality belly meat is used in making strips of *la rou*. Fatty and lean meat can be minced and made into sausages, and even the pig's head can be cured as a whole (Visit Beijing 2023).

Preservation of meat may well have been a practical outcome in areas of greater population, but in remote mining camps frugality and carefully considered outcomes from producing a large roast probably ranked highly.

Pig oven sites in Australia

During the late twentieth century, historians and historical archaeologists were beginning to look more closely at Australia's cultural diversity and Australian Chinese history in particular. In 1977, Owen Tomlin recorded two "ceremonial ovens'", one extant and one destroyed; on the Jordan Goldfield, Victoria (Tomlin 1979, 100). Historian Noreen Kirkman (1984, 193) recorded an oven at Byerstown on the Palmer Goldfield (Figure 6.3) in the same year; and, in 1982, Ian Jack and others noted an unusual but "substantial rectangular stone oven" near Lone Star Creek on the Palmer (Jack et al. 1984, 53). Howard Pearce's 1982 study of the Pine Creek, NT, area was the earliest to describe oven-like structures in that region, and soon after Helen Vivian (1985) noted similar structures in north-east Tasmania.

During the early 1990s, additional ovens were recorded across north-east Australia (Alfredson 1988; Bell 1983; Comber 1991; Grimwade 1988, 1990; McCarthy 1986, 1989; Van Kempen 1987) while Ian Jack noted three ovens in New South Wales (Bell 1995, 213). Interest in better understanding the purpose of these unusual structures was clearly increasing. Papers presented at the *Conference on the History of the Chinese in Australasia and the South Pacific* in Melbourne in October 1993 by Peter Bell, Justin McCarthy and Denise Gaughwin were the first to publicly discuss these reports and to contemplate their function (Bell 1995, Gaughwin 1995, McCarthy 1995).

Bell set about synthesising data that emerged from that conference regarding the existence, primarily on Australian Chinese mine sites, of 46 large domed stone ovens: 19 in the Northern Territory, 16 in Queensland, seven in Tasmania, three in

Figure 6.3 The remains of an oven at Byerstown on the Palmer Goldfield, Queensland. Photo: Noreen Kirkman 1979.

New South Wales and one in Victoria. He noted, "the oddest aspect of the oven's geographical distribution in Australia is not where they are, but where they are not" (Bell 1995, 223). What was surprising was that the areas where Chinese settlement had been the greatest – Victoria and New South Wales – were underrepresented in the initial inventory. The obvious question, "Why?" was postulated by Bell, who suggested that the use of ovens came after the south-east Australian gold rushes of the 1850s. By 1996, he wrote that ovens were confined to "relatively large numbers on the Palmer and Pine Creek Goldfields, a small cluster on the north-east Tasmanian tinfields, and hardly anywhere else in the country", further noting that "this is a reasonably complete and certainly representative sample of most of the ovens in Australia, and that the data is not a product of the research methods" (Bell 1996, 15). Since then, however, a wider distribution of oven sites has become apparent.

Several ovens have been identified with links to temples. A single photograph of an oven at Hou Wang Temple, Atherton, Queensland (Figure 6.4) emerged during unrelated research and in 1999, the author recorded another alongside the temple foundations in Croydon in Queensland's Gulf Country (Figure 6.5) (Grimwade 2003). Soon after, further Queensland ovens had been noted at Ravenswood, near Charters Towers, and there were reports of a long-abandoned oven at Darwin's temple site. Ovens at Thornborough, on the Hodgkinson Goldfield, Queensland and Woods Point, Jordan Goldfield, Victoria also have possible associations with

Figure 6.4 Two European visitors standing at the top of the ramp alongside the Atherton oven circa 1920. Photo: collection of Gordon Grimwade.

temples. A decade later Burke and Grimwade indicated ovens were once integral to other regional temples including Etheridge (Georgetown), Innisfail and Port Douglas (Burke and Grimwade 2013, 125). Evaluation of how many of the approximately 150 other former temple sites across the country may have had ovens attached is ongoing, with at least 15 being credibly identified as having ovens.

Bjornskov (2001, 121) discussed 10 oven sites in the Pine Creek, NT, area including several recorded previously by Bell and McCarthy, also claiming, incorrectly as further research has shown, that ovens are "only found in association with sites where Chinese undertook mining." Other ovens, particularly in south-east Australia, extending from a relatively small structure at Mitta Mitta in north-east Victoria to Cape York have been noted in ensuing years, to the point where there are now over 80 known nationwide, although information on several remains limited.

The late Professor R. Ian Jack (1935–2019) photographed a collapsed oven at Mookerawa, NSW, in the late twentieth century (possibly the Stuart Town oven recorded in Bell 1995, 227). Juanita Kwok and the late Barry McGowan (1945–2018) reported an oven on a former market garden in nearby Wellington (Juanita Kwok, email, 15 June 2017). A photograph of Chinese gardeners in Bathurst (n.d.), supplied to Kwok by Tony Bouffler, shows a rectangular brick oven in the

Figure 6.5 Croydon pig oven adjacent to temple site. Photo: Gordon Grimwade 2001.

background. These, along with two ovens at Windeyer (RNE Place No 468 and Bell 1995, 227), form a distinct geographical cluster.

Early in 2021, a large oven near Mt Misery, Victoria, was reported by Richard McNeil (Richard McNeil, email, 19 March 2021). In 2023, four more ovens were noted by the author near Uhrstown and two at Doughboy Creek on the Palmer Goldfield in north-east Queensland. Michael Williams noted references to another at Nerrigundah, NSW (Michael Williams, email, 18 Dec 2023), and Kwok (2023, 107) has noted 12 locations in New South Wales including Bell's original three. At Timbarra, Kwok notes that three ovens possibly existed (Kwok 2023, 104). It is clearly premature to state that all Australian ovens have now been identified.

Historical records, particularly early newspapers, provide invaluable evidence of pig ovens, again helping us to understand the scale of their spread and density. Looking across sources and evidence, the distribution remains skewed in favour of Queensland and the Northern Territory, with Tasmania having the third greatest number of ovens (Table 6.1 and Figure 6.6). These results are biased to some extent as they reflect the intensity of research rather than any cultural factors.

Table 6.1 Number of pig ovens identified by state and territory.

STATE / TERRITORY	Bell 1995	Current	Comments
New South Wales	3	12–14	Predominantly in Bathurst/Wellington area
Northern Territory	19	19	Pine Creek area
Queensland	16	31	Predominantly in North Queensland (Palmer, Atherton, Ravenswood and Gulf)
South Australia	0	0	
Tasmania	7	10	North-east Tasmania. Two known destroyed
Victoria	1	8	Widespread. Limited data on several
Western Australia	0	1	Perth
Total	46	81–83	

DISTRIBUTION OF PIG OVENS 2021

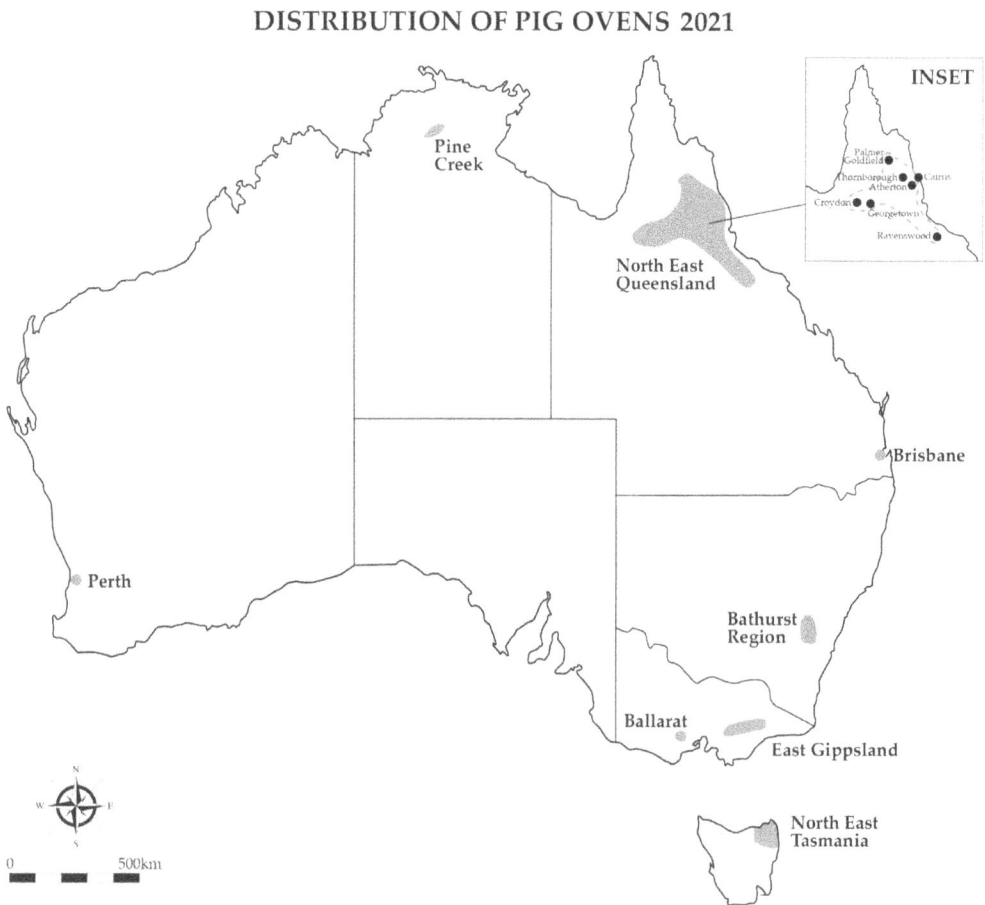

Figure 6.6 Map showing main areas of pig oven sites in Australia. Map: Gordon Grimwade.

Global context

In any discussion of the Australian experience of pig oven sites, it is also appropriate to consider the use of pig ovens overseas. In New Zealand, three oven sites are known in the South Island: Lawrence (Ng, personal communication, 2007), Ashburton (Grimwade, personal observation, 2007) (Figure 6.7) and Alma (2 ovens) (Bauchop, 2019). In the North Island, Bell noted the presence of ovens in Lower Hutt and Whangarei (Bell 1995, 225), although the latter appears to have been destroyed sometime before 2007 (Grimwade, personal observation, 2007). There is one operational oven at Riverhead, north of Auckland, and at least 12 in the Pukekohe area south of Auckland, some of which are still used infrequently (Ginny Sue, personal communication, 2019). The original Lawrence oven (post-1867) is believed to be the oldest but was destroyed during the twentieth century and since rebuilt. No clear construction dates are available for the other South Island ovens, but most appear to date from a resurgence in pig roasting in New Zealand during the 1950s–1970s (Bernie Lim, Ted Young and Ginny Sue personal communication, 2019). Notably, Neville Ritchie reported no ovens during his extensive study of the Clutha Valley, Otago (Ritchie 1986). With the possible exception of the original Lawrence oven, the known New Zealand ovens, therefore, postdate the gold rushes of the 1870s.

Examples of ovens have also been identified in North America. Wegars (1991, 55) concluded that many so-called "Chinese ovens" on the United States railway network were actually erected by Italians and Greeks for baking bread. Maniery (2001) and others have since, however, identified oven sites, particularly in California, that do have clearly identifiable Chinese origins.

It is critical of course to look beyond diaspora sites and consider pig ovens in countries of origin. In many historical archaeological research projects opportunities may also exist to examine contemporary practices and even to undertake experimental projects not only to validate assumptions but to also test feasibility – together these elements strengthen the validity of excavations, informant interviews and documentary research. During a research visit by the author to Guangdong, China, in 2006, enquiries were made about the use of pig ovens among several archaeologists, none of whom were aware of their use. Social media, however, has since indicated anecdotal and factual evidence about contemporary practice does, in fact, confirm historic and contemporary uses of pig ovens in China and Southeast Asia. For example, YouTube has intermittently, provided video examples of operational ovens in Vietnam, Hong Kong and in an unspecified Central Asian city. Similarly, in Islamic Central Asia, *tandir* style clay ovens are used to bake bread, cook *plov* and roast joints (other than pork) in a manner reminiscent of the larger Chinese pig ovens.

Figure 6.7 Pig oven with gantry and side steps, Ashburton, New Zealand. Photo: Gordon Grimwade 2007.

The possibility of technological adaptation and transfer is beyond the scope of this chapter, but worthy of further research.

Oven construction and typologies

Ovens were the product of communal activity for community benefit. Not only was there the need for skilled stonemasons to ensure physical integrity, but the acquisition of raw material would have required significant labour over several days. Physically, five oven variants have been defined in Australasia:

1. ramped access to the oven top (Atherton, Croydon, Qld)
2. a free-standing oven accessed by a gantry sometimes with steps up for access (Ashburton, NZ and possibly the Palmer Goldfield, Qld and Pine Creek, NT)
3. an oven built into a steep bank with ground level top opening (Thornborough and Uhrstown, Qld and Riverhead, NZ)
4. "mini-ovens", possibly used for roasting smaller joints of meat (Mitta Mitta, Vic)
5. rectangular ovens (Lone Star Creek, Palmer Goldfield, Qld, and Bathurst, NSW).

Structurally, pig ovens must meet the following key criteria:

1. built of stone capable of retaining heat for several hours
2. built of stone that will not crack or explode when heated
3. large enough to hold a substantial fire capable of heating the walls for the entire cooking time
4. fitted with a bottom vent to generate draft and from which ashes could be raked easily with minimal heat loss and which could be plugged during cooking
5. provided with a top access wide enough to feed in firewood and to lower in at least one pig
6. fitted with a heat-retaining lid for the top access vent.

Topography and geology played significant roles in determining the style of oven and its structure. For example, it would be a foolhardy group that would risk using stone that might explode and embed fragments in the roasting pig. Carefully selected local stone sources were thus important considerations. Sloping terrain, such as creek banks, was an obvious prerequisite for the ground level access ovens. Although early examples of ovens were built using available unworked rock, many later structures used kiln fired clay bricks. In some cases, like Thornborough, Queensland, brick was used in the lower internal courses and stone near the top (Figure 6.8). Access to refractory (fire) bricks was relatively difficult in nineteenth-century Australia. Their superior ability to retain heat made them favoured for later structures as is evident in the numerous mid-twentieth-century North Island New

Figure 6.8 Pig oven constructed on sloping terrain, Thornborough, far north Queensland. Photo: Gordon Grimwade 2013.

Zealand ovens (personal observation, 2019). This tendency was also favoured in California (Maniery 2001, 3).

The archaeological evidence of most Australian ovens indicates they were usually circular, built of unmodified locally sourced rock and, in northern regions at least, mortared with ant bed: pulverised termite mounds mixed with water. Elsewhere, clay soils were preferred which, when mixed as slurry and allowed to dry, formed a hard, almost impervious, bond – particularly after being subjected to intense heat. It is generally considered that the oven "cores" – the (almost) cylindrical stone structures that are all that now remain at many early oven sites – were probably covered with a generous outer coating of clay or concrete plaster to assist with heat retention. Over the years, this has eroded, leaving only the core (Wegars 1991, 37). This is consistent with the concrete mortar rendered Ashburton oven and the Vietnamese example noted previously.

The larger and most common Australasian ovens comprise a core burning chamber approximately 1.8 to 2.5 metres high (many are now significantly shorter due to deterioration). This is sufficient to enable a prepared carcass to be suspended from the top vent so that the snout is about 300 mm above the oven floor. In Perth, it was reported that "pigs are roasted, but in an oven ten feet [three metres] deep, and by way of variety, mutton occasionally meets with a similar fate"

(*Sunday Times* 1922, 17). Internally, the chambers are tubular, barrel-shaped or cone-shaped. A vent at the base – opposite the ramp or at right angles to the gantry steps depending on the construction style – enhances the draught and generates rapid combustion of the timber with which it is fuelled. Although there is currently no archaeological evidence to indicate the preferable species of fuel timber, personal experience suggests that small logs of eucalyptus species provide optimal heat in a relatively short period. Large logs burn too slowly to provide the desired rapid heat increase needed to achieve optimal cooking temperatures.

There is little evidence of metal grates being built into the ovens. Most are simple chambers into which fuel is dropped, ignited and burnt quickly to then retain the heat for as long as possible. Rules have their exceptions of course. The oven at Wellington, NSW, is the only known extant Australian oven where it has been established:

> 12 –15 inches (300–375 mm) up a round steel mesh laid between brick wall for holding fire logs up, sometimes unwanted steel pieces would also be (br)ought in, charcoal and ash from burnt log fall through (the) mesh, a camp oven would be put on the steel mesh after fire wood burnt down to catch the fat drippings (Sing Lee 2017).

The top vent opening is generally around 650 to 700 mm wide, which is sufficient to lower a pig carcass into the cooking chamber. Some have larger openings to accommodate two or more pigs at a time. As recently as 2019, the Red Season Aroma Restaurant, Hong Kong, could fit up to five pigs in one oven, with the cookhouse utilising several ovens at once. The ovens at both Lit Sung Goong, Cairns, and Holy Triad, Breakfast Creek, Brisbane, may also have been capable of cooking multiple pigs at once. The top vent, as noted earlier, remains fully open during the firing/heating period to maximise draft and to allow additional fuel to be added quickly. After the pig is lowered into position the top is covered to provide a rudimentary seal.

So-called "mini-ovens" have been recorded in several Australian locations; for example, at Mitta Mitta, Victoria, which, in 2004, was 550 mm high and 900 mm wide at the top vent and had a base diameter of 1200 mm (Kaufman and Swift 2004, 37). Bell (1995, 219) also notes the existence of several Queensland ovens around 800 mm high. Their function is less certain as they would only be capable of roasting joints of meat or small animals (rabbits, bandicoots or chickens) or to heat a large wok positioned over the top vent.

Figure 6.9 Spiked baton used to perforate skin before roasting as an aid in development of crackling. Photo: Gordon Grimwade 2019.

Ancillary tools

Beyond the ovens themselves, it is important to recognise that a suite of artefacts was used, and continues to be used, in pig roasting. Tools associated with the cooking process include sharp knives to "butterfly" the carcass and a preparation table. The practice of forcefully striking the carcass with a baton, through which nails have been driven, is common in New Zealand and effectively pierces the skin to maximise fat discharge during cooking and develop the much sought after crackling. Various YouTube video clips indicate this is also considered important by present day Hong Kong chefs. Ray Chong (New Zealand) strikes the carcass with the baton before lowering the pig into the oven while chefs at the Red Seasons Aroma Restaurant cook the pig for a quarter hour, remove it, pierce the carcass and then return it to the oven (Grimwade 2008).

Present day operators, like their forebears, use long handled ash rakes that can be pushed into the bottom vent to scoop out the wood ash and charcoal once the oven has reached the required temperature. These rakes comprise a rectangle of steel plate, slightly smaller than the bottom vent, secured to a long rod about two metres long, to allow the operator to reach ash on the far side of the oven floor. Ash dispersal patterns observed at Atherton Chinatown's original oven site suggest the practice has historical origins. Darwin resident Lily Ah Choy recounted in the early 1990s to historian Peter Bell, that "when the oven was very hot the coals were cleaned out" (Bell 1995, 220).

Before lowering the pig into the oven, a wok or camp oven, full of water, is lowered to the oven floor as a means to prevent dripping fat from catching fire and to generate moisture during cooking (Ray Chong, personal communication, 2007). Bell (1995, 22), however, notes in the historical context, "a tray was put in the bottom to catch the fat", clearly demonstrating that there were wide ranging personal preferences at work within broad societal norms. Again, personal preferences are evident and there is no reason to suspect variations of this kind were uncommon.

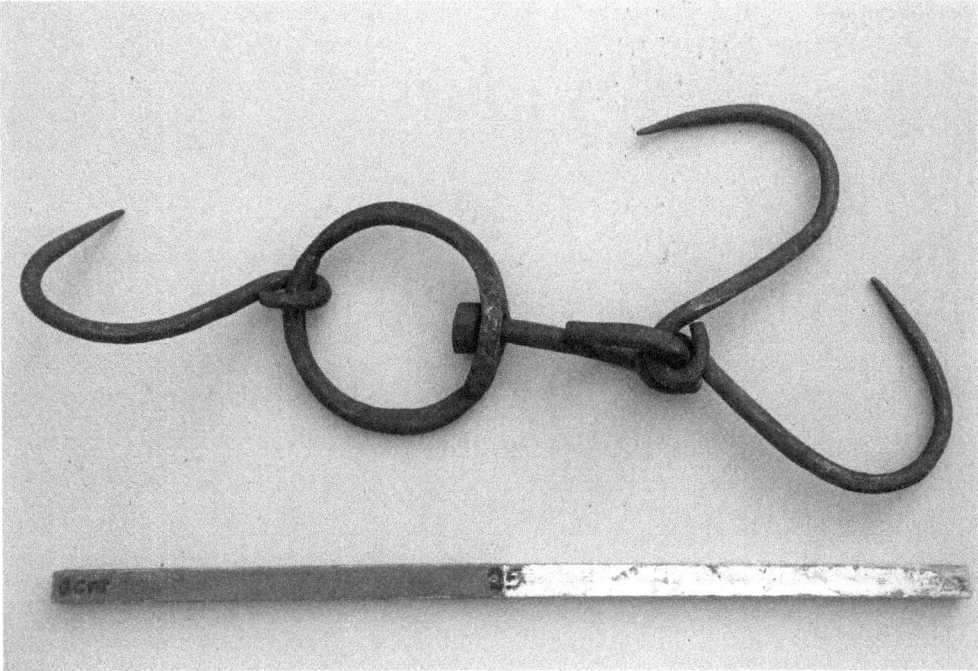

Figure 6.10 Hooks used to suspend the pig from its hindquarters during roasting process. Photo: Gordon Grimwade 2007.

Elaborate multi-ring hooks have long been used to secure the hindquarters of the pig during cooking. Nineteenth-century examples are held in the collections of the former Lit Sung Goong (Cairns), the Cooktown Museum and at Wellington, NSW. They show some similarities to the stainless-steel hooks used by Red Seasons Aroma Restaurant, Hong Kong around 2023.

In an experiment using scale drawings and photographs, three blacksmiths produced a wrought iron replica of the Cairns example in approximately six hours (Figure 6.10). No doubt the production rate would have been faster in the past. The single top hook is hung over the metal pole, supporting the carcass during cooking, while the other two hooks secure the hindquarters.

A plug inserted in the bottom vent helped control the draft and minimised heat loss during cooking. Present day plugs range from metal plates with welded handles to thick blocks of hardwood around 200 mm thick, suggesting, historically, such fittings were created opportunistically depending on locally available resources and skills. The top vent was, at least in more recent examples, covered with a variety of fireproof material with corrugated iron or steel caps and "sealed" with wet hessian sacks. There are inferences that large rocks may have been used opportunistically in lieu of metal caps, although firm evidence of this has yet to be found.

Cooking process

Early Australian investigators have suggested a cooking process similar to those used in ground ovens:

> A fire would be lit in the base of the oven and fed from the opening at the base, then large stones would be lowered and allowed to become red hot. A whole pig would be lowered onto the stones and a brass or metal cover placed over the opening until the meat was thoroughly cooked (Victorian Heritage Database, n.d.).

Such a process would, in practice, have been unworkable. First, the bottom vents were intended to provide draft and were too small to insert fuel. Secondly, there would have been insufficient space for both the pig carcass and enough stones to provide adequate heat.

Contemporary practices of pig cookery using ovens of this nature, however, provide a more probable indication of past practices. Current methods involve the dressed pig being "butterflied", to expose the fleshiest parts more evenly to the heat. Care is needed to avoid cutting too deeply and thus increase the risk of the pig disintegrating during cooking. The hooks are then secured into the hindquarters and, if it considered necessary, fencing wire added as extra security (Ray Chong, personal communication, 2007) (Figure 6.11). The widespread existence of the hooks, described above, suggest that they have been used for many years and are clearly designed to accommodate a butterflied carcass.

The pig is then marinated, with many cooks having their own closely guarded recipe. Tim Sing Lee's father used "a mix of five spice and soy sauce with a small amount of saltpetre to help colour the meat" (Tim Sing Lee, personal communication, 2017). It is worth noting that saltpetre also reduces the risk of botulism and has a long history of use as a meat preservative (Berk 2013, 591–606). Sing Lee further notes, "a trough would be cleaned and filled with a mixture of salt, water, spice of something, homemade sprite spirit] to marinate the pig for overnight, in the morning the pig would be hang up [sic] to dry before being lowered down to the oven". Bell writes, "Frank Chin from Tasmania and Lily Ah Toy from Darwin both describe how the pig carcass was dressed and marinaded in sauces (soy sauce with garlic and ginger)" (Bell 1995, 220). In New Zealand, Ray Chong (personal communication, 2007) uses a "mix of Chinese 'five spice', soy sauce and Chinese whisky". Chong states that some cooks added cochineal to get a red (lucky) colour to the meat, unlike Sing Lee who was adamant that cochineal was not used to develop a red colour to the pork (Grimwade 2008, 26; Sing Lee, personal communication, 2017). Other accounts are silent on the marinating process but there is good reason to believe

Figure 6.11 Butterflied pig carcass ready for oven. Note hooks in hindquarters, Riverhead, New Zealand. Photo: Gordon Grimwade 2007.

Figure 6.12 Ray Chong and assistant haul roast pig from oven, Riverhead, New Zealand. Photo: Gordon Grimwade 2007.

it was, and is in its various incarnations, an essential part of the cooking process; although, in some instances, it was secondary to the delights of the final product. In pre-war Atherton, John Fong On (1915–2001) noted that for the *Qing Ming* festival, Hung Mun, a Chinese cook working at the nearby Lake Eacham Hotel, "would get a day off and barbecue a large pig at the barbecue pit [sic] at the rear of the Hou Wang temple. He was an expert at barbecuing and the pork would come out crackling. It was delicious, but we kids preferred the pork fillets" (Lee Long 1996, 30). Fong On's reference to the "barbecue pit" is the original oven, indicating it was still operational during the late 1920s.

Several hours before the feast, a large fire would be started in the oven with the vent plug completely removed to maximise the draught. The fire was kept burning strongly until it was considered the oven chamber was hot enough. As soon as practical, the hot ash was raked out and the vent plug fully inserted. In line with present day practices, the water-filled wok and the pig were lowered into the oven so that the snout was just clear of the wok. The top vent was then covered and the contained heat left to do its all-important work.

Cooking takes from two and a half to four hours, depending on the size of the pig, the oven temperature and heat loss (Grimwade 2008, 26) (Figure 6.12). If poultry was also to be cooked it was lowered in later on in the cooking period and usually hung near the top to maximise use of available heat (Grimwade 2008, 26). Historical accounts infer a similar process was followed.

Several oral sources suggest that if the pig was not fully cooked it was removed, the fire rekindled and the pig returned to the oven once the bricks were reheated. Once cooked, the roast was carefully removed and carried on a rudimentary bier – a discarded door is ideal – to the feast, for carving and distribution.

The absence of pork bones in the vicinity of the original Atherton oven tends to confirm that the carving was not conducted near the oven and possibly had ceremonial relevance. In the past, a strict code of conduct ensured distribution of the meat was carefully controlled. This protocol has been modified through evolving cultural traditions. Mrs Sing Lee noted that the family, originally from the Loong Dhu region of Guangdong, would select portions by weight based on pre-sold tickets. She further noted, "Money raised went to the butcher for the slaughter and dress the pig. All work were [sic] done by men, women were not permitted to handle all those sacred things. The cost and size of portion differ each year" (Mrs Sing Lee, personal communication, 2017). Cairns resident, Bishop George Tung Yep (born 1927) recounts being punished when, as a lad, he "stole the tail of the roast pig before it could be offered in the temple and was punished severely for this misdemeanour" (Grimwade in press). Those practices and repercussions have mellowed over time. At a family reunion in Atherton in 2018, the meat was simply carved and portions handed out on a "first come, first served" basis (Grimwade, personal observation, 2018).

Oven reconstruction

In 2015, the opportunity was afforded to undertake both an excavation and a reconstruction of the Atherton oven, with funding provided by the National Trust and the Queensland Government's Everyone's Environment Grant scheme. The original oven had been bulldozed in the mid-twentieth century (John Fong On, personal communication, 1987). Its location was identifiable from a single photograph and ground truthed to where a patch of charcoal-stained soil and some rocks were identified, south-west of the temple.

While the original site was previously bulldozed, relict evidence indicated that the oven was about two metres wide at the base and had faced north. An extensive ash deposit covering about 15 metres square from near the lower vent confirmed that the ash had been raked out and spread, which was consistent with reported cooking practices (Grimwade 2016). Among the diverse and largely unrelated artefacts recorded there was only one piece of pig bone recovered. Machinery and other ferrous metal artefacts were concentrated adjacent to the ramp indicating that, as use of the oven waned, it became a convenient storage facility.

An archaeologically sterile area was identified nearby and a new, north facing, ramped oven was constructed. Given the minimal evidence of the original oven, the project team decided that the experimental oven would be ramped (consistent with the photographic evidence) and of similar proportions scaled from the original photograph. The ultimate design was based on field research of other ovens and the need to provide a more durable resource that the owners, the National Trust, could use for educational and entertainment purposes.

Given the annual rainfall of the region is around 1,200 mm, the ramp sides were protected with basalt rock walls to minimise erosion and improve longevity, instead of simply being left as a compacted soil ramp. A plywood template guided the stonemasons in the construction of the tapered cylinder for the actual cooking chamber.

The two-metre-high oven, with a 700 mm top opening, was constructed using second-hand firebricks to provide optimal heat retention and longevity (Figures 6.13–6.15). Initially, it had been intended to use local rock and to mortar the joints with crushed termite nests similar to that which had been used in ovens like Croydon, however this did not prove to be practical. The oven was subsequently cured by lighting a small fire in the base to reduce the risk of cracking and then fully heated. Volunteers were provided with meat from a "test fired" leg of pork.

Conclusions

Archaeological research is an ongoing process. Definitive outcomes are as dynamic as the environment in which archaeological sites exist. The ongoing research into the large stone ovens that started over 40 years ago has, fortuitously, enabled much to be learnt about the structures, their use and how they fitted into the cultural landscape. In the process, it has become clear they were often associated with temples and part of long-standing culinary cultural practices, and were not simply associated with large-scale mining settlements.

The technique of roasting whole pigs in a socio-religious setting is demonstrably a dying art. This historically important element of Chinese migrant life in Australia and elsewhere in Pacific Rim countries has, however, been progressively documented to show that the distribution of ovens and, by extension their significance, is far more widespread than was initially thought. In 1995, Bell (1995, 6) had hypothesised "the oddest aspect of the oven's geographical distribution in Australia is not where they are, but where they are not". Decades later, we have been able to demonstrate

Figure 6.13 Oven core of replica oven, Atherton, Queensland. Photo: Gordon Grimwade 2016.

Figure 6.14 Oven completed with partially constructed ramp later filled with rock and soil, Atherton, Queensland. Photo: Gordon Grimwade 2016.

Figure 6.15 Completed replicated oven, Atherton, Queensland. Photo: Gordon Grimwade 2021.

not only a wider spatial distribution – though still absent from South Australia – than initially envisaged but have also acquired a greater appreciation of how much work was involved in constructing ovens as well as the links to ceremony and celebration that they helped forge. Archaeological fieldwork combined with historical research, interviews and experimental archaeology have made it possible to correlate contemporary and past practices to produce a more definitive record reinforcing the value of multi-faceted research.

Chinese pig ovens have played important roles around the Pacific Rim as a component of both religious and secular activities. Current research suggests that, while the focus has moved from cooking at the rear of a temple to specialist kitchens supplying restaurants and private dwellings, this food still plays a significant role in modern Chinese culinary art. In the process, the move from religious ceremony to commercial exploitation demonstrates the dynamic forces that affect cultural change and development.

Acknowledgements

Inevitably when dealing with research that spans around four decades countless people have assisted in providing assistance. To list everyone is "mission impossible" and I apologise to those I have omitted; your contribution was no less important. My thanks to: my reviewers, Dr Peter Bell, Prof Heather Burke, Ray Chong, Melissa Dunk, Denise Gaughwin, Prof Martin Gibbs, Rev Christine Grimwade, Prof Manying Ip, Dr Juanita Kwok, Vicky and Max Lake, Prof Susan Lawrence, Paul Macgregor, Justin McCarthy, Dr Kevin Rains, Dr Sandi Robb, Dr Neville Ritchie, Martin Rowney, Dr Madeline Shanahan, Kym Stotter, Sherri du Toit, Dr Priscilla Wegars, Dr Michael Williams, Rhonda Micola and Friends of Atherton Chinese Temple Inc., Hans Pehl (blacksmith), John and Nola O'Boyle (stonemasons),Ginny Sue, Ted Young, Tim Sing Lee, Bernie Lim and Federation of NZ Chinese Commercial Growers Inc. and the late Mary Low and Henry Chan, John Fong On, Prof Ian Jack, Dr Barry McGowan and Dr James Ng.

References

Adamson, J. and H-D. Bader (2013). Gardening to prosperity: The history and archaeology of Chan Dah Chee and the Chinese market garden at Carlaw Park, Auckland. *Finding our recent past: historical archaeology in New Zealand*, 143–65. Auckland: NZ Archaeology Association.

Alfredson, G. (1988). *Draft Report on the Initial Archaeological Survey of the Doughboy Creek Gold Project for Australian Groundwater Consultants*. Chapel Hill: Alfredson Consulting Pty Ltd.

Associated Press (2019). *Last remaining pig roaster busy ahead of Year of the Pig (2019)* [video], YouTube, accessed 5 December 2021. https://www.youtube.com/watch?v=NKzZaU9pVy4.

Baldwin, J.A. (1986). Pre-Cookian Pigs in Australia? *Journal of Cultural Geography* 4(1): 17–27.

Bauchop, H. (2019). *Heritage item summary report: Chinese pig roasting oven and gantry. 513 and 579 Fortification Road, Alma*. Unpublished typescript, Oamaru, NZ.

Bell, P. (1996). Archaeology of the Chinese in Australia. *Australasian Historical Archaeology* 14: 13–18.

Bell, P. (1995). Chinese ovens on mining settlement sites in Australia. In P. McGregor, ed. *Histories of the Chinese in Australasia and the South Pacific*, 213–29. Melbourne: Museum of Chinese Australian History.

Bell, P. (1983). *Pine Creek: report to the National Trust of Australia (Northern Territory) on an archaeological assessment of sites of historic significance in the Pine Creek district.* Report to National Trust of Australia, Northern Territory.

Bengsen, A., P. West and C. Krull (2017). Feral pigs in Australia and New Zealand: range, trend, management, and impacts of an invasive species. In M. Melletti and E.R. Meijaard, eds. *Ecology, conservation and management of wild pigs and peccaries,* 325–38. Cambridge: Cambridge University Press.

Berk, Z. (2013). *Food process engineering and technology.* London: Academic Press.

Bjornskov, M. (2001). Rock, mortar and traditions: an archaeological study of Chinese "ovens" in the Northern Territory. In C. Fredericksen and I. Walters, eds. *Altered states: material culture transformations in the Arafura region,* 121–47. Darwin: Northern Territory University.

Brown, A. (2017). *Stoked: cooking with fire.* Auckland: Random House.

Burke, H. and G. Grimwade (2013). The historical archaeology of the Chinese in Far North Queensland. *Queensland Archaeological Research* 16: 121–40.

Clarke, C.M.H. and R.M. Dzieciolowski (1991). Feral pigs in the northern South Island, New Zealand: origin, distribution, and density. *Journal of the Royal Society of New Zealand* 21(3): 237–47.

Comber, J. (1991). *Palmer Goldfield Heritage Sites Study (Stage 2).* Report to Queensland Department of Environment and Heritage, Brisbane.

Cuff, T. (1992). A weighty issue revisited: new evidence on commercial swine weights and pork production in mid-nineteenth century America. *Agricultural History,* 66(4): 55–74.

Darwin, C. (1868). *The variation of animals and plants under domestication.* London: John Murray.

Department of Sustainability, Environment, Water, Population and Communities (2011). *The Feral Pig.* Canberra: Australian Government.

Gaughwin, D. (1995). Chinese settlement sites in north east Tasmania: an archaeological view. In P. McGregor, ed. *Histories of the Chinese in Australasia and the South Pacific,* 230–48. Melbourne: Museum of Chinese Australian History.

Giuffra E., J.M.H. Kijas, V. Amarger, O. Carlborg, J.T. Jeon and L. Andersson (2000). The origin of the domestic pig: independent domestication and subsequent introgression. *Genetics* 154: 1785–91.

Grimwade, C. (in prep). Barrow boy to bishop.

Grimwade, G. (2024). Worshipping the North: early Chinese temples in mainland tropical Australia. *International Journal of Historical Archaeology.* DOI: 10.1007/s10761-024-00762-6.

Grimwade, G. (2016). *Pig oven excavation and reconstruction, Atherton Chinatown.* Report to Friends of the Atherton Chinese Temple Inc., Atherton.

Grimwade, G. (2008). Crispy roast pork: using Chinese Australian pig ovens. *Australasian Historical Archaeology* 26: 21–8.

Grimwade, G. (2003). Gold, gardens, temples and feasts: Chinese temple, Croydon, Queensland. *Australasian Historical Archaeology* 21: 1–8.

Grimwade, G. (1990). *Palmer River Goldfields cultural resources [3 vols].* Report to Queensland Department of Environment and Heritage, Brisbane.

Grimwade, G. (1988). *Historical site survey: Fortuna Pty Ltd, Palmer River, Qld.* Report to Fortuna Pty Ltd, Cultural Resource Services Pty Ltd, Cairns.

Hollis, G. (2002). *Swine* [video], Livestock Trail by University of Illinois website, accessed 27 July 2021. http://livestocktrail.illinois.edu/porknet/questionDisplay.cfm?ContentID=4696.

Hum Lee, R. (1960). *The Chinese in the United States of America.* Hong Kong: Hong Kong University Press.

Jack, R.I., K. Holmes and R. Kerr (1984). Ah Toy's garden: A Chinese market garden on the Palmer River goldfield. *Australian Journal of Historical Archaeology* 2: 51–8.

Kaufman R. and Swift A. (2004). *Historic mining sites survey: Mt Wills and Mitta Mitta area goldfields,* unpublished report, LRGM Services.

Kirkman, N. (1984). The Palmer Goldfield 1873–1883. Honour's thesis, James Cook University, Townsville, Qld.

Kim, S-O, C.M. Antonaccio, Y.K. Lee, S.M. Nelson, C. Pardoe, J. Quilter and A. Rosman (1994). Burials, pigs, and political prestige in Neolithic China [and comments and reply]. *Current Anthropology* 35(2): 119–41.

Kwok, J. (2023). A reassessment of Chinese pig ovens in Australia. *Journal of Australasian Mining History* 21: 95–113.

Lamb, C. (2013). *A Dissertation upon Roast Pig,* Project Gutenberg, accessed 7 May 2025. https://www.gutenberg.org/files/43566/43566-h/43566-h.htm.

Lee Long, W. (1996). Recorded interview with John Fong On. Post-war Chinese Australians Oral History Project TRC 3447 [audio file], Oral History Section, National Library of Australia, accessed 24 May 2023.

Maniery, M.L. (2001). Fuel for the fire: Chinese cooking features in California. Paper presented to Society for Historical Archaeology, annual meeting, Long Beach.

McCarthy, J. (1995). Tales from the Empire City: Chinese miners in the Pine Creek region, Northern Territory, 1872–1915. In P. McGregor, ed. *Histories of the Chinese in Australasia and the South Pacific*, 191–202. Melbourne: Museum of Chinese Australian History.

McCarthy, J. (1989). *Would be diggers and old travellers: the Chinese of Union Reefs and the Twelve Mile in the Northern Territory 1876–1910.* Report to National Trust of Australia, Northern Territory.

McCarthy, J. and P. Kostoglou (1986). *Pine Creek Heritage Zone Archaeological Survey.* Report to National Trust of Australia, Northern Territory.

Morris, S. (1984). *Oriental cooking.* Sydney: Doubleday.

Raw Street Capture (2016). *Vietnam street food – Crispy Roast BBQ Whole Pig Pork in Charcoal Oven – Street food in Vietnam 2016* [video], YouTube, accessed 5 December 2021. https://www.youtube.com/watch?v=E0v8RGVD68Y.

Register of the National Estate (archived material), accessed December 2021. https://www.awe.gov.au/parks-heritage/heritage/places/register-national-estate.

Ritchie, N. (1986). Archaeology and History of the Chinese in Southern New Zealand during the Nineteenth Century, PhD thesis, University of Otago, Dunedin.

Ruvinsky, A. and M.F. Rothschild (1998). Systematics and evolution of the pig. In A. Ruvinsky and M.F. Rothschild, eds. *The genetics of the pig,* 1–16. Oxford: CAB International.

Tomlin, O. (1979). *Gold for the finding: a pictorial history of Gippsland's Jordan Goldfield.* Melbourne: Hill of Content.

Tsang, K.B. (1996). Chinese pig tales. *Archaeology* 49(2): 52–7.

Van Kempen, E. (1985). *Survey of historic Chinese sites in Queensland and the Northern Territory.* Report to the Australian Heritage Commission, Canberra.

Victorian Heritage Database (n.d.) Chinese pig oven. Victorian Heritage Database Report. https://vhd.heritagecouncil.vic.gov.au/places/10792/download-report.

Visit Beijing (2017). *Cured meats are the preserve of Spring Festival.* Visit Beijing website, accessed November 2023. https://english.visitbeijing.com.cn/article/47ONkGcUhWV.

Wang, S. (2004). *Chinese Gods of Old Trades.* Beijing: Foreign Languages Press.

Wegars, P. (1991). Who's been working on the railroad? an examination of the construction, distribution, and ethnic origins of domed rock ovens on railroad related sites. *Historical Archaeology* 25(1): 37–65.

Newspapers

Ovens and Murray Advertiser, 5 December 1872.
Portland Guardian and Normanby General Advertiser, 14 April 1873.
Queenslander (Brisbane, Queensland), 30 January 1886.
Sydney Mail and New South Wales Advertiser, 7 May 1887.
Sunday Times (Sydney, NSW), 5 March 1922.
Weekly Examiner (Launceston, Tasmania), 17 August 1872.

7

Baked, boiled, roasted, steamed and stewed
Kitchens and cooking appliances as artefacts of domestic life in colonial Australia

Jacqueline Newling

Introduction

The art of cookery – generally accepted as the practice of heating or treating organic substances to turn them into "food", that is, safely edible and palatable substances – has evolved through time, and with it, the development of different techniques and subsequently, cooking appliances. Shaped by geographical and environmental factors, and cultural transmission, each culture has its own culinary particularities, influencing what and how foods are grown, processed, cooked, eaten and consumed. From the first arrival of colonists from England in 1788, Australian culinary culture was by-and-large transferred from Britain, and in many instances, adapted to local conditions (see Newling 2021; for British context see Pennell 2016 and Lehmann 2003.)

It is rare, however, to find historic kitchens intact. Kitchens tend to be upgraded more than any other part of a house, with new technology and changing lifestyles. Kitchens altered significantly from the mid-nineteenth century. Open hearth fires, where the majority of cooking once took place, were modified or replaced with safer and more fuel-efficient iron "ranges" (open, enclosed and semi-enclosed) fired with wood, manufactured coal (which emitted highly noxious fumes) or preferably, cleaner-burning charcoal. These solid-fuel appliances were gradually eclipsed in urban settings after gas was piped into homes from the late 1800s, and later, electric "cookers", which did not begin to dominate until after the Second World War

(Delroy 1990, 268–70). Gas lighting and artificial refrigeration became available during this time but were not always affordable, and piped hot water cannot be assumed until the 1950s; even later in some households. And yet, as the hundreds of recipes in nineteenth-century cookery books demonstrate, a vast array of dishes could be produced without what are now regarded as basic essentials.

This chapter explores the cooking methods employed in Australian households before gas and electric appliances came into common use in the early twentieth century. It is by no means a comprehensive history of nineteenth-century kitchens, cookery or culinary technology. Instead, it approaches the kitchen as an artefact, or more-so an assemblage of artefacts, with an aim to providing an understanding of cooking facilities and the types of apparatus, vessels and implements used in domestic settings, and the practices involved in using them. Sources of information include extant kitchens (original or reinstated) in heritage sites and house museums, trade catalogues, household manuals and cookbooks, and depictions of domestic kitchen technology in artworks. By illuminating the less tangible aspects of colonial cookery this chapter aims to add dimension to these material objects and built environments so they can be recognised in relational terms, in contexts of both food production and social activity.

The chapter is in two parts. The first looks at kitchen facilities in both large estate-style houses and humbler cottage dwellings, offering surviving examples that are publicly accessible where possible. The examples are by no means exhaustive and are limited to my own encounters, predominantly in Sydney, Canberra and Tasmania. The second part of the chapter looks more closely at the types of cookery performed in these spaces.

Part one: the kitchen

Today we think of kitchens as one room with multiple fittings and appliances, from the simple toaster and electric kettle to a sink and fridge. The functions of these culinary conveniences were once (and still are in some cultures) the responsibility of the cook, as necessary components of household management. Access to water was integral, and temperature, light and moisture needed to be carefully managed. The general principles of their management were based on longstanding European practices, as was domestic architecture, including the placement of the kitchen (Sambrook and Brears 1993). Conditions in Australia were often more extreme than those experienced in cooler climes, and although houses ostensibly followed northern hemisphere design conventions, these practical considerations were often incorporated into, or indeed, dictated, the design of food preparation and storage areas in colonial dwellings.

Many large estates produced much of their own meat, milk, bread, garden and orchard produce, requiring a slaughterhouse and butchery, and possibly a smokehouse, a dairy, bakery and fruit stores. Closer to townships and urban areas these foods could be purchased from local markets and providores. Even so, many households maintained vegetable gardens and fruit trees, and some kept goats for fresh milk and made their own bread. Houses of all kinds needed some kind of pantry store for dry goods, cool spaces for perishables, a scullery or washing up area, in addition to the main cooking facilities. We will look first at these facilities in large and affluent houses, and then how their functions were addressed in smaller households.

Expansive kitchens

It was not uncommon for kitchens of large affluent houses, especially if they were once some distance from towns and markets or supported an estate or farm, to feature a series of inter-related apartments or offices, each with its own function, as part of the kitchen (Sambrook and Brears 1993; Pennell 1998). Easily accessible metropolitan examples include Vaucluse House and Lindesay in Sydney, Rippon Lea in Melbourne, Ayers House in Adelaide, Newstead House in Brisbane, and Lanyon near Canberra.

Scullery

The principal function of a scullery was for washing up and other activities involving water such as scrubbing vegetables. The scullery was usually in close or immediate proximity to the main kitchen, but might also service the larder and dairy (discussed shortly). If not plumbed, the scullery needed to be in easy access to a water source. Some sculleries had a fire or cooking range to heat water for culinary use, and prior to plumbed washrooms, might also provide hot water for other household requirements, including personal ablutions in bedrooms.

Dry-store

Dry goods needed to be close at hand to the kitchen, but positioned away from light, heat and damp to prevent them becoming musty, stale or rancid, and minimise pest infestations. Houses in remote areas kept bulk stores and drew from them in smaller amounts according to weekly or daily needs, keeping the ready supply in bags, wooden tubs and ceramic crocks in a well-ventilated pantry or cupboard in the kitchen. Bottled preserves and condiments could also be kept in a pantry store.

Larder and dairy

Meat and milk products were traditionally stored separately and needed to be kept as cold as possible. The larder, or meat-locker, and dairy, or milk room, were usually located in the coolest parts of the kitchen complex, ideally in a southern location. They were often dug into the ground or in a basement or cellar, screened from sunlight, and well-ventilated to encourage airflow and allow warm air to escape (Beeton 1861, 1006). Surviving sunken or below ground larders and dairies can be seen at Vaucluse House museum and Government House in Sydney, and at Parramatta, the archaeological remains of the dairy that once served Old Government House.

The larder housed processed and preserved meats and animal products for use in the short-term, such as flitches of bacon and ham, either hanging from hooks in the ceiling or kept in ventilated cabinets. The latter was also used to store potted meat, fish and cheese preparations preserved in clarified butter; and sweet and savoury jellies such as brawn. Glazed vats or tubs were used for brine-pickled pork, corned beef and tongue. Cured meats that required little intervention could also be stored in cellars for longer periods of time. Eggs would also be stored in the larder in boxes lined with straw.

The dairy or milk room was both a storage space and processing area. Generally fitted out with stone benches, freshly drawn milk could cool in wide open dishes on the top of the bench without conducting heat to the storage bays below. Cream that naturally rose to the top of the milk as it cooled would be churned into butter, and the skimmed milk used for other purposes. Several nineteenth-century cookery texts offer detailed instructions on the care and management of the dairy and the domestic production of butter and cheese (e.g. Rundell 2009 [1816], 259–69; Beeton 1861, 1006–8).

Although it was imperative that the dairy and larder be kept cool, ideally there would be access to water and a cooking stove nearby. The science behind pasteurisation was not identified until the late 1800s but it was understood that scalded – not boiled – milk would stay "sweet" for longer (Rundell 2009 [1816], 267–8). Milk also needs to be heated to certain temperatures to make different cheeses and yoghurt-style curd, and pickling solutions for meat preparations, such as corned beef, needed to be replaced or refreshed by re-boiling. It was also understood that equipment and utensils must be immaculately cleaned after and before use to prevent food spoilage. Drainage channels along the floor were a common feature of milk rooms, used to conduct away waste products such as whey (though this was often saved for animals) therefore indicating the liberal use of water for cleaning in these rooms.

Produce stores

Various techniques were used to keep fruit and vegetables beyond their natural seasons. Soft leafy greens would not store well but root vegetables, hardy greens (such as cabbage) and some kinds of fruit (especially if picked unripe) could be kept for extended periods in tubs of sand in a cellar or other cool space. Fruit could also be sundried, preserved as jam or in sugar syrup, or made into chutney. Apples and flavourless "jam melons" were popular fillers for jams of expensive and exotic fruit such as stem ginger and pineapples, while apples, marrows (giant zucchinis), and chokos (from the late 1800s) were used to add bulk to chutneys and relishes, or fruit pie fillings that were preserved in jars for later use. Beans and cauliflower were made into Indian piccalilli or mustard pickles, and from the mid-1800s, tomatoes were combined with fruit for various savoury sauces and condiments. Vegetables were also pickled in brine or vinegar, or fermented as sauerkraut in earthenware jars or later, in glass bottles. English cookery author Maria Rundell (1816) advises that vinegar be boiled in a jar, as acids dissolve the lead in the tin lining of saucepans, and similarly, that unglazed jars be used to store pickles "as salt and vinegar penetrates the glaze, which is poisonous" (Rundell 2009 [1816], 178). The vessels could be sealed with cork or parchment, perhaps with a coat of wax or whipped egg white, and kept in a cool and dry cupboard or pantry-store (see Shepherd 2000, 187–91). Glass mason jars with porcelain screw caps were advertised from the early 1880s. These shelf-stable preserves were generally kept in a pantry in or near the kitchen, or in a cellar for longer-term or bulk storage.

Household management

These rooms and spaces were tended by kitchen staff under the direction of the cook, who followed in turn, the instructions of the mistress of the house, or in a very well-staffed household, a housekeeper. The relationship between their various functions is important on both practical and social terms, requiring careful administration of staff and resources or in nineteenth-century vernacular, domestic economy. Good household management involved knowledge and skills in a range of culinary arts and practical sciences now largely lost in domestic settings, to ensure the supply of particular foods and minimise waste by taking advantage of seasonal produce and climatic conditions to maximise fuel efficiency, time, energy and cost of labour.

Social interactions between the people who worked in these spaces, and the ways they interacted with different members of the household, whether servants or family, are equally important as the material functions of these areas. Television series such as Downton Abbey highlight the social hierarchy of servants, from lowly scullery maid to housekeeper or butler, and lines of communication with the master and mistress of the house. They, and their duties, were all part of the rhythm of a household, and some employers formed close and caring relationships with their staff.

With the rise of the middle class in the 1800s, many of the *nouveau riche* had to learn these systems (including the art of social dining and entertaining) and the proliferation of published household manuals, menu books and cookery texts subsequently produced are useful sources for researchers today (e.g. Anon. 1857; Beeton 1861; Pierce 1857).

Colonial development grew rapidly in New South Wales and Victoria after the discovery of gold in the 1850s. New townships were established and roadways and rail networks expanded, and once-remote properties became better connected to supply services, lessening the need to be self-supporting. Artificial refrigeration meant fewer people needed to salt down large quantities of meat or make bread, butter and cheese. These, along with fresh meat, could be purchased on regular trips to town or delivered on regular bases, meaning that householders could manage with pantries, food-safes and, in warmer months, ice chests. The reduction in the number of servants in households was another contributing factor in these service rooms and the work performed in them becoming redundant. As a result, many service wings and outbuildings were demolished or repurposed, and kitchens were integrated into the main part of the house, offering more convenient access to dining areas and allowing closer connection and interaction with social and family activity. This had been standard practice in smaller and more modest houses that operated without dedicated service rooms and in many cases, without household staff. In many historic houses that are now museums, surviving kitchens and servants' spaces are used as reception areas, administrative offices, refreshment rooms, and, less-so, as bathroom facilities (Shanahan, personal communication, 2022). This indicates how little value these working spaces have been given when interpreting historic houses, compared with the often grander living areas.

Simple kitchens

In smaller and more modest households (which does not necessarily mean small numbers of residents) equivalent procedures to those outlined above took place in modified forms and at reduced scales, the duties generally performed by family members rather than servants. A "tuckerbox" and a mesh-sided food-safe set against a south-facing wall in the kitchen or veranda may be all that was necessary for protecting dry-goods and perishable foods from heat, light, insects and vermin. Tin boxes with perforated sides, hung from a hook to catch the breeze, acted as a mini larder for small households.

Even humble cottages sported fireplaces and sometimes bread ovens made of brick or stone, clad inside and out with mud or clay – for example, Calthorpes House and Mugga-Mugga Cottage, both in Canberra (see also Baglin and Baglin 1979). Alternatively, small bread loaves, buns and biscuits could be cooked in a portable "American" oven. Essentially an open-faced, three-sided box made of reflective tin with a tray shelf or two within, which could be set in front of the hearth-fire at the appropriate distance for the job (see Acton 1855, 164; 1857). Bread could also be made in a "Dutch" oven, an iron pot distinguished by a closely fitted flat lid with raised sides upon which coals could be piled, while the body of the pot was nestled into the coals of the hearth fire to bake. In urban areas, bakeries not only supplied bread, but following an age-old tradition, also baked pies, pastries and meat that customers brought in ready-prepared for cooking, for a small service fee. Households could therefore manage without an oven and/or avoid the discomfort of using a hot oven in the summertime.

Some householders, even when living in towns where milk could be bought, kept a milch-goat. They were hardy animals that were cheaper and easier to feed and required less space than a cow. Goat-milk could be processed into cottage-style cheese but is not ideal for butter making. Butter might therefore be bought in, or homemade from purchased dairy cream.

Other daily needs – dry-goods, meat, fresh fruit and vegetables (if not grown at home) – could also be purchased from local grocers, butchers and street vendors. Buying small quantities at regular intervals eliminated the need for extensive storage space. Some houses had a basement and/or cellar store, however they were often used to store coal rather than food.

Perishables (and drinks) could be kept cool for short periods of time in lead-lined "sarcophagi" or cheaper tin-lined "refrigerator boxes", insulated with tightly packed straw or sawdust. A predecessor to today's chillybin or esky, they were cooled by filling with cold water drawn from a deep well. It was also common practice to chill drinks, set jellies and moulded creams by suspending them in a bucket just above the waterline in the well, where it was coldest. Commercial manufacture of ice began in the 1850s but it took some time for the industry to benefit householders. Domestic ice chests were available from the 1860s but they were costly to buy and only useful for those who could access and afford regular deliveries of ice, which remained a concern for decades (Muskett 1893, 59). The obvious benefits of domestic refrigeration saw the rapid development of icemaking technology. Iceworks were quickly established in regional towns, and newspapers featured instructions for making homemade iceboxes for food storage. Rural households were clearly disadvantaged until kerosene-powered refrigerators became available in the late 1920s. For many householders, a refrigerator was a significant purchase, and ice chests were still in demand in the 1940s.

Artificial lighting

Improvements in artificial lighting changed the way people ate and cooked. Due to the cost of clean-burning candles or whale oil, only wealthy people could afford to light their dining rooms at night. Their kitchens were often lit with cheaper tallow, which was greasy and smoky. For the majority of people, the main meal of the day took place at lunchtime, to make practical use of daylight as an economic measure, and to take advantage of the cooler hours of the morning for hot and laborious work. Supper, or "tea" as it was known in some households (not to be confused with the beverage, though tea may be served with the meal) was a quickly-cooked affair, perhaps leftovers from the day's main meal, or for some, bread and cheese. Even the middling or leisure classes who had staff to cook for them took dinner during the day, and a simpler, though similarly styled, evening meal of fewer courses (for detailed study on mealtimes and social status see Lehmann 2003).

Gas lighting was increasingly adopted in private homes from the 1870s (in metropolitan areas), and evening dining became prevalent for "white collar" workers whose workdays followed set operating hours. Their children may have eaten at an earlier hour. For those who did not have money to burn either candles or gas, workday meals were taken according to the demands of the day. Factory or retail workers might come home for lunch if practicable, as might schoolchildren, but for many, the hot meal of the day, which may be relatively simple, was now taken in the early evening. Stories abound of the lights going out mid-meal in homes that used coin-operated gas meters in the early 1900s, and the scramble to find pennies to reactivate the service. Sunday was often reserved for a more formal family meal, often a lunchtime or evening roast, when the meal could be prepared in daylight hours if necessary, and the family could spend more time at the table.

Local adaptation

If not within the living area of a dwelling, the kitchen was almost invariably at the rear of the house or beneath the house in the basement. Quite often, kitchens in the colony were in a detached building. Risk of fire spreading into formal areas is the common *tropos*, but as Clara Aspinall explained, "Kitchens are detached from the houses, to keep the latter as cool as possible" (Aspinall 1862, 102). A separate kitchen also minimised the likelihood of noise, cooking smells, greasy smoke and steam permeating the living areas. For basic hearth-side cookery, a chimney that functioned properly would draw heat and smoke up from the fire, the constant draught preventing the kitchen from overheating (Baglin and Baglin 1976, 7).

However, enclosed iron ranges and ovens were designed to hold heat and would almost certainly raise the ambient temperature of the kitchen. As warm air rises, they would also warm the room/s above.

Some houses, such as Elizabeth Bay House (now a museum) in Sydney, had two kitchens – one in a detached wing at the rear of the house and the other in the basement, conveniently installed underneath the family room, which would benefit from passive heat emanating from cooking activity below. The skeletal remains of the basement kitchen and other service rooms survive in the house; however, the detached wing was demolished to make way for a road and building development in the 1930s.

At Susannah Place, a row of four "two up, two down" terrace houses built in 1844 in The Rocks in inner-Sydney (now also a museum), the original kitchens were in the east-facing basements. In three of the four houses, the kitchens were relocated to the ground floor, providing easier access to living areas and better light. In two of the houses, enclosed balconies added later in the century became make-shift kitchens. This was made possible with the advent of free-standing gas or electric cookers in the early 1900s, thus freeing up the original back room for living space. In the wintertime, however, some tenants chose to cook with the iron range that remained in the back room fireplace, which warmed the house as well as producing a hot meal. These examples demonstrate the ways that residents adapted British-designed houses to suit the local environment for comfort and convenience.

The uses of and necessity for the spaces outlined above evolved quite rapidly through the second half of the nineteenth century. Technological breakthroughs can be dated to particular decades, but by no means were they uniformly available or adopted. Whether and when traditional methods were replaced by new, more industrial ones depended on location, financial means and personal preference, however most were obsolete by the mid-twentieth century. Many of the products and processes these spaces facilitated have been outsourced to commercial and usually industrialised providers. Some of the foods produced in these spaces have become all but lost. Domestic freezers have made ice cream a household staple but chilled desserts such as blancmange and sago pudding have disappeared from family menus. Similarly, deli-bought charcuterie has replaced home-cured meat. While timesaving for cooks, these changes have altered our relationship with food by distancing us from our food sources and the knowledge and skills involved in food production and preservation. More familiar might be basic cooking methods suggested in the title of this chapter, that were employed primarily in the main part of the kitchen, which centred around the fire or stove.

Part two: cooking methods

The transference of heat is recognised as the principal cooking medium, and is the main focus of this second part of the chapter, which moves from open hearth cookery to manufactured iron ranges. There are three basic means of heating food – radiation, convection and conduction – which manipulate the molecular composition of the food. Their reactions are often facilitated by added water or fats. Grilling, broiling and roasting expose food to radiant heat. Boiling, simmering and steaming are forms of convection using heat conducted through water or vapour. Deep-frying also uses convection by immersing food in oil, while pan-frying or sautéing use conducted heat from an oiled pan. Baking uses both air convection and radiated heat (McGee 2004, 780–7).

Open hearth cookery

The vacant cavities so often seen in historic houses and museums, perhaps displayed with an inchoate array of old cooking implements, belie the versatility the original hearth fire offered. In the hands of a competent cook, and with the right equipment, all forms of cookery (grilling, roasting, steaming, frying, etc.) could be achieved with this single facility – regardless of whether it was part of the living area or in a designated kitchen. A variety of pots, pans, griddles, plates and grid-irons could be placed in, on or in front of the fire, or over it, suspended from an iron bar fitted across the inside of the fireplace beneath the chimney. Some fireplaces featured a safer and more convenient crane attached to the side wall. A hinge allowed the jib-arm to swing out so that cooks could tend pots suspended from it, without reaching over the fire. Cooking temperatures were controlled by manipulating exposure to the heat. This could be achieved by adjusting the number of hooks or length of chain that held the cooking vessels, changing their distance above the fire. Many recipes instructed that food should be cooked "before the fire", that is, in front of the fire itself, to cook from the radiant heat rather than directly over a flame. Pots could be placed directly on the hearth or raised up on a stand or trivet.

Frying and sauteeing

A secondary cooking area could be created for delicate dishes by scooping some coals from the fire onto the outer hearth or kitchen floor, over which a grid-iron would be placed to support a pot, sauté pan or earthenware chafing dish. Better equipped kitchens featured a separate structure with cavities in which small fires could be set. These "stewing stoves" had been used in England since the early sixteenth century. By the 1800s, they were fitted with iron fire baskets to hold the hot burning coals, over which trivets were placed, acting as hobs. When not

Figure 7.1 The kitchen at Monticello, Charlottesville, Virginia, USA, showing clockwise from left: a bank of stewing stoves, set kettle, fireplace with crane, roasting jack on the wall above, and beehive baking oven (closed). Photo: Jacqueline Newling 2018.

connected to a flued chimney system, these stoves would ideally be positioned near a window or well ventilated part of the kitchen to minimise the risk of toxic fumes being emitted, especially when manufactured coal came into use. These small, fuel efficient hobs had the benefit of individual heat control and could be lit for small or delicate quick-cooking dishes such as omelettes or sautéed offal – ideal for breakfast or light suppers. With the use of a grid-iron, fish or steaks could also be grilled without the need for the main fuel-hungry fire. Expansive banks of hobs can be seen in kitchens at Kew Palace near London and Thomas Jefferson's Monticello in Virginia, USA (Figure 7.1), and a smaller example with three hobs remains in the basement kitchen at Elizabeth Bay House in Sydney.

Roasting

The traditional English-style roast dinner maintained in many Australian households today is not typical of the roast enjoyed by our forebears before the mid-nineteenth century. True roasting is a form of radiant heat, transferred to food by direct exposure to the fire. A spit positioned across the front of the fire, from which large cuts and

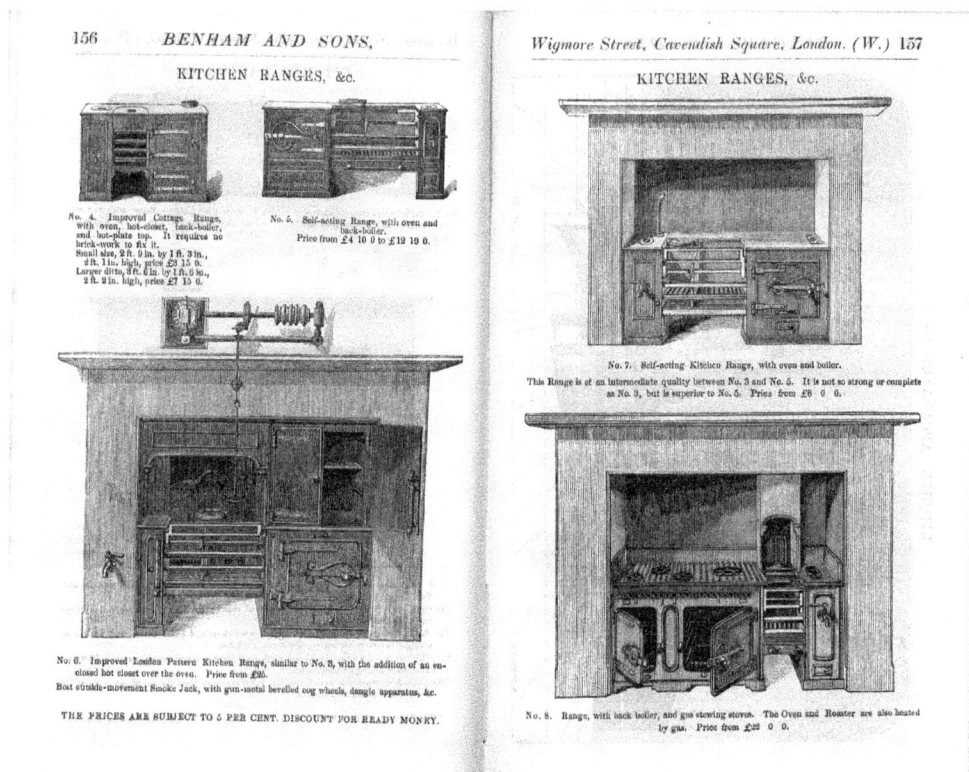

Figure 7.2 Benham and Sons (1868), illustrated catalogue. London: Benham and Sons. Caroline Simpson Library Collection, Museums of History NSW.

"joints" of meat or whole birds were roasted, could be turned manually to ensure even cooking. In more sophisticated setups, spits were driven by mechanical means using a "smoke-jack" generated by hot air drawn up into the chimney that worked gears which rotated the spit-bars (an early mechanical spit can be seen in Figure 7.1, and a more sophisticated example in illustration "No. 6" in Figure 7.2).

Even without these fittings, meat could be roasted in front of the fire using a "dangle spit" formed by cords or chain suspended from the mantle above the fireplace. The cords would be twisted and tensioned periodically by the cook, allowing the meat attached to spin around as the cord unfurled. Brass and japanned tin "bottle jacks", advertised for sale in the colony from at least 1816, automated the process somewhat by means of an internal key-wound mechanism that turned a spool which the meat hung from. A bottle jack is one of the implements recommended in Isabella Beeton's *Book of Household Management* in 1861 (Beeton 1861, 31). A depiction of an "Australian kitchen" in 1880s editions of Beeton's tome shows a cook tending a roast suspended from a bottle jack with a drippings tray below (Figure 7.3).

AUSTRALIAN KITCHEN,

Figure 7.3 Australian kitchen, *Mrs Beeton's Book of Household Management* (c. 1888, 1256). London: Ward, Lock and Co. Rouse Hill Estate Collection, Museums of History NSW.

A pan positioned beneath the joint caught rendered fat and meat juices, which could be used to baste the meat, or to cook roast potatoes or Yorkshire-type puddings in the drippings. Additional economy could be achieved by a freestanding "tin kitchen" or "tin roaster" positioned in front of the fireplace, its reflective tin-plate providing extra radiant heat as the jack rotated. These could be homemade or manufactured (see for example, Benham and Sons 1852, 74). Bottle jacks appear in household auction lists in the 1860s, but an 1868 article in a regional newspaper suggests that the apparatus was by then quite novel for Australians living outside the metropole, if not more broadly, "as it is an almost universal custom ... to bake [meat] in an oven" (J.P. 1878, 18). It appears, therefore, that the 1880s edition Mrs Beeton was wryly mocking life in the Antipodes, suggesting that people were using antiquated technology.

Boiling

Many Australians would be aghast at the thought of boiling a leg of mutton, even more-so a calf's or pig's head or ox-tongue, but these were popular dishes even in early twentieth-century Australia. Tongue and calves' heads were quite prestigious, sheep derived alternatives less-so. Pigs' heads were also boiled to make brawn. Boiling of such food items was done in large oval-shaped iron cooking pots which are now often seen in museums and antique shops.

Boiling, which in historical cookbooks could also mean lower temperature simmering, was available to anyone with access to a heat source and a watertight vessel that could withstand direct exposure to heat. Lightweight and versatile, the now iconic Australian "billy" or tin "kettle" was ubiquitous for more than a century before Banjo Patterson wrote "Waltzing Matilda" in the 1890s. Synonymous with camp fire cookery, they could be nestled in hot coals, and when fitted with handles could be lifted from the fire with a stout stick, or suspended from a tripod or a rod supported by a frame. Heavier and more durable was the round-based cauldron-style iron pot, usually equipped with three small feet so it could stand on the ground without rolling about.

A great variety of dishes can be made in such kettles and pots, including soups, stews and grain-based gruels (often maligned but porridge and congee are still readily consumed today). Nutrients are retained in the cooking liquid, which could be served as broth, or thickened with rice, barley, stale bread or biscuit.

Cloth-boiling

Cloths were used to bundle up a variety of sweet and savoury foods to boil for puddings. Christmas plum pudding is probably the best known survivor of this style of cooking in Australia, but pease pudding was made with dried split-peas, and hasty puddings were made with flour and suet, sometimes enriched with fruit ("spotted dick" style). The technique was popularised in the late eighteenth century and almost exclusively limited to the British culinary diaspora, including Australia (see Leach 2008). A savoury pudding could be boiled in the pot with the meat and vegetables with which it would be served, adding flavour to the pudding and to the cooking broth, which might be served as soup. A miniature form of flour-and-suet pudding remained in the repertoire as dumplings, which were boiled without a cloth in stews towards the end of cooking. This was an economical way to add substance and texture, thickening the broth and making the dish more filling. Savoury puddings were gradually eclipsed with the increasing use of potatoes as accompaniments to meat dishes, as they were easier and quicker to cook, and more versatile (Wilson 1973, 217–18).

Steaming

With Christmas plum pudding perhaps the exception, basins have largely replaced cloths for steaming puddings, being easier to serve from and to clean. The basin could be lined with pastry, filled with meat and gravy and covered with a pastry top, sealed with a plate, and steamed, semi-immersed, in a pot of boiling water. A "sea pie" could also be made in a kettle or iron pot with or without a basin, by covering a prepared stew with a layer of dumpling dough which formed a scone-like crust as the pie simmered in a well-sealed pot.

Casserole-style dishes could also be made without an oven, by filling a glazed earthenware jar with prepared meat, vegetables and herbs, sealing it tightly with a "bung" of cork or leather and setting the jar in a pot of water to simmer for several hours. This technique was known in the nineteenth century as "jugging" but in Australia the term "steamer" was adopted, as the ingredients steamed in their own juices. The kangaroo or wallaby steamer, layered with salt-pork or bacon and flavoured with onions, aromatics and port wine, is a localised version of the older English jugged hare (Santich 2012, 39). In *The English and Australian Cookery Book for the many as well as the upper ten thousand* (1864), the name steamer was retained but the dish was cooked in a saucepan, in the same way as a stew. The book includes three versions of the kangaroo steamer, one which could be preserved "for twelve months or more" by packing the cooked steamer tightly into an "open-mouthed glass bottle; the bung … sealed down, and the outside of the bottle washed well with white of egg, beaten" (Abbott 1864, 83). When required for eating, the jar was boiled in a pot for half an hour to reheat. Glazed earthenware jars were also used to make more delicate melted butter sauces, egg dishes, milk puddings, custard and fruit "cheese" (lemon curd-style) in the way that we might use a double boiler. They were also used to reheat delicate dishes, to prevent them scorching or sticking to a metal pot.

Water "on tap"

Before clean potable water was plumbed into homes, water filters, coolers and "fountains" were common domestic features. Large hand-hewn limestone dripstones from the early–mid nineteenth century, through which water was poured to remove impurities, can be seen at Vaucluse House and Elizabeth Farm (also a museum, near Parramatta). Smaller, sometimes decoratively designed, ceramic water dispensers fitted with filters and a tap near the base (much like modern versions) also helped keep drinking water cool (see for example Anthony Hordern and Sons Ltd general catalogue, 1914, 636). For hot water, large iron kettles sealed with a lid and fitted with a brass tap near the base were almost permanently suspended over the hearth fire for a ready supply. These vessels eliminated the need for a "set kettle" which were once a fixture in kitchens that serviced large households (see Figure 7.1). Akin to the "copper" commonly associated with laundries, they were set into a mud-and-stone or bricked surround adjoining the main fireplace, so that the fire beneath the structure that heated the copper could be vented into the chimney. The presence of a set kettle can lead to confusion as to whether the room was a kitchen or laundry, as they were used in both facilities. The room the Swann family used as a laundry at Elizabeth Farm in the early 1900s also has a substantial open fireplace, and evidence of an oven cavity that was bricked over at an unknown time, suggesting that the room was previously a kitchen.

Bread baking

Bread ovens with domed or beehive (skep) shaped interiors were often installed next to the cook's fire in the main kitchen, with the oven's flue connecting into the chimney. Good examples remain in Culthorpe's Cottage, the detached kitchen of Mugga-Mugga in Canberra, and 10 Quality Row at Kingston on Norfolk Island (all now museums). Archaeological remains have been reconstructed in the 1820s kitchen at Parbury Ruins, Millers Point, Sydney. At Rouse Hill House in north-western Sydney, the bread oven (c. 1855) is separate to the kitchen, built into a wall in the service wing, while some properties, such as Brickendon in Longford, Tasmania, have a dedicated bakery building – in this case adjoining a smokehouse (Clive Lucas, Stapleton and Partners 2008, 62, 67).

Beehive ovens work with radiant heat, held in the oven's internal brick lining. To heat the oven, a fire is lit inside and the door is left open, for airflow and to draw away any smoke, which is generally conducted up through a flue positioned in front of the oven door. Once the oven has reached the desired temperature, the coals are raked out and the oven floor swept with a damp broom. Only then is the door closed, trapping the heat within. An experienced baker knew the temperature of the oven by how quickly a handful of flour browned when thrown onto the oven floor, or, less safely, by the length of time they could hold their forearm in the oven. It could take up to two hours to reach bread-baking temperature, but once heated, the oven could retain its heat for several hours, and a series of dishes of varying types, from pies to meringues and delicate custards, could be cooked in the residual heat (Nylander 1994, 197–8; for detailed explanation about bread baking and types of apparatus available in the mid-1800s, see Acton 1857). A nineteenth-century innovation was the "Scotch" oven, where heat was drawn from a firebox set into a smaller chamber next to the baking oven, eliminating the need to set a fire inside the brick oven and rake out the coals (Haden 2006, 61–73). This style of oven – several of which are still in use today in regional towns in New

South Wales, South Australia and Victoria – was used for commercial baking rather than domestic situations.

Enclosed and semi-enclosed range cookery

Open hearth fires and beehive ovens are fuel hungry, and in places where wood was scarce, particularly in metropolitan areas, coal had to be purchased. Manufactured "ranges" for fireplaces were in use in England from the late 1700s, but became more commonplace and increasingly elaborate as the nineteenth century progressed (see for example, General Iron Foundry Company Limited catalogue, 1862*)*. A relatively simple cooking range may comprise two vertical side panels, often in the form of water tanks, which were heated by the fire set between. An iron fender or crossbars were positioned in front of the fire between the panels to prevent coals falling out, and adjustable "cheeks" – flat plates of iron – could be moved inwards to create smaller fire-beds. Swivelling trivets affixed to the vertical plates allowed vessels to be moved over or away from the fire. Open exposure to the central fire allowed for roasting from some form of jack, as discussed above.

The absence of an inbuilt oven in these type of ranges suggests that they serviced kitchens with separate baking ovens. These were not necessarily brick beehive ovens, more often small pastry ovens, in the form of an iron box set into a cavity in a wall beside the fireplace, with its own small fire space and ash-pit below. Such is consistent with the setup at Elizabeth Bay House. Heat could circulate around the oven and any smoke from the fire was drawn into a flue behind or to one side of the oven and vented into the main chimney. Though a poor substitute for a brick beehive bread oven, they were suitable for baking small "cottage" loaves and soda bread, tarts, pies, and small batches of rolls, buns, scones and biscuits.

More compact semi-enclosed "self-acting", "cottage" or "cottager" ranges offered an open-faced fire for roasting, albeit of smaller scale, and retained features such as adjustable cheeks and swivelling trivet (Figure 7.2). A boiler or water tank was generally on one side of the fire, and on the other, a pastry oven. An early example dating to the mid-1840s survives at Vaucluse House. The oven can be lit from below as well as receiving heat from the central fire. Later models had the advantage of a flue system that conducted heat behind the oven, and by the 1860s, the ovens featured inbuilt plates that could be rotated to enable even cooking.

These multi-function appliances could be installed in existing fireplaces, replacing hearth-fire cookery. Publications from the 1860s indicate that this style of range remained in use for some time, even though more advanced models such as the Leamington Kitchener, which took the first prize and medal at the Great Exhibition in London in 1851, were available on the market (General Iron c.1862, 18; Benham and Sons 1868, 146, 157, 160). Originally imported from Britain or America, they were costly for some householders, but an increasing number of local foundries made them more affordable.

Much simpler and less expensive was the basic iron box oven (Figure 7.4). Available from the 1840s, they were fully enclosed and easy to install. Colonial illustrations and museum reconstructions show the box oven variously heated from above and below, the chimney drawing away any smoke from behind the box. A fire set on top of the oven provided a heat source for vessels hung directly over the fire, or an iron sheet could be positioned above the fire as a hotplate, supported by bricks on either side of the oven-top. Examples include S.T. Gill's 1857 depiction of the kitchen in Monsieur Noufflard's house in Sydney (Historic House Trust of NSW 1983), Frederick McCubbin's (1896) *Kitchen at the old King Street Bakery* and Hardy Wilson's (c. 1920) *Kitchen and fireplace at Berrima*. Similar setups can also be seen in the basement kitchen of 64 Gloucester Street at Susannah Place, The Rocks, Sydney; the Commandant's House, Port Arthur, Tasmania; and as shown in Figure 7.4 at Sovereign Hill in Ballarat, Victoria.

Oven "roasting"

Today, a traditional "roast" dinner is generally baked in an oven rather than true roasting, where meat is directly exposed to a flame. Offering detailed advice on dressing and tending meat to assure the best possible outcomes and circumventing common mistakes when roasting, cookery authority Eliza Acton (1855) conceded that the technique "requires unremitting attention on the art of the cook rather than any great exertions of skill" (157–9). While suitable for cooking various types of fish, pork, ham and pickled beef if well-covered with a "course paste" or layers of buttered paper, she deemed oven-baking "both an unpalatable and an unprofitable mode of cooking joints of meat in general" (Acton 1855, 165). Nonetheless, she recommends that when oven-baking, meat should be raised from the baking dish by placing it "properly skewered, on a stand, so as to allow potatoes or batter pudding to be baked under it" (Acton 1855, 165).

Acton does, however, advocate other types of cooking in the domestic oven, generally of the more delicate kind, through "slow oven-cookery". With enough cooking liquid, calf's feet, rolled heads and soup bone reductions could be effectively made in the oven. Cooking in a jar (casserole-style) with its lid "well pasted down, and covered with a fold of thick paper" was deemed ideal for rice "slowly baked with a certain proportion of liquid, either by itself or mingled with meat, fish or fruit" (Acton 1855, 164). Similarly, oven-braising, where meat dishes prepared on the stovetop are transferred into the oven to finish cooking in a sealed dish, is offered as an alternative to stewing (Acton 1855, 165). In effect, these techniques could replace boiling, jugging, steaming and stewing on a stovetop, relieving the

Figure 7.4 Iron box oven in a recreated cottage kitchen at Sovereign Hill, Ballarat (hotplate not shown). Photo: Jacqueline Newling 2019.

need for the cook to ensure their pots would not boil dry. For safety, comfort and fuel-economy, roasting before a fire eventually gave way to baking in fully enclosed ranges.

The range of techniques employed by a cook would depend on their taste and skills (often derived from their social background or *habitus*, training or work experience), available time and financial means for requisite ingredients and equipment. Trade catalogues and some cookery texts provide extensive lists of equipment, or *batterie de cuisine*, but a variety of dishes and meals could be produced with a relatively few implements. English chef Alexis Soyer advises in *A Shilling Cookery for the People* (1854), that "nearly one half of the receipts" in the book could be "cooked to perfection" with a "[sauce]pan, grid-iron, and frying pan" (Soyer 1854, 174). A stove with oven and boiler was highly recommended. The lists of kitchen requisites in Beeton (1861, 31) and *The Commonsense Cookery Book* (NSW Cookery Teachers Association 1914) hardly vary in terms of pots, pans and basic utensils, but absent in the twentieth-century text is the need for a cinder-sifter, coal-shovel and bellows, which were necessary for hard-fuel cooking apparatus. Regardless, kitchens large and small provided numerous options for people to adapt their tastes and needs to the resources at hand, whether plentiful or constrained. As culinary artefacts, the scope and potential of historic kitchens can only be fully appreciated as the sum of their many parts, assemblages that include elements that are not materially evident.

Conclusion

Over time, kitchens have become safer and healthier spaces, and generally better integrated into the social areas in the home – coming the full circle if we consider small houses where the kitchen was part of the eating, working, recreational and sometimes sleeping area. Cooks continue to prove themselves resourceful and creative, adapting to changes in technology, and taking advantage of improved access to and affordability of an expanding variety of ingredients, education and health advice, and greater exposure to other cultures' cuisines and cooking styles.

Recalling the phrase, "the past is a foreign country: they do things differently there" (Hartley 1953), this chapter has attempted to fill in some of the gaps in reading and interpreting a colonial kitchen by illustrating some of the intangible aspects of large and small kitchens in culinary and social contexts. Much of the cooking we do today would be recognisable to colonial cooks – a baked dinner may have replaced the roast, but the barbeque is not a distant stretch from the grid-iron or spit, with direct exposure to a flame. Our forebears may be surprised that we are more likely to own a wok than a pudding cloth. We can assume they would envy the ease with which we can heat our stoves, and the relative speed at which we can prepare a meal. Even when we think we are cooking "from scratch", the food we purchase is partly or fully processed – cleaned and gutted, free of feathers and scales, and increasingly, skinned, deboned and filleted, perhaps marinated. Cuts of meat are smaller, as are the pots and pans we use to cook them (which also reflects a reduction in the number of residents in many households). These conveniences have obscured these once-standard operations, diminished our understanding of the processes involved, and our appreciation of the (mostly unseen) labour required for us to eat well. It comes as little surprise that kitchens from the past hold so much mystery for modern cooks and consumers. While attempting to make sense of colonial kitchens as historical artefacts and assemblages, this work by no means reduces the wonder that can be can found in those that survive.

Acknowledgements

This work was prepared on Wangal Country upon which I am privileged to live and work. I acknowledge that this land has never been ceded by Australian First Nations and pay respects to Elders past and present.

Much of my knowledge has been developed during my long-standing tenure at Museums of History NSW (MHNSW), formerly Sydney Living Museums/Historic Houses Trust NSW, as a house museum guide and then curator. This chapter has been produced independently, however, and does not necessarily reflect or represent the views of the institution.

I am indebted to the University of Sydney for travel grants for research in England and Virginia, USA, and Sydney Living Museums for sponsoring further research in America funded by the Ruth Pope Bequest.

I extend my thanks to the anonymous peer reviewers whose advice and recommendations have greatly added to the quality of this work.

References

Abbott, E. (1864). *The English and Australian cookery book, for the many as well as the upper ten thousand.* London: Samson, Low, Son and Marston.

Acton, E. (2003 [1855]). *Modern cookery for private families*, facsimile edition. East Sussex: Southover Press.

Acton, E. (1857). *The English bread-book for domestic use.* London: Longman, Brown, Green, Longmans, & Roberts. https://archive.org/details/b21531006.

Anon. (1857). *The home book of household economy: or, hints to persons of moderate income; containing useful directions for the proper labours of the kitchen, the house, the laundry, and the dairy; including the best receipts for pickling, preserving, home brewing, and also sick-room management and cookery.* London: G. Routledge & Co.

Anthony Hordern and Sons Ltd (1914). General catalogue. Sydney: Anthony Hordern and Sons. https://archive.org/details/Hordern15027.

Aspinall, C. (1862). *Three years in Melbourne.* London: L. Booth. https://archive.org/details/threeyearsinmelb00aspirich/mode/2up.

Baglin, E. and D. Baglin (1979). *Australian chimneys and cookhouses.* Sydney: Murray Child and Company.

Beeton, I. (1861). *Beeton's book of household management.* London: S.O. Beeton. https://archive.org/details/b20392758/mode/2up?

Beeton, I. (c. 1888). *Mrs Beeton's book of household management.* London: Ward, Lock and Co.

Benham and Sons (1868). Illustrated catalogue. London: Benham and Sons. https://archive.org/details/Benham14191.

Clive Lucas, Stapleton and Partners, Pty. Ltd (2008). Brickendon Conservation Management Plan, for Department of the Environment, Water, Heritage and the Arts.

Delroy, A. (1990). Domestic gas cooking appliances in metropolitan Perth, 1900–1950. *Western Australia Museum Records and Supplements*, 14(4): 461–81.

General Iron Foundry Company Limited (1862). *Drawings of ranges, stoves, pipes, ornamental and general castings made by the General Iron Foundry Company Limited.* London. https://archive.org/details/GenIron30636/page/n21/mode/2up.

McCubbin, F. (1896). *Kitchen at the old King Street bakery* accessed 6 March 2025. https://commons.wikimedia.org/wiki/File:Frederick_McCubbin_-_Kitchen_at_the_old_King_Street_Bakery,_1884.jpg.

Hartley, L.P. (1953). *The go-between.* London: Hamish Hamilton.

Haden, R. (2006). Australian history in the baking: the rebirth of a Scotch Oven. *Journal of Australian Studies*, 30(87): 61–73. DOI: 10.1080/ 14443050609388051.

Historic Houses Trust of NSW; Shar Jones and Michel Reymond (1983). *Monsieur Noufflard's house: watercolours by S.T. Gill, 1857.* https://first.mhnsw.au/#record/4742.

Leach, H. (2008). Translating the 18th century pudding. In F. Leach, G. Clark and S. O'Connor, eds. *Islands of inquiry: colonization, seafaring and the archaeology of maritime landscapes*, 29: 381–96. Canberra: ANU Press.

Lehmann, G. (2003). *The British housewife, cookery books, cooking and society in eighteenth-century Britain*. Totnes, UK: Prospect Books.

McGee, H. (2004). *On food and cooking, an encyclopedia of kitchen science, history and culture*. London: Hodden & Stoughten.

Muskett, P. (1893). *The art of living in Australia*. London: Eyre and Spottiswoode.

Newling, J. (2021). First Fleet fare: food and food security in the founding of colonial New South Wales, 1788–1790. Doctoral thesis, The University of Sydney, Sydney, NSW. https://hdl.handle.net/2123/24785.

NSW Cookery Teachers Association (1914). *The commonsense cookery book*. Sydney: Angus & Robertson.

Nylander, J. (1994). *Our own snug fireside: images of the New England home, 1760–1860*. New Haven, CT: Yale University Press; Alfred A. Knopf, Inc.

J.P. (1878). The ball at O'Squiffey's. *The Albury Banner and Wodonga Express,* 18 May, 18.

Pennell, S. (1998). Pots and pans history: the material cultural of the kitchen in early modern England. *Journal of Design History* 11(3): 201–16. Oxford University Press on behalf of Design History Society.

Pennell, S. (2016). *The Birth of the English Kitchen 1600–1850*. London: Bloomsbury.

Pierce, C. (1857). *The household manager: being a practical treatise upon the various duties in large or small establishments, from the drawing-room to the kitchen*. London; New York: Geo. Routledge & Co.

Rundell, M. (2009 [1816]). *A new system of domestic cookery*, facsimile edition. Bath, UK: Persephone Books [London: John Murray].

Sambrook, P.A. and P. Brears, eds (1993). *The country house kitchen*. The National Trust (UK). Stroud: Sutton Publishing Ltd.

Santich, B. (2012). *Bold palates*. Kent Town, SA: Wakefield Press.

Shepherd, S. (2000). *Pickled, potted and canned*. London: Headline Book Publishing.

Soyer, A. (1854). *A shilling cookery for the people,* London: Geo. Routledge & Co.

Wilson, C.A. (1973). *Food and drink in Britain*. London: Cookery Book Club.

Wilson, H. (1920). *Kitchen and fireplace at Berrima* [artwork]. National Library of Australia call number PIC Drawer 10571 #PIC/11872/104. http://nla.gov.au/nla.obj-147889358.

8

Food in bottles
What they can tell us

E. Jeanne Harris, Bronwyn Woff and Peter O'Donohue

Introduction

The art of preserving food dates back millennia. It enabled our ancestors – Indigenous and settlers alike – to take advantage of seasonal surges in production and times of plenty to plan for leaner periods, but it also allowed travellers to take food with them to sustain them on their journeys. By the time non-Indigenous settlers landed on Australian soil, they were well-versed in preserving methods and they brought these cultures and technologies with them. By the early nineteenth century, colonial communities in Australia were regularly supplied with familiar foods from their homelands. These new foodstuffs, introduced from around the world, relied on preservation and so there is a need to understand storage technologies as a critical component of early colonial food and foodways.

Importantly though, by analysing bottles from artefact assemblages closely, we can also understand the complexity of colonial Australians' food and dining experiences. Food and food experiences were shaped by a range of factors such as ethnicity, socio-economic status, change over time and location. Looking closely at bottle collections helps us to understand the food and food cultures across colonial Australia. In order to interrogate artefact collections fully, however, it is necessary to understand key issues around food preservation, change over time, emerging technologies and other cultural influences such as class and ethnicity. This chapter provides an outline of the range of issues that historical archaeologists should be aware of in order to meaningfully analyse bottle collections and optimise our understanding of food cultures in colonial Australia.

Central to understanding the role of bottles in food and foodways is to understand the importance of food preservation in the past. Food preservation technologies are varied, including smoking, salting, pickling, dehydration and a range of other techniques. Each of these techniques has its own associated range of tools and utensils. This chapter focuses on the use of bottles in food preservation and explores the range of types and uses in colonial Australia.

Colonial Australian dietary patterns ultimately had their roots in eighteenth- and nineteenth-century European cuisine and, in particular, traditions of Britain and Ireland. Goody (2019, 263) has argued that the British diet "went straight from medieval barbarity to industrial decadence during the eighteenth and nineteenth centuries". While the reality of this transition was more nuanced and phased than Goody implies, the rapid development of industrial preservation technologies and the role they played in colonisation and expansion of the Empire is undeniable. Critical factors in this transition were improvements in the mechanisation of preserving techniques, marketing and transportation. In Britain, commercially preserved foods did not reach the market until the 1830s due to their high price, but they soon became a critical part of the diet – and remain so to the present. By extension, these products also became an important part of colonial dietary patterns, where the tyranny of distance and a much warmer climate only served to increase their value and necessity.

It is also important to note that colonial Australian assemblages include a range of goods connected to Asian diaspora communities and their trade networks. The diverse range of preservation techniques represented by assemblages associated with Asian, and more specifically Chinese, communities will be explored in some detail below. These goods highlight the diversity of both the colonial Australian community and our food cultures from an early chapter post-colonisation.

Presented here is not a case study of food bottles from selected sites for comparative analysis. Rather, the aim is to provide a background of preserving technologies that contributed to the improved supply, quality and variety of foods available in the colonial market. Furthermore, this chapter gives the reader the tools needed to identify bottle forms and product content, and demonstrates how the interpretation of foodways contributes to identifying patterns in the colonial diet.

Glass and ceramic bottles represent the most durable packaging for many foodstuffs and are the primary commercial packaging found in the archaeological record. Archaeologists meticulously record data on the bottles recovered from excavations. They identify their form and function, manufacturing technologies and physical attributes. In most collections, alcohol bottles (wine, beer, whisky, gin/schnapps and other spirits) and soft drink bottles (aerated water, cordial and mineral water) represent most recovered glass and ceramic bottles. The results of artefact analyses often include beverage preferences, market access and socio-economic factors. However, beyond identifying the original contents of food bottles, little analysis of Australian collections generally addresses the interpretation of the cultural affiliation, lifestyles and dietary patterns of the people who used and discarded these bottles. Providing background on preserving technologies for food in bottles, identification of basic bottle forms and colonial dietary patterns serves as a foundation for archaeologists to build their interpretive analysis of foodways in a colonial setting.

Food storage and preservation in Australia

Refrigeration of foods was not available in Australia until 1839, when the shipment of iceblocks from North America (Canada and the United States) first arrived. This trade of natural ice continued until the 1860s, when James Harrison of Geelong developed a prototype based on an 1834 British design for vapour-compression refrigeration, which he patented in 1856 (Selinger 2013, 20; Roberts n.d., 11). In 1860, he formed The Sydney Ice Company, which brought patented ice to Sydney for the first time (Roberts n.d., 3). While the domestic refrigerator was yet to come, people in metropolitan areas could now have regular visits from the iceman, and ice chests became a fixture in many suburban homes. The first iceboxes were insulated wooden boxes lined with tin or zinc and used to hold iceblocks to keep the food cool (see also Chapter 7). A drip pan collected the meltwater – and had to be emptied daily.

In the absence of widespread refrigeration, colonial Australians needed to rely on a range of preservation techniques – some ancient in origin, while others harnessed the advantages of scientific and technological innovations of the nineteenth century. The preservation of foods has taken many forms over time. Preservation methods include drying, smoking, salting, fermenting, pickling in vinegar, dehydration, canning and freezing. When commercially packaged, evidence of these preservation methods is found within Australian contexts, but their representation at different points in time and in different regions was influenced by a range of factors, including demographics, cultural preference and tradition, and economic and technological developments. This section will briefly outline some of the major developments and influences on food preservation in the colonial period.

Perhaps the richest spread of preservation techniques is found within collections associated with Asian communities in Australia. Preservation methods for Asian foodstuffs in colonial contexts include pickling, drying, smoking, salting, sugaring, steeping and fermentation. All these preserving methods aim to remove the air and create an anaerobic environment for the storage of foods (Drummond and Wilbraham 1994, 313). Drying and smoking, two of the earliest methods, involved removing the moisture from vegetables and meats to limit microbial growth and spoilage (Metheny and Beaudry 2015, 7). Salt was also used as part of most preservation, including drying, smoking, dehydrating and pickling, by drawing the liquid out of food (Shephard 2000, 54). Chinese traditions incorporated elements of Chinese herbal medicines as antimicrobial agents into food preservation methods as well. Most common of these agents are spices – cinnamon, mustard, vanilla, clove and allspice – and some herbs – specifically oregano, rosemary, thyme, sage and basil – which all confer strong antimicrobial activity (Hintz et al. 2015, 1–2).

Many of the innovations in food preservation were also achieved out of the necessities of the times. For example, prior to the development of refrigeration, meat preservation was a major concern. This was true for all people, but the long distances, climate and distribution networks meant that meat preservation was particularly important for travellers, explorers and armed forces on the move in colonial Australia. In the 1840s, the fall in the price of meat from sheep produced a glut of freshly butchered meat in the Australian market. This prompted Sizar Elliot's rediscovery of tinned meat production, and the market for Australian tinned meats gained much success during the 1860s cattle plague in England (Shephard 2000, 243). Connected to this, commercial packaging of beef extract also began in the late 1840s, with Baron Justus von Liebig's portable soups. Von Liebig established his company in Uruguay, where vast quantities of Uruguayan and Argentinian beef were a by-product of the hide and leather industries (Shephard 2000, 173–5), selling the product under the name Bovril. The product became popular amongst travellers and explorers, such as Henry Morton Stanley, who reportedly took Bovril's meat extract on his 1865 African exploration and subsequently endorsed the product (Driver 1991, 134). However, the real commercial success of meat extracts was due to its successful promotion as a soup concentrate to the generals in the Franco-Prussian war (1870–1871) who were looking for a way to nourish the army while on the move (Shephard 2000, 173–5).

Over the course of the nineteenth century, ongoing improvement in food science also had an impact on preservation and, by extension, the categories of material culture that archaeologists find on sites. New and enhanced methods to store foods in sealed containers (bottles and tins) improved the anaerobic conditions needed for preservation and in turn changed the range of types and wares available. Preserving in glass bottles was first achieved in the late eighteenth century when Nicholas

Appert successfully developed a method that involved the exposure of food-filled glass bottles to a heated water bath or under steam pressure at temperatures of 116–121°C (240–250°F) (Drummond and Wilbraham 1994, 317; Gruetzmacher et al. 1948, 4; Shephard 2000, 229). Appert's development was in response to the need to supply wholesome foods to the French armed forces in battle; however, its application ultimately led to increased domestic and commercial food storage in bottles (Milner 2004, 30). Preserving foodstuffs in bottles in the home, also known as "canning", gained popularity by the mid-nineteenth century when improved closure methods were developed. The two most successful closures were the porcelain-lined zinc lid or the glass lid jointed by a rubber ring gasket (Arnold 1983, 6).

Bottle forms and materiality

Identifying common food-related bottle forms, their contents and their use in food preparation is the first step in analysing bottles as indicators of foodways. The majority of bottle forms identified as glass food containers are of European origin. Wooden casks and ceramic food containers found on colonial sites can be of both European and Chinese origins, again highlighting the diversity of both colonial communities and their distribution networks. This section charts the development of some of the main container forms found.

Global glassmaking history

Glass has been manufactured and used to make vessels for many thousands of years, and glass bottles are one of the most common objects found on historical archaeological sites (Smith 2008, 16–17). The use of glass for storage of everyday products accelerated from the seventeenth century as more shapes were created and standardisation of storage sizing occurred (Jones and Sullivan 1989, 2; Lerk 1971, 4). The prosperity triggered by the Industrial Revolution in England, and the relative affordability of increasingly mass-produced glass, had an impact on the increase in the presence of glass vessels in assemblages throughout the modern period (Vader and Murray 1975, 1).

Glass blowing was originally a highly skilled trade, where boys as young as 12 were taken on as apprentices to learn the skill over years (Handford Henderson 2016; Schulz 2016). Bottle and container making for food storage and other products remained a primarily handmade process into the late eighteenth century. Soon, advances in glass moulding methods took over the handmade process, eventually followed by semi-automatic and fully automatic bottle-making machines. These advancements increased the production capacity of factories, from one team making up to 200 dozen (2,400) bottles per day by hand (Handford Henderson 2016, 81) to at least double that with the introduction of the semi-automatic machine. The production rate increased a further 180 per cent with the introduction of the fully automatic machine (Miller and Sullivan 2016, 189). These advancements lowered the price of manufacturing as less-skilled workers were hired to run machines. The fully automatic system employed by bottle makers today finds its roots in the methods of the semi-automatic machines of the late nineteenth century and the fully automatic machines of the early 1900s.

Glassmaking in Australia

Before the late nineteenth century, very few glassmaking factories existed in Australia. Most often, bottles were ordered from overseas factories and shipped to the colonies empty, to be filled upon arrival (Smith 2008, 19). The first glass factory in Sydney is believed to be a short-lived one owned by Simeon Lord and Francis Williams, which opened in Pyrmont in 1812. The factory closed in 1813 due to clashes in staffing between workers and management (Jones 1979, 35). The first successful bottle manufacturer in Australia was J. Ross of Sydney (1867–1919). The first successful bottle manufacturer in Melbourne was Melbourne Glass Bottle Works Company, a firm owned by Felton and Grimwade. They were an established pharmaceutical and importer company (1866), but they opened the glassworks in 1872 due to supply and cost issues that were having an impact on the primary business. By the 1910s, Felton and Grimwade acquired and amalgamated several bottle works companies and formed the now well-known Australian Glass Manufacturers Company (Moloney 2012; Vader and Murray 197, 14).

Ceramic containers

As well as glass bottles and containers, commercial commodities were packaged in ceramic containers, pots and bottles made mainly from stoneware and earthenware. Plain brown utilitarian ceramics of Chinese origin are generally characterised as brown-glazed stoneware (CBGS). The vessels contained preserved foods and liquids from the southern areas of China, particularly from the Guangdong province, which is inland to the west of Hong Kong. Foodstuffs contained within these vessels were mainly vegetables, meats, sauces, oils, condiments and alcohol.

The different forms of the CBGS were indicative of their contents; the four most common types are wide-mouthed, shouldered jars (*Fut How Nga Peng*) for non-viscous foodstuffs; "tiger whiskey" (*Ng-Ka-Py* liquor) bottles (*Mao-Tai* or *Tsao Tsun*); spouted jars (*Nga Hu*) for liquids; and globular jars (*Ching*) for bulk shipment of liquids and preserved items (Figures 8.1 and 8.2).

Wide-mouthed shouldered jars were wheel formed, made of coarse grainy stoneware, usually 130 to 150 cm in height with unglazed bases.

Figure 8.1 Chinese utilitarian vessels: (L) wide-mouthed shouldered jar, (M) spouted jar, (R) liquor jar. Photo: authors.

Figure 8.2 Large globular jar. Photo: authors.

Figure 8.3 Ceramic marmalade pots. Photo: authors.

Liquor bottles were made from finer clay, formed in moulds in three separate pieces, then joined together; they are 155 to 160 mm in height. Spouted jars are 130 to 140 mm in height with wheel-formed bases joined to mould-formed top sections and unglazed bases. Globular jars vary in height from 280 to 360 mm. They were probably completely wheel formed; they have lugs on the shoulders for securing capping pieces (Muir, 2003).

There is a high degree of standardisation in the forms of these CBGS, suggesting that their manufacture was to a basic design for each form, repeated across large numbers of independent potters. The firing of the ceramic containers was predominantly done in large "Dragon" kilns. The size of the containers ranged from 10 cm to over 1 m in height, with corresponding variations in their diameters and wall thicknesses. Correct placement in the kilns was critical to ensure proper firing temperatures of between 1100 and 1300 degrees Celsius was achieved to produce a stoneware ceramic.

The primary commercial use for ceramic bottles of European origin was for the stoneware packaging of beverages; however, foods, such as condiments, were also packaged in earthenware pots and jars for shipment to Australia from European sources (Figure 8.3). Most ceramic storage vessels recovered in Australia are either salt-glazed or Bristol-glazed stoneware (Brooks 2005b, 33). While the Bristol-glazed bottles and jars were mostly imported from Britain, salt-glazed containers were made in the colonies from the early nineteenth century. During the 1820s, the introduction and instant popularity of locally manufactured ginger beer and spruce beer led to an increased demand for bottles (Figure 8.4). As there were no successful glass bottle manufacturers in Australia, the increased demand for bottles

Figure 8.4 Stoneware ginger beer bottle. Photo: authors.

was filled by local potters (Ford 1995, 27). Prior to this, potters had been mainly producing utilitarian wares. The first successful stoneware bottle manufacturer is regarded as Sydney's Jonathan Leak, who started a stoneware bottle tradition that was followed by other Sydney potters, including Thomas Field (1846–1880) and Enoch Fowler (Ford 1995).

Wooden casks

It is important to note that other materials were used to store foods and beverages. Certain products manufactured overseas were often transported to Australia in bulk containers such as wooden barrels and casks. Sizing produced by coopers ranged from the largest, called a "tun" (252 gallons = 954 litres) to the smallest, called a "pin" (4 gallons = 15 litres). All types of foods were transported in these large containers, from salted meats to beverages and dry foods like grains. Once these commodities arrived in Australia, the bulk products were often decanted into smaller volumes or, in the case of alcohol, were transported to the venue at which they would be sold.

Bottle availability and reuse

In the eighteenth early to mid-nineteenth centuries, bottles were seen as a product and commodity themselves, rather than simply packaging as they are seen today. Australian-based product manufacturers ordered bottles from overseas bottle manufacturers, however, high transport costs and long wait times for bottles to arrive made it difficult to acquire new bottles (Woff 2014; 2019). The few Australian-made bottles were a poorer quality product than those manufactured overseas,

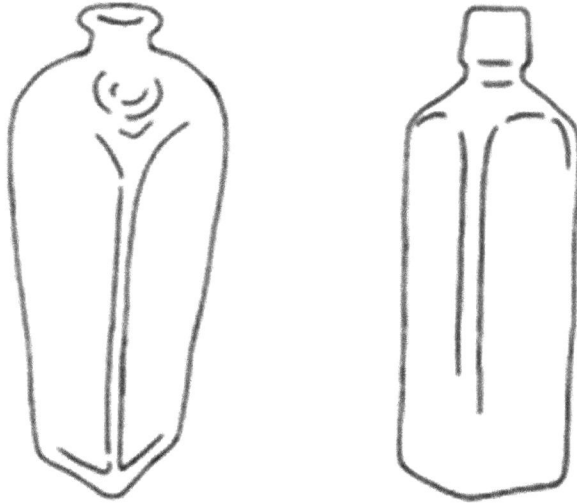

Figure 8.5 Late eighteenth to twentieth century gin/schnapps bottles. Illustration: E. Jeanne Harris.

and product manufacturers preferred not to use them. This changed in the late nineteenth century, with the decrease in the number of imports received from Britain due in part to what is known as "The Long Depression" (1870s–1890s). In the 1890s, glass factories in Melbourne and Sydney were working around the clock to keep up with the demand (Graham and Graham 1981, 56; Lucas 2002, 10).

As bottles were seen as owned by the product manufacturer who bought them, they were expected to be returned after being emptied to be washed and reused (Ellis and Woff 2017; 2014, 11–26; 2019). However, this did not always occur and caused enough stress to product manufacturers that in The *Australian Brewers' Journal,* they labelled this issue "The Bottle Question". Brewers in this journal discussed instances of loss, breakages and use by other manufacturers, and attempted to seek solutions (*Australian Brewers' Journal* 1887, 8; Ellis and Woff 2017). Despite this system increasing the use-life of bottles up to decades (Adams 2003; Busch 1987, 68), the quantities of bottles available in the Australian colonies were still less than the demand required by product manufacturers (Graham and Graham 1981, 56; Lucas 2002, 10).

Adding to this problem was the issue of ownership, with embossing not becoming popular worldwide until the 1840s (Boow 1991, 1), although this continued to be prohibitively expensive into the late nineteenth century. Often, manufacturers could not justify adding this cost to the already high price of bottles (Woff 2014, 44; 2019). They used paper labels pasted to bottles to denote their ownership and advertise their product; however, once these were removed, it was impossible to tell who the un-embossed bottles belonged to (Woff 2014; 2019).

Figure 8.6 Late eighteenth to early nineteenth century British types. Illustration: E. Jeanne Harris.

Additionally, product manufacturers were using whichever bottles they could acquire, and consequently, bottles were being used for products other than those they were intended for. Archaeological examples include case bottles usually used for gin and schnapps being used to hold medicines (Crook and Murray 2006), sarsaparilla and rum (Carney 1998), paint tint and cordial (Carney 1998) (Figures 8.5 and 8.6). These documented cases of bottles reused for other products highlight the need for reuse to be considered when analysing historical and archaeological collections (Boow 1991, 24; Woff 2014; 2019).

Eventually, manufacturers offered to pay for returned bottles and in response, began charging for bottles sold with their product inside. During the early 1800s, empty wine bottles were sold for as much as six shillings per dozen, and by the 1850s were still being sold for four shillings per dozen (Boow 1991, 24). In comparison, an average labourer's weekly wage in the early 1800s was five shillings (Boow 1991, 24), preserved fruit and pickles cost as much as five shillings per bottle (Boow 1991, 18), and in the 1850s, eggs were seen as a luxury item, costing about four shillings per dozen (Biagi 2019; *Argus* 1856, 4).

Similarly, secondary and adaptive reuse of Chinese, brown-glazed stoneware (CBGS) frequently occurred. According to oral histories collected in the USA in the early years of the twentieth century (Hellman and Yang 1997), jars were reused for storage, cooking and rainwater collection – they were the Chinese equivalent of the traditional "Mason" preserving jar or, more recently, disposable containers that are reused for storage purposes. The final disposal of a CBGS jar could have been immediate or occurred years after its functional utility had been exhausted.

The standardisation of glaze, form and sizes over many centuries in China makes it difficult to date CBGS by typology or evolution of a form.

Bottle forms and functions

Over time, archaeologists have created an association between bottle shapes and their uses, and these relationships are applied to artefacts from historical archaeology collections. Within archaeology, such associations began in North American archaeological discussions (Brooks 2005a). These associations have been and continue to be influenced and informed by the language of bottle collectors and other interested parties (Vader and Murray 1975, 2).

At its most basic level, form refers to what the object is, i.e. "bottle". Categorisation of bottle forms may be recorded using descriptors for shape such as "beer bottle". Function refers to the use of the bottle, such as "food storage" (Brooks 2005a). It is important to note that some forms existed that were used for a range of things, especially panelled light green and light blue bottles, which were used for foods, medicines and a range of other domestic and personal products, and so cannot be ascribed to a specific function (Woff 2014; 2019). Archaeologists and artefact specialists use form and function as interconnected ways to identify, describe, record, interpret and assign meaning to objects within historical archaeology collections. Form and function are ascribed by identifying particular profiles and characteristics of bottles, such as the colour, shape, style or decoration. These are used to identify and characterise a collection so that the information we record can be further interrogated, analysed and interpreted. Although form and function seem like straightforward ways to classify bottles, issues arise where these methods are solely used to identify objects (Brooks 2005a), including bottles. Due to the multitude of options for products contained within bottles, understanding the ways in which humans use and reuse objects along with further context about the excavation site and the people who interacted with this place are required to ensure that the interpretation of a collection of bottles or a broader archaeological collection can be as correct as possible. This approach can be seen in Carney's 1998 article "A Cordial Factory in Parramatta, New South Wales".

Dietary patterns

Whether free settlers or transported convicts, European immigrants in colonial Australia were predominately from Britain and Ireland. Throughout Europe, each of the distinct nations, cultures and regions had their own food traditions and practices, although there were also shared tenets and common staples that underpinned food and foodways. Many of these traditions came with these immigrant communities to Australia, although once here, the availability of foodstuffs, supply, climate and shared experience meant that some food practices were maintained (and remain part of Australian food cultures today), while others ceased in a new environment and context. Gradually, the diet of immigrant communities expanded and adapted to include locally available foodstuffs, such as *Smilax glycophylla* plant, whose leaves were brewed for "sweet tea" and whose red berries provided much-needed vitamin C to cure scurvy (Davey et al. 1977, 32–3), and meat obtained from local fauna such as kangaroo. According to Newling (2021, 150), "Some local resources were adopted more readily than others, for reasons including familiarity, taste, perceived health benefits, availability and accessibility and compatibility with culinary and cultural practices, or habitus". There was also variability in habits for how foods were stored, prepared, and consumed (Wood 1977, xi).

The food patterns of the colonists were also reflected in the condiments and foods they used in the preparation and consumption of meals. Evidence of commercially packaged food products is found in the bottle assemblages recovered from archaeological sites. Some condiments (i.e. salt and oil) have such wide-ranging use in cuisines of all cultures that they contribute little to the interpretation of dietary patterns. Other condiments and foods (vinegar, sauces, potted meats, meat drinks, coffee, milk) provide an opportunity to understand how these foods were used in Australian cuisine and provide insight into dietary habits during colonial times. The following products represent some of the main foods and condiments found in glass bottles from archaeological contexts. They are discussed in relation to how they were made and how they were used in the preparation, service and consumption of foods, and other day-to-day uses.

Vinegar

Vinegar was ubiquitous in colonial cuisine. It was one of the staples in the First Fleet's weekly ration, with each convict receiving 1/4 pint of vinegar, which was thought to prevent scurvy (Davey et al. 1977, 25). Early colonists also brought with them the preferences for foodstuffs preserved in vinegar. Preserving in vinegar gained prominence in Britain during the sixteenth century, replacing salting as a preservative, initially to meet the need for more nutritious foods for sea travel. As the population moved towards urban centres, the need to preserve foodstuffs for transport increased.

Vinegar making is a culinary process that is probably as old as brewing alcoholic beverages, and is a powerful preservative commonly used to promote fermentation (Shephard 2000, 85). Fermentation is "a natural process by which yeast or bacteria feed off sugars to produce alcohol or lactic acid" (Metheny and Beaudry 2015, 208). Fermentation as a process for food preservation has been used since before recorded times. This fermentation process, typically called "pickling", preserved various foods, such as vegetables, fruits, meats and eggs in liquid-tight vessels such as stoneware and glass containers. Vinegar also figured prominently in colonial dishes. Recipes in *The English and Australian Cookery Book,* considered the first Australian cookbook, often included vinegar as an ingredient in the preparation of savoury pies and puddings, sauces and gravies (Abbott 1864). Popular in many Victorian Era British and Australian households was *The Book of Household Management* (Beeton 1861). It included an extensive recipe section, and besides the use of vinegar for pickling (preservation), vinegar was often an ingredient used in the preparation of meats, salads, sauces and flavoured vinegars used to enhance taste. Therefore, it is not unusual that vinegar is an oft-found ingredient in Australian cookery.

Medicinal uses of vinegar were numerous and varied. Doses of vinegar were used to treat scurvy cases, especially on ships during the voyage to the colonies (Clements 1986, 30). It also figures prominently in concoctions to counteract poisons (Beeton 1861, 1080). Topically, vinegar was used as an eyewash, in poultices and diluted in baths to reduce fever.

Non-corrosive and heat-resistant properties make glass bottles the ideal receptacles for storing vinegar and foodstuffs preserved in vinegar (Shephard 2000, 189) (Figure 8.7). Once the colonies were stably established, settlers began to process their own vinegar for the preservation of foods. However, an 1885 article in the *South Australian Register* (1885, 6) entitled "Colonial and Imported Vinegars" was a comparative assessment of the quality of colonial vinegar in relation to those imported from Great Britain. Colonial vinegars used in this assessment were mainly those from South Australia, including Seppelts, Lomes, Barton and Co, and Waverley Vinegar Works. Imported vinegars include those made by Champion, Crosse and Blackwell, Potts, and Hill, Evans and Co. The author's findings suggest that colonial vinegars, except those made by Seppelts, were all inferior to British vinegars and too weak to be used for pickling. Furthermore, vinegar for pickling is only about half the strength of ordinary vinegar. This weakness of colonial vinegars may account for the continued popularity of imported vinegars in the colonial market throughout much of the nineteenth century.

Chutneys

The term chutney is applied to anything preserved in sugar and vinegar and generally includes fruits, vegetables and/or herbs (Figure 8.8). English chutney is a strong-tasting condiment based on Indian cuisine, used to enhance the flavour of dishes. First introduced into the British diet by eighteenth-century officials returning from postings in India, chutney was gradually adapted to the British palette and had peak popularity during the mid-nineteenth century (Rolfson 2017, 3–4). Evidence of

Figure 8.7 Champion vinegar bottle. Photo: authors.

Figure 8.8 Pickle/chutney jar. Photo: authors.

this popularity is demonstrated by the variety of chutney recipes listed in cookery books of the time (Abbott 1864; Beeton 1861).

Sauces

During the nineteenth century, Australian dietary patterns were characterised by a preponderance of meat (Clements 1986, 34) due to an abundance of fresh and inexpensive meat as a by-product of the wool industry and increasing numbers of cattle ranches in the 1850s (Ashcroft 1977, 14). In British culinary tradition of the period, sauces accompanied most meat dishes, so they naturally became a significant part of Australian colonial cuisine. This traditional dietary pattern dates back to the British cuisine of the Middle Ages when meats were never eaten dry (Beeton 1861, 118). Most prominent by the colonial period was the "one sauce of England" (Acton 1859, 105), which consisted of melted butter thickened with egg yolks or cream (Freeman 1989, 124). Fish sauce was also a favourite, with its own long history in English cuisine. Initially, fish sauces were a culinary solution to preserving fish in hot, humid climates (Smith 1998, 299). In the colonial period "English ketchup" (also, catsup) was not a tomato-based condiment but a homemade spiced vinegar and anchovy sauce (Sydney Living Museum, n.d.). The English first encountered this condiment during their seventeenth-century settlement in Sumatra (today known as Indonesia) (Smith 1998, 302). This condiment's first successful commercial development was Lee and Perrin's Worcestershire sauce during the nineteenth century. At the time, the main ingredient of Worcestershire sauce was soy sauce with other ingredients including anchovies, shallots, garlic, tamarind, salt and vinegar (Shurtleff and Aoyagi 2012, 5). Worcestershire sauce was served with fish, hot and cold meats, steaks, gravies, soup, etc. By the 1850s, Lee and Perrin's sauce was distributed worldwide and was eventually imitated by others, such as English firm Holbrooks from 1872 and Australian firm Neumans from 1909 – who also imitated the Lee and Perrin's bottle shape (Figure 8.9). Bottled sauces, such as Worcestershire sauce, were a staple condiment in Australian households, with many consuming more than a bottle of sauce each week (Walker and Roberts 1988, 64).

Potted meats/spreads

Meats and fish are kept longer if mashed into a paste and/or potted. The concept of potted meats evolved from the ever-popular pastry pie-cased dish of the seventeenth century. As a mainstay of "pocket foods", the meat pie had one shortcoming – the lack of preservation. Consequently, by the mid-1600s, the pastry crust gave way to the earthenware pot. Earthenware pots could be sealed by a layer of oil, butter or fat, making them airtight and watertight,

Figure 8.9 Worcestershire sauce bottle. Photo: authors.

resulting in potted meats becoming a viable foodstuff for seasonal preservation, travellers and transported military (Shephard 2000, 182). This method is still used in modern preservation and commercial packaging of meats and fish, generally sold in metal or glass containers.

The process of potting meats was often an in-home activity. This is especially true in colonial Australia, where there was an abundance of meat. Potted meats were also sold by the local grocer and while they did not publish advertisements for the sale of potted meats, there are numerous accounts of theft and/or shoplifting noted in newspapers throughout the colonies (*Tasmanian and Austral-Asiatic Review* 1845, 3). Imported potted meats from European companies, such as in England

Figure 8.10 Strasbourg paté de foie gras pot lid from the University of South Australia's City West Learning Centre Site, Adelaide (Harris 2013, 38).

and France, were also sold and advertised (*Sydney Morning Herald* 1847, 4; *Argus* 1853, 5); most advertised of these was Strasbourg paté de foie gras (Figure 8.10).

Fish paste bottles are a commodity commonly found in the archaeological record. Fish paste was a common household condiment made by pounding fish and mixing with butter (or other fat) and various spices, including mace, cayenne and nutmeg (Beeton 1861, 226; Monro 1922, 202). Common fish pastes include anchovy, herring kippers, salmon and prawns. While often made in the home, commercially potted fish pastes, such as essence of anchovies, were available during the early 1800s. An early imported fish paste to Australia was Fine Yarmouth's bloater paste, which was first advertised in Hobart in 1837 (*The Hobart Town Courier* 1837, 1). An often-found commercial fish paste jar in the Australian/ New Zealand archaeological collection is Peck's (Figure 8.11). Peck's large-scale commercial packaging began in the 1890s and was a common commodity in an Australian pantry from the early 1900s (Australian Food History Timeline, n.d.).

Meat drinks

Beef extract is a nineteenth-century food preservation innovation that served to advance food storage technology. As mentioned earlier in this chapter, Baron Justus

Figure 8.11 Examples of common fish paste bottles: (L) Peck's; (R) unspecified. Photo: authors.

von Liebig successfully developed commercially packaged beef extract in the 1860s, which was subsequently sold as "invalid soup" under the trademark Bovril (Shephard 2000, 175) (Figure 8.12). While advertised as a means to rebuild muscle strength in the infirm, twentieth-century research indicates that the only beneficial ingredients were the essential ingredients (B vitamins, riboflavin and nicotinic acid) that, in combination, served to stimulate the flow of gastric juices, promote appetite and be a digestive aid (Shephard 2000, 174).

Coffee

Coffee was introduced to Europe and North America about the same time as tea, however, coffee was far more affordable than tea (Ellis 2004, 123–4). The first British coffee house was opened in London in 1652 by a Turkish merchant and was an instant success. Soon after, coffee houses sprang up throughout the country (Drummon and Wilbraham 1994, 116). The last two decades of the nineteenth century saw Australian "Coffee Palaces" established. Modelled on the European and North American coffee house, these businesses were temperance hotels that served no alcohol (Denby 2002, 174).

Instant coffee for in-home consumption, in the form of a cordial concentrate, was available in the 1820s but was an imported luxury, so much so that the theft of two dozen bottles of expensive coffee essence was reported among the items

Figure 8.12 Bovril's beef extract bottle. Photo: authors.

taken from the household stores of Mr R. Howe's Sydney residence (*The Sydney Gazette and New South Wales Advertiser* 1827, 3). The development of Symington's Essence of Coffee and Chicory in 1882 provided a convenience food. Symington's concentrate allowed for coffee in a minute by adding the product to boiling water (Figure 8.13).

Dairy

Milk and cream are both beverages and condiments used to prepare culinary dishes. The history of dairy in Australia began with the colonisation of New South Wales in 1788, which included plans to establish a dairy. These plans were thwarted shortly after landing when the four cows and one bull escaped and were not recovered until years later in 1795 (Clements 1986, 32). The first commercial dairies were established in the early 1800s, and included Dr John Harris' Ultimo dairy (1805) and the Van Diemen's Land Company dairy/factory (1820s). Hindered by the nineteenth century's slow transport methods and the lack of refrigeration, "loose" milk was only sold locally. In the 1890s, the introduction of pasteurisation improved milk preservation; however, commercially bottled milk was not generally available until the 1920s (Farrer 2001, 100). Until the mid-1940s, milk was mainly served

Figure 8.13 Symington Essence of Coffee and Chicory bottle. Photo: authors.

at the local shop from 20-gallon cans into household containers provided by the buyer (Kameny 2008, 20).

Chinese dietary patterns

Thus far, the discussion of dietary patterns has focused on foodstuffs consumed by the predominant Australian population of European heritage. The nineteenth-century migration of Chinese people throughout the Pacific Rim represents one of the world's largest population movements (Voss and Allen 2008, 6). By the 1860s, there were approximately 40,000 Chinese immigrants in the Australian colonies, most of which had arrived to prospect in the goldfields, and comprised 3.8 per cent of the colonial population.

Spier's study of shipping invoices identified more than 130 specific Chinese foodstuffs that were imported into the USA in the mid-nineteenth century. The list of items includes:

> oranges, pumelos [sic], dry oyster, shrimps, cuttlefish, mushrooms, dry bean curd, bamboo shoots, narrow-leaved greens, yams, ginger, sugar rice, sweetmeats, sausage, dry duck, eggs, dry fruit, salt ginger, salt eggs . . . tea oil, dry turnips, beetle nut, orange skins, kumquat, duck liver, melon seed, dried duck kidneys, minced turnips, shrimp soy, chestnut flour, birds' nests, fish fins, arrowroot, tamarind, dried persimmons, dried guts, bean sauce, lily seed, beche de mer, Salisburia seed, taro, and seaweed (Spier 1958, 80).

A similar range of food products likely made their way to Australia. The range of products provided diverse flavourful additions to colonial fare, while also supplementing vitamin and mineral intake.

CBGS vessels, discussed earlier in this chapter, are a type of consumer product that is an aspect of foodways evidencing "culturally distinctive performances of status and social relations" (Mullins 2011, 138). The sharing of food may also have drawn the Chinese diaspora community closer together in the face of marginalisation as the products were uniquely Chinese and reinforced significant elements of cultural identity. Chapter 6 outlines the importance of roast pork and feasting in diaspora identity, but it is important to recognise that assemblages associated with imported products may also have been a focal point for community and cultural practice. The foods in CBGS allowed the Chinese to maintain pre-existing foodways and dietary habits along cultural lines. For the Chinese, it was traditionally important to maintain a balance not only between *fan* (starch) and *ts'ai* (meat and vegetables) in their culinary practices but also by providing "hot" and "cold" humoured foods in balanced proportions (Chang 1977, 6–7). Adding preserved, fermented and pickled foods allowed the maintenance of the enduring principles necessary for constructing a healthy meal.

The importation of CBGS and their associated contents was part of a complex trade network that operated within and outside the primary European transportation networks in Australia, New Zealand, the USA and Canada. Originating as they did in mainland China, both the contents and the containers would have had a long journey to their recipients, passing through the hands of farmers, potters, manufacturers, merchants, cargo handlers, entrepreneurs and middlemen along routes that included traffic by foot, cart, wagon, ship, pack animal and railroad.

Table 8.1 Relative frequencies of condiment bottles recovered from Parramatta households and the Red Cow Hotel.

Condiment	8 Parramatta Households (%)	Red Cow Hotel (%)
oil/vinegar	39.5	25.0
pickle/chutney	48.5	35.4
sauce	8.6	25.0
soy sauce	1.9	0.0
fish paste	1.5	4.2

Discussion

Bottles and bottle fragments are common finds on historical archaeological sites. Archaeologists exert considerable energy to measure and date these, but it is critical to remember that they represent an important part of the food cultures of colonial Australia and so we need to understand them in this wider context. This chapter provides the background and tools needed for archaeologists to assess bottles in artefact collections more holistically and to understand their role in food culture. To do this, we need to understand contextual matters such as the background history of preserving methods, improved bottling technologies and an introduction to uses of package commodities. This context contributes to our understanding of the range of factors that influence dietary patterns, such as market access, ethnicity and socio-economic status of individuals, households and communities.

Engaging with the nature of the site also helps us to understand how and why certain preserves were being eaten in different locations and can shed light on the nuanced dining experiences of people in the past. Artefact collections show us that the patterns of meals consumed in a private residence varied considerably from those enjoyed in a public house or hotel. For example, a comparative study of condiment bottles from nineteenth-century Parramatta, NSW, households (Harris 2021) with a Penrith, NSW, hotel of the same period (Harris 2005, 4) indicates that while the types of condiments used in both settings were the same, there was a considerably higher relative frequency of sauces such as Worcestershire and tomato found in the hotel assemblage (Table 8.1). Combined with other data from these artefact collections, such as cuts of meats or table-service forms, these results may establish differences in dietary patterns between the two settings. This helps us to understand the varied experiences of dining during the nineteenth century, and with the benefit of historical records, we can more fully appreciate colonial food cultures in their entirety.

There is a possibility of a multi-cultural household, perhaps with servants who dine separately and have a different dietary pattern than their employers. Additional research is essential before drawing any conclusions regarding the constituents of the household. For example, Chinese export porcelain tableware and CBGS food-storage bottles were in the artefact collection from a wealthy household on Hindley Street, Adelaide, SA (Harris 2013, 45–6). However, several factors led to inconclusive results as to whether the household included Chinese servants. First, from the eighteenth century, Chinese export porcelain was inexpensive utilitarian ware. The East India Company's trade monopoly on the Indo-Pacific region and the colony's rising needs for such commodities contributed to the increased presence of this ware in the colonial market (Staniforth and Nash 1998, 5). Therefore, Chinese export porcelain in the artefact collection was not necessarily indicative of a Chinese presence in the household. The association of the CBGS bottles was clouded by the fact that there was an early concentration of small Chinese businesses east of the project area, including a general importer and a tea importer. Whilst there are no documented Chinese residents within the project area, the presence of ceramics of Chinese origin suggests some interaction between European and Asian factions of the community (Harris 2013, 45–6).

Conclusions

The purpose of this chapter is to emphasise the importance of identifying food bottles and understanding foodways as foundational steps to further our understanding of dietary patterns. These tools, considered with historical documentation, contribute to an understanding of foodways and aid the interpretation of the complex nature of colonial Australia's food and dining experiences.

One of the first steps presented is a discussion of common food bottles and their intended contents. Assigning a date to a bottle, which is achieved by researched data on documented manufacturing techniques, bottle manufacturers or products, follows bottle form and is useful as an aid in its placement in the documented timeline for a site. Once these steps have been achieved, analysis of a bottle collection can lead to an understanding of who the bottles belonged to and their food and dining habits. Food bottles can assist in the interpretation of dietary patterns, cultural affiliation and, to some extent, the status of the people associated with these bottles. A main use for data generated for a collection of bottles is that it can contribute to a comparative analysis with other collections. This includes comparison of similar site collections, such as the example of Parramatta and Penrith condiment bottles, or a comparison with historical documentation, such as the example of CBGS bottles and Chinese residents and business.

References

Abbott, E. (1864). *The English and Australian cookery book*. London: Sampson Low, Son and Marston.

Acton, E. (1859). *Modern cookery*. London: Longman, Brown, Green and Longmans.

Adams, W.H. (2003). Dating historical sites: the importance of understanding time lag in the acquisition, curation, use, and disposal of artifacts. *Historical Archaeology* 37(2): 38–64.

Argus (1856). The Melbourne produce market, 21 January, 4. http://nla.gov.au/nla.news-article4828753.

Arnold, K. (1983). *Australian preserving and storage jars pre-1920*. Bendigo, VIC: D.G. Walker.

Arnold, K. (1990). *A Victorian thirst*. Bendigo, VIC: Crown Castleton.

Arnold, K. (1991). *Australian glass, 1900–1950: valuation guide*. Maiden Gully, VIC: Crown Castleton Publishers.

Ashcroft, E. (1977). Introduction. In B. Wood, ed. *Tucker in Australia*. Melbourne: Hill of Content.

Australian Food History Timeline (n.d.). *Australian Food Timeline*, accessed 8 February 2021. https://australianfoodtimeline.com.au/pecks-pastes-australia/.

Australian Brewers' Journal 1887 (1882–1921), Melbourne.

Baugher-Perlin, S. (1982). Analysing glass bottles for chronology, function, and trade networks. In R.S. Dickens, Jr., ed. *Archaeology of urban America: the search for pattern and process*. New York: Academic Press.

Beeton, I. (1861). *Beeton's book of household management*. London: S.O. Beeton.

Biagi, C. (2019). In for a penny, in for a pound: faunal analysis of the Jones Lane Archaeological Precinct, Honours thesis, Archaeology Department, La Trobe University, Bundoora.

Boow, J. (1991). *Early Australian commercial glass: manufacturing processes*. Sydney: The Heritage Council of NSW.

Brooks, A. (2005a). Observing formalities – the use of functional artefact categories in Australian historical archaeology. *Australasian Historical Archaeology* 23: 7–14.

Brooks, A. (2005b). *An archaeological guide to British ceramics in Australia*. The Australasian Society for Historical Archaeology and La Trobe University Archaeology Program.

Busch, J. (1987). Second time around: a look at bottle reuse. *Historical Archaeology* 26: 67–80.

Carney, M. (1998). A cordial factory in Parramatta, New South Wales. *Australasian Historical Archaeology* 16: 80–93.

Chang, K.C., ed. (1977). *Food in Chinese culture: anthropological and historical perspectives.* New Haven, CT: Yale University Press.

Clements, F. (1986). *A history of human nutrition in Australia.* Melbourne: Longman Cheshire.

Crook, P. and T. Murray (2006). *An archaeology of institutional refuge: the material culture of the Hyde Park Barracks, Sydney 1848–1886.* Sydney: Historical Houses Trust of New South Wales.

Davey, L., M. MacPherson and F.W. Clements (1977). The hungry years 1788–1792. In B. Wood, ed. *Tucker in Australia.* Melbourne: Hill of Content.

Denby, E. (2002). *Grand hotels: reality and illusion.* London: Reaktion Books.

Drummond, J.C. and A. Wilbraham (1994). *The Englishman's food: a history of five centuries of English diet.* London: Pimlico.

Ellis, A. and B. Woff (2017). bottle merchants at A'Beckett Street, Melbourne (1875–1914): new evidence for the light industrial trade of bottle washing. *International Journal of Historical Archaeology* 22(1): 6–26.

Ellis, M. (2004). *The coffee house: a cultural history.* London: Weidenfeld & Nicolson.

Farrer, K.T.H. (2001). Food technology. In *Technology in Australia 1788–1988.* Melbourne: Australian Academy of Technological Sciences and Engineering. https://www.austehc.unimelb.edu.au/tia/100.html.

Freeman, S. (1989). *Mutton and oysters: the Victorians and their food.* London: Victor Gollancz.

Ford, G. (1985). *Australian pottery: the first 100 years.* Wodonga, Victoria: Salt Glaze Press.

Goody, J. (2019). Industrial food: towards the development of a world cuisine. In A. Julier, C. Counihan and P. Van Esterik, eds. *Food and culture*, 263–82. New York: Routledge.

Graham, M. and D. Graham (1981). *Australian glass of the 19th and early 20th century.* Sydney: David Ell Press.

Gruetzmacher, L.C., T. Onsdorff and M. Mack (1948). *Canning for home food preservation.* Corvallis, OR: Oregon State System of Higher Education, Federal Cooperative Extension Service, Oregon State College.

Handford Henderson, C. (2016). Glassmaking: III – The evolution of a glass bottle. In P. Schultz, R. Allen, B. Lindsey and J.K. Schulz, eds. *Baffle marks and pontil scars: a reader on historic bottle identification*, 71–89. Germantown, MD: Society for Historical Archaeology.

Harris, E.J. (2021). Cleanliness is next to Godliness: the influence of Victorian values on health concerns in nineteenth-century Parramatta, NSW. PhD thesis, University of New South Wales, Armidale.

Harris, E.J. (2013). *UniSA City West Learning Centre Site, Adelaide, SA: Analysis of Artefacts.* Report to Austral Archaeology Pty Ltd.

Harris, E.J. (2005). *Specialist Glass Report: Red Cow Inn and Penrith Plaza, Penrith.* Report to Casey and Lowe Pty Ltd, Leichhardt.

Hellman, V.R. and J.K. Yang (2007). Previously undocumented Chinese artifacts. In M. Praetzellis and A. Praetzellis, eds. *Historical archaeology of an overseas Chinese community in Sacramento, California; Volume 1: Archaeological Excavations.* Rohnert Park, CA: Anthropological Studies Center Sonoma State University Academic Foundation, Inc.

Hintz, T., K.K. Matthews and R. Di (2015). The use of plant antimicrobial compounds for food preservation. *BioMed Research International*, 1–12. DOI: 10.1155/2015/246264.

Hobart Town Courier (1837). Advertising, 8 September, 1.

Jones, D. (1979). *One hundred thirsty years: Sydney aerated water manufacturers from 1830 to 1930.* Deniliquin, NSW: Reliance Press.

Jones, O. and C. Sullivan (1989). *The Parks Canada Glass Glossary for the description of containers, tableware, flat glass and closures.* Ottawa: Environment Canada.

Kameny, R. (2008). *Australian milk and cream bottles and dairy related items.* Bendigo, VIC: Crown Castleton Publishers.

Lerk, J.A. (1971). *Bottles in Australian collections.* Bendigo, VIC: J.A. Lerk.

Lucas, L. (2002). Glass bottle recycling in Victoria. Honours thesis, Archaeology Program, La Trobe University, Melbourne.

Metheny, K.B. and M. Beaudry (2015). *Archaeology of food: an encyclopedia.* New York: Rowman & Littlefield.

Miller, G. and C. Sullivan (2016). Machine-made glass containers and the end of production for mouth-blown bottles. In P. Schultz, R. Allen, B. Lindsey and J.K. Schulz, eds. *Baffle marks and pontil scars: a reader on historic bottle identification*, 189–204. Germantown, MD: Society for Historical Archaeology.

Milner, M. (2004). Fruit jars…a history worth remembering. *Bottles and Extras*, winter(2): 30–3.

Moloney, D. (2012). *A history of the Melbourne glass bottle works site including its industrial context: Spotswood, Victoria.* Report to Museum Victoria.

Monro, A.M. (1922). *The practical Australian cookery.* Sydney: Dymock's Book Arcade, Ltd.

Muir, A.L. (2003). Ceramics in the collection of the Museum of Chinese Australian History. *Australasian Historical Archaeology* 21: 42–9.

Mullins, P.R. (2011). The archaeology of consumption. *Annual Review of Anthropology* 40: 133–4.

Munsey, C. (1970). *The illustrated guide to collecting bottles.* New York: Hawthorne Books.

Roberts, B. (n.d.). *James Harrison refrigeration pioneer.* CIBSE Heritage Group online website, accessed January 2022. http://www.hevac-heritage.org/built_environment/pioneers_revisited/harrison.pdf.

Rolfson, T. (2017). Curries, chutneys, and Imperial Britain. *Constellations* 8(2): 1–9. DOI: 10.29173/cons29329.

Schulz, P. (2016). The American glass bottle industry – a brief history. In P. Schultz, R. Allen, B. Lindsey and J.K. Schulz, eds. *Baffle marks and pontil scars: a reader on historic bottle identification*, 11–23. Germantown, MD: Society for Historical Archaeology.

Selinger, B. (2013). Refrigeration: an Australian connection. *Chemistry in Australia* May: 20–21.

Shephard, S. (2000). *Pickled, potted and canned: how the preservation of food changed civilisation.* London: Headline Book Publishing.

Shurtleff, W. and A. Aoyagi (2012). *History of Worcestershire Sauce (1837–2021); extensively annotated bibliography and sourcebook.* Lafayette, CA: Soyinfo Center.

Smith, A.F. (1998) From garum to ketchup: a spicy tale of two fish sauces. In H. Walker, ed. *Fish: Food from the Waters: Proceedings from the Oxford Symposium on Food and Cookery 1997*, 299–307. Devon, UK: Prospect Books.

Smith, F.H. (2008). *The archaeology of alcohol and drinking.* Gainesville, FL: University Press of Florida.

Spier, R.F.G. (1958). Food habits of nineteenth-century California Chinese. *California Historical Society Quarterly* 38: 79–136.

Sydney Living Museums (2017). *Let's katchup sometime*, accessed 1 February 2021. https://blogs.sydneylivingmuseums.com.au/cook/lets-katchup-sometime/.

Sydney Morning Herald (1847). Advertising, 7 June, 4.

Tasmanian and Austral-Asiatic Review (1845). Advertising, 19 June, 3.

Twiss, K. (2012). The archaeology of food and social diversity. *Journal of Archaeological Research* 20: 357–95. DOI: 10.1007/s10814-012-9058-5.

Vader, J. and B. Murray (1975). *Antique bottle collecting in Australia.* Sydney: Ure Smit.

Voss, B. and R. Allen (2008). Overseas Chinese archaeology: historical foundations, current reflections, and new directions. *Historical Archaeology* 42(3): 5–28.

Walker, R. and D. Roberts (1988). *From scarcity to surfeit: a history of food and nutrition in New South Wales.* Kensington, NSW: New South Wales University Press.

Woff, B. (2014). Bottle reuse and archaeology: evidenced from the site of a bottle merchants' business. Honours thesis, Archaeology Department, La Trobe University, Bundoora.

Woff, B. (2019). The reliability of bottle form for ascertaining function: bottle reuse and archaeology. *Australasian Historical Archaeology* 37: 37–42.

Wood, B., ed. (1977). *Tucker in Australia.* Melbourne: Hill of Content.

Zumwalt, B. (1980). *Ketchup pickles sauces: 19th century food in glass.* Fulton, CA: Mark West Publishers.

Conclusion

Madeline Shanahan

Food is everything we are. It's an extension of nationalist feeling, ethnic feeling, your personal history, your province, your region, your tribe, your grandma. It's inseparable from those from the get-go.

Anthony Bourdain

The quote above, by the late great chef and writer Anthony Bourdain, summarises something that most of us intrinsically understand about food. Whether it is connection to a traditional dish underpinning a wider communal identity, or simply something you loved (or loathed) in your lunchbox each day at school, most of us will appreciate that food forms part of who we are. This is the cultural and anthropological dimension to cuisine, but the concept that "we are what we eat" is also true in physiological terms. Indeed, as we have seen in this volume, archaeology shows us that our individual food story is written in our very bones.

This volume has presented just eight food stories from Australia's past. These have covered stories looking at change over many millennia, from deep time to the relatively recent past. They have also included distinct places, distant from one another in time and space, from over 47,000 years of plant use in the Kimberley to the nineteenth-century Victorian goldfields. Chapters have also addressed diverse cultural and ethnic identities, from a range of Aboriginal nations represented within the chapters, to convicts and Chinese diaspora. They have also covered a range of foodstuffs, from plant foods, to fish, mutton, roast pork and bottled preserves. Collectively, these chapters have highlighted the potential for Australian archaeologies of food, both in terms of the sheer diversity of stories to tell here and the depth of scholarship being undertaken across a range of disciplinary approaches. It is this depth and breadth of both history and geography, as well as the scholarship being undertaken here, that means that this volume really needs to be seen as just a starting point for the archaeology of food in Australia.

To begin with the first of these issues, the sheer scale of Australia as a continent and the almost inconceivable length of human occupation here means that there is really no limit to the food stories that archaeology can contribute to. While First Nations peoples have long understood their Ancestors' deep connection to this place, for many other people it is hard to properly comprehend the timescales we operate within in Australian archaeology. Within this timescale there were also multiple phases of climactic and environmental shifts, in which Country would have changed many times over. Of course, for First Nations people this depth of connection to Country is highlighted through oral traditions – preserving knowledge of changing sea levels and now extinct species. It is critical, then, that we recognise that this sheer time and geographic depth, not to mention the cultural and linguistic diversity, would be matched by change and diversity of food and foodways. This means that there is almost limitless potential for food stories connected to these many millennia, and these are stories which archaeologists working in collaboration with Traditional Owners are uniquely well placed to tell. The chapters by Owen (Chapter 1), Dilkes-Hall, Davis and Malo (Chapter 2) and Disspain, Manne and Lambrides (Chapter 3) grapple with this vast time period and diversity of foodstuffs, but they are just the beginning of the contribution that the discipline can make.

Of course, adaptation continued in the colonial and postcolonial periods for First Nations peoples. We know from both community knowledge and historical records that, post-1788, Aboriginal peoples' food and foodways display both change and continuity as they survived and adapted to the impact of colonisation. Traditional food gathering and hunting practices were disrupted, as access to resources were increasingly restricted. New foodstuffs, such as flour, sugar and tea, replaced or substituted traditional foods, some of which had a detrimental impact on health, and some of which were also weaponised by colonists in our most painful chapters of history. New tools, materials and weapons also became part of Aboriginal food procurement in this next phase – all of which changed food cultures and left material markers. Importantly, we also know the role that Aboriginal peoples played in nineteenth- and twentieth-century food industries – as stockmen, cooks and dock workers, among other professions. This volume has not addressed contact archaeology and Aboriginal food stories in the colonial period substantially, but this should be a critical area for future research; an area which has not substantially progressed since earlier studies in the discipline (Birmingham and Wilson 2010). Contact period stories addressing food directly could contribute to better understandings of change, continuity and adaptation. They could explore the maintenance of traditional food staples, as well as the development of shared cross-cultural dishes important to Aboriginal communities (such as damper). Much has been written about the use of new materials such as glass in the production of tools, and it is important to integrate this into archaeologies of food consistently. Of course, the contribution of Aboriginal peoples to farming, trade and industry could also be a key theme for future archaeologies of food, drawing on the work of scholars already pursuing these subjects.

Of course, colonisation also led to new people, cultures and cuisines coming to Australian shores. From 1788 on, waves of colonists, convicts and migrants from every corner of the globe have brought new foodstuffs, dishes, festivals and traditions with them. This volume has just scratched the surface of these stories. It has looked at colonial relationships with meat and the Australian love of sheep (Nussbaumer and Filios, Chapter 4), colonial fishing practices (Disspain, Manne and Lambrides, Chapter 3), experiences of institutionalisation (Connor, Chapter 5), the development of kitchens and cookery (Newling, Chapter 7) and the importance of bottling in the nineteenth century (Harris, Woff and O'Donohue, Chapter 8). The majority of these chapters focus on the food cultures and experiences of predominantly British and Irish migrants, but Grimwade's chapter on the Chinese diaspora's food traditions (Chapter 6) is a critical contribution highlighting the diversity of food experience in nineteenth-century Australia. Recognition of the diversity of culture and cuisine should be a key focus for future archaeologies of food. Research on this issue is currently limited as historical archaeologists have not pursued ethnicity and identity as consistently as the discipline has elsewhere. A key reason for this is Australian historical archaeologists' fixation with artefact assemblages and quantitative analysis, a general lack of engagement with cultural landscapes, a reluctance to focus on synthesis of varied datasets and a general disdain for qualitative analysis. Grimwade's chapter demonstrates the progress that can be made by engaging with landscape and comparative site analysis for the study of ethnicity when situated within a broader contextual understanding of cuisine and culture. The search for a securely stratified artefact assemblage has, to date, limited studies of ethnicity in our recent past, but there is no reason that historical archaeologists cannot engage with cultural landscapes including restaurants, market gardens, docklands, pubs, retailers, bakeries, wineries and homes to understand the material experiences of food here. To reflect the diversity of Australia's many food cultures, archaeologists will also need to be prepared to engage more consistently with the post-war period.

While we have touched on temporal, geographic and cultural diversity, the other key opportunity for the archaeology of food in Australia stems from the demonstrable disciplinary diversity across academia and consulting. This volume demonstrates just a selection of the range of techniques and methodologies and has included archaeobotany, zooarchaeology, archaeomalacology, stable isotope analysis, artefact analysis and studies of buildings, domestic space and landscapes. Within each of these subfields, and among the range of expertise not represented as outlined in the Introduction, there is unlimited potential for further collaborative research on the archaeology of food here. As this volume has demonstrated, it is within this diversity that the true value of archaeology to contribute to thematic discussions of our many pasts is found.

And so, this series of eight food stories from Australia's past should be seen as opening the door to a new thematic line of inquiry for Australian archaeology rather than an end point. This is a thematic line of discussion that rests on collaboration within the discipline – crossing the lines of industry and the academy – and draws together a vast range of datasets, sources and perspectives on the past. Importantly, the wider Australian community has demonstrated a deep interest in both food heritage and the archaeological discipline. Australian archaeology, both within universities and consulting, is an expensive endeavour, and it is also one that has an impact on a non-renewable resource. It is therefore critical that we engage with the wider community's desire to understand Australian culinary pasts in all their glorious complexity.

Index

Index

Australia
- British food traditions, adoption 109, 113, 116, 117, 228
- changes to over human occupation 19–20
- diversity of food offerings 3
- Holocene period, south-eastern 21
- lack of scholarship on food archaeology 4, 11
- settlement 81

Barrow Island site 94, 159
Beeton, Isabella
Book of Household Management 208, 214, 240
biomolecular identification techniques 88
- aDNA (ancient DNA) 88
- ZooMS (Zooarchaeology by Mass Spectrum) 88
bones
- animal *see* animal bones
- fish bones 83, 84–7
- human skeletons 8
bottles and glass
- Australia, glass and bottle making in 232, 236
- availability, 18th and mid-19th centuries 235–6
- beef extracts (Bovril) 230, 244–5
- chutneys 240, 242
- closure methods 231
- coffee 245–6, 247
- collections, importance of analysis of 227, 228–9, 249
- comparative analysis 250
- condiment bottles Parramatta and Red Cow Hotel, Penrith 249
- dating 250
- durability 228
- embossing 236
- fish pastes 244, 245
- forms, identification 231, 238, 250
- function, ascribing 238
- glass, first food preservation using 230–1
- glass blowing 231
- glass moulding 231
- glass production, history 231–2
- green panelled 238
- heat resistance 240
- historic 14

light blue 238
- mass-production and affordability 231, 232
- milk 246–7
- non-corrosive quality 240
- ownership, issues as to 236
- payment for returned bottles 237
- potted meats/spread 242–4
- purchase price 237
- re-use 236, 237
- sauces 242
- vinegar, use of 239–40
- Worcestershire sauce 242
Bourdain, Anthony 257
bread ovens 209, 218–19
Brewarrina fish trap network 91
Brooking Gorge 1 57, 59, 62
Budj Bim Cultural Landscape
- fish traps 91
buildings and landscapes 10–11
Bunuba 57, 69

Cadigal people 22, 39
capitalism xiv, xvi, 10
- waged labour 149, 151, 159
carbon and nitrogen, stable isotopes
- animals, fish and shellfish, in 24
- humans, in 25
- plants, in 24
Carpenter's Gap 1 57, 59, 62, 66, 67
ceramic food containers 9, 231, 232–5
- adaptive reuse 237–8
- Bristol-glazed stoneware 234
- Chinese brown-glazed stoneware (CBGS) 232–4, 248, 250
- European origin, of 234
- locally made 234–5
- salt-glazed stoneware 234
chaff 5, 39
chemical analysis 9
Chinese
- Chinese brown-glazed stoneware (CBGS) 232–4, 248, 250
- dietary patterns 247–8
- domestication of pigs 172
- feasts, unifying role 177
- immigrants to Australia, 19th century 173, 247

263

Index

www.ingramcontent.com/pod-product-compliance
Lightning Source LLC
Chambersburg PA
CBHW061234270326
41929CB00031B/3485